ACCLAIM FOR JOAN JACOBS BRUMBERG'S

THE BODY PROJECT

"A fascinating and important book which tracks girls and their bodies from the era of repression to the culture of obsession. . . . A tough-minded analysis."
—*Newsweek*

"A troubling report from the trenches of adolescence." —*USA Today*

"A delightful and painful history [that] allows us to eavesdrop on a wonderful assortment of teenage diaries. . . . *The Body Project* draws the crucial connection between bad body images and bad choices, between how girls feel about their bodies and what they do with them." —*Boston Globe*

"An excellent and startling book . . . that urges us as a society to acknowledge and respond to the vulnerability of adolescent girls without returning to regressive eras." —*Memphis Commercial Appeal*

"A necessary read for adolescent girls, women, and the parents of girls."
—*San Diego Union-Tribune*

"A wonderful book for a mother-daughter study group. . . . Brumberg came up with the fine idea of mining diaries as a source for girls' history."
—*Women's Review of Books*

"Reading *The Body Project* is a step forward in The Freedom Project."
—*Gloria Steinem*

"The voices emerging from these diaries provide a poignant, realistic, and often funny framework for Brumberg to explore changes in girlhood. *The Body Project* is a book to read with pen in hand in order to scribble down the margins."
—*Ms.*

JOAN JACOBS BRUMBERG

THE BODY PROJECT

The author of *Fasting Girls: The History of Anorexia Nervosa,* Joan Jacobs Brumberg is a Stephen H. Weiss Professor at Cornell University, where she holds a unique appointment teaching in the fields of history, human development, and women's studies. Her research and sensitive writing about American women and girls have been recognized by the Guggenheim Foundation, the National Endowment for the Humanities, the Rockefeller Foundation, and the MacDowell Colony. She lives in Ithaca, New York.

Awards Brumberg has received include the Berkshire Book Prize for the best book by a woman historian, given by the Berkshire Women's History Conference (1988); the John Hope Franklin Prize for the best book in American Studies, given by the American Studies Association (1989); the Eileen Basker Memorial Prize for the best book in the area of gender and mental health, given by the Society for Medical Anthropology (1989); and the Watson Davis Prize for the best book in translating ideas for the public, given by the History of Science Society (1989).

ALSO BY JOAN JACOBS BRUMBERG

Fasting Girls: The History of Anorexia Nervosa

Mission for Life: The Judson Family and American Evangelical Culture

THE BODY PROJECT

4
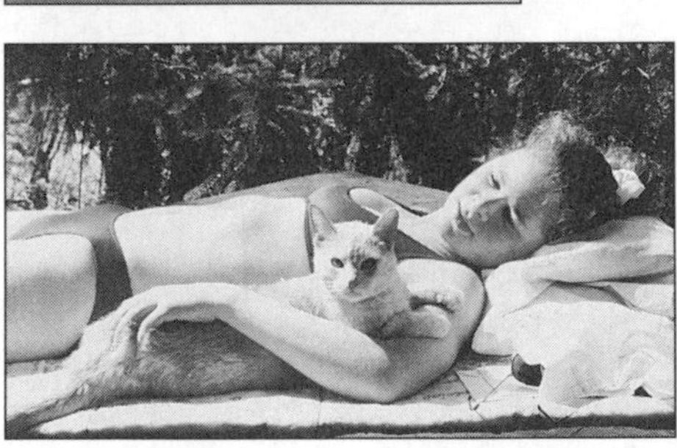

THE BODY PROJECT

An Intimate History of American Girls

JOAN JACOBS BRUMBERG

VINTAGE BOOKS
A DIVISION OF RANDOM HOUSE, INC.
NEW YORK

FIRST VINTAGE BOOKS EDITION, SEPTEMBER 1998

 Published in the United States by Vintage Books, a division of Random House, Inc., New York, and simultaneously in Canada by Random House of Canada Limited, Toronto. Originally published in hardcover in the United States by Random House, Inc., New York, in 1997.

Owing to limitations of space, acknowledgments of permission to use illustrative material will be found on page 268.

Library of Congress Catologing-in-Publication Data
Brumberg, Joan Jacobs.
The body project : an intimate history of American Girls / Joan Jacobs Brumberg.
p. cm.
Originally published: New York : Random House, 1997.
Includes bibliographical references and index.
ISBN 0-679-73529-1
1. Teenage girls—United States—History. 2. Young women—United States—History.
3. Body, Human—Social aspects—United States—History. I. Title.
HQ798.B724 1998
305.235—dc21 98-8098
CIP

Book design by Caroline Cunningham

Random House Web address: www.randomhouse.com

Printed in the United States of America
11 13 15 17 19 18 16 14 12

For Madeline Rand Brumberg and

Isabel Fenwick Brumberg

"I would have girls regard themselves not as adjectives but as nouns. . . ."

—Elizabeth Cady Stanton, "Our Girls"

"My hopes of the future rest upon the girls. My patriotism clings to the girls. I believe America's future pivots on this great woman revolution."

—Dioclesian Lewis, *Our Girls*

Acknowledgments

Acknowledgments always serve as an important review of an author's intellectual and personal debts. When the going was rough, and I was uncertain about the direction of my writing, I turned repeatedly to two important people in my life, David Brumberg and Faye Dudden, both of whom provided consistent moral support as well as savvy and prompt historical judgments. Although I made enormous demands on them both, they remained good-humored and thoughtful in their responses. In the same way, Ellen Grebinger was a critic-on-demand, willing and able to read pages of copy even on an undulating dock at Tupper Lake.

I am fortunate to have a wide circle of professional colleagues who have supported my goal to bring meaningful women's history to an audience beyond "the profession." Many of them are also important friends who sustained my spirit as well as my scholarship. Allan Brandt, Carol Groneman, Ann J. Lane, Heather Munro Prescott, Barbara Sicherman, Nancy J. Tomes, and Susan Ware deserve special thanks for their timely, highly individualistic readings of portions of the book, or for their phone and E-mail responses to particular queries or intermittent expressions of my frustration. Closer to home, at Cornell, the intellectual acuity and the warm friendship of Lois Brown, Jacqueline Goldsby, Phyllis Moen, and

Cybele Raver have been critical to the completion of this book, as has the long-standing personal support of Helen Johnson and Jan Jennings. Carol and Michael Kammen's keen interest in my pursuit of unconventional historical subjects is also appreciated.

Like many scholars, I am indebted to organizations outside my own university that saw potential in my work: the John Simon Guggenheim Foundation, the National Endowment for the Humanities, and the American College of Obstetricians and Gynecologists all provided me with critical financial support that translated into extra time for research and writing. No place, however, has been so important to my evolution as a writer as the MacDowell Colony, where I had both exquisite space and uninterrupted time to develop a form and cadence for this particular narrative. At MacDowell, I made many friends whose reactions to my stories about American girls confirmed my faith that history remains an important literary endeavor. My agent, Georges Borchardt, has been a wise and kind adviser as well as a smart and enthusiastic advocate of my work; Kate Medina, my editor, taught me a great deal about accessibility and told me bluntly when I needed to shed the girdle of academese that shapes so many professional historical accounts of the past. Renana Meyers, Page Dickinson, and Molly Stern, all at Random House, made smart and helpful suggestions. I'm particularly indebted to Sybil Pincus and Caroline Cunningham for calm and competent production advice.

A good history book requires creative use of sources as well as detective work in libraries. I am grateful to Carmen Blankenship, Amy Blumenthal, Julie Copenhagen, Lance Heidig, Judith Holliday, Robert Kibbee, Fred Muratori, Susan Szasz Palmer, Donald Schnedeker, Nancy Skipper, and Caroline Spicer, all in the Cornell Library system, for their dedicated and informed assistance over the years; and I thank Jenny Daley at the Duke University Special Collections. Laurie Todd helped me with all kinds of research matters and organized my correspondence with diarists in a superbly competent way. Renee Kaplan, Susan Matt, Debra Michals, Shelly Kaplan Nickles, and Margaret Weitekamp also provided competent short-term research assistance when the burdens of teaching, writing, and administration slowed me down. And there were many Cornell undergraduates—especially Karen Cooperman, Alison Halpern, Lori Karin, Aliza Milner, Erica Sussman, and Haruka Yamashita—whose papers on aspects of "girl culture" added to my storehouse of knowledge about the adolescent experience in the past and present. I cannot name all the women who shared their adolescent diaries with me, because I must respect their privacy, but I can convey my deepest appreciation to them for their generosity and the trust that these loans implied. I am also indebted to Kirsten Mullen for her generosity with photographs from her collection.

Dr. Lawrence Charles Parish, Dr. Rebat Haldar, and Rima Apple generously answered questions about dermatology; Peter Zollo of Teenage Research Inc. provided information on adolescent consumer behavior. There are also a number of archivists who deserve my thanks: Mary Degenhardt, Girl Scouts of America; Elaine Engst, Kroch Library, Cornell; Dale Meyer, Herbert Hoover Presidential Library; Eva Mosley, Schlesinger Library, Radcliffe College; Sarah Partridge, Bettmann Archive; Susan Rishworth, American College of Obstetricians and Gynecologists. Over the years I have also relied heavily on Jolan Balog for all kinds of secretarial support, which she continues to provide with competence, good humor, and grace; for the third time, Roberta Ludgate gave my book manuscript its final polish; and Amber Cohen in Photographic Services at Cornell skillfully coordinated my many requests for slides and prints.

Finally, writing this book was punctuated with a great deal of personal loss—both my parents, as well as a number of friends. I emerged whole and optimistic, with a completed manuscript that I believed in, because of a circle of friends and family who held me especially close to their hearts: Marshall Blake and Faye Dudden, Catherine and John Eckenrode, Ellen and Paul Grebinger, and Joel and Midge Kerlan have been the siblings I never had. My husband, David, my son, Adam, and my daughter-in-law, Sarah, continue to fill my life with love, probably too much good food and wine, and the simple joy and laughter that come with nurturing another generation—Madeline and Isabel.

Contents

INTRODUCTION

The Body as Evidence

At the close of the twentieth century, the female body poses an enormous problem for American girls, and it does so because of the culture in which we live. The process of sexual maturation is more difficult for girls today than it was a century ago because of a set of historical changes that have resulted in a peculiar mismatch between girls' biology and today's culture. Although girls now mature sexually earlier than ever before, contemporary American society provides fewer social protections for them, a situation that leaves them unsupported in their development and extremely vulnerable to the excesses of popular culture and to pressure from peer groups. But the current body problem is not just an external issue resulting from a lack of societal vigilance or adult support; it has also become an internal, psychological problem: girls today make the body into an all-consuming project in ways young women of the past did not.

A century ago, American women were lacing themselves into corsets and teaching their adolescent daughters to do the same; today's teens shop for thong bikinis on their own, and their middle-class mothers are likely to be uninvolved until the credit card bill arrives in the mail. These contrasting images might suggest a great deal of progress, but American girls at the end of the twentieth century actually suffer from body problems more pervasive and more dangerous than the constraints implied by the corset. Historical forces have made coming of age in a female body a different and more complex experience today than it was a century ago. Although sexual development—the onset of menstruation and the appearance of breasts—occurs in every generation, a girl's experience of these inevitable biological events is shaped by the world in which she lives, so much so, that each generation, at its own point in history, develops its own characteristic body problems and projects. Every girl suffers some kind of adolescent angst about her body; it is the historical moment that defines *how* she reacts to her changing flesh. From the perspective of history, adolescent self-consciousness is quite persistent, but its level is raised or lowered, like the water level in a pool, by the cultural and social setting.

Back in the 1830s, Victoria, the future queen of England, became intensely self-conscious about her body at the age of fifteen and sixteen, and although her first menstrual period was never announced officially, it was generally known that Victoria crossed the threshold into womanhood at about that time. At age eighteen, before she became queen, Victoria expressed general dissatisfaction with her looks. She mused over her hair, which was getting too dark; her hands, which she considered ugly; and her eyebrows, which she thought so inadequate that she considered shaving them off in order to encourage their growth. She also made awkward attempts to disguise her physical flaws: she tried covering up her stubby fingers with rings, but then found she had difficulty wearing gloves, which were obligatory for someone of her status. Some of Victoria's self-consciousness was a response to the attention she received as a future monarch. But it also had to do with the biological changes of adolescence, changes that breed both awkwardness and awe. The American poet Lucy Larcom, who tended looms in the textile mills of nineteenth-century New England, lived a life vastly different from Victoria's, but she, too, became "morbidly self-critical" in adolescence. When her body began to change visibly, her older sisters insisted that she lengthen her skirts and put up her hair—markers of sexual maturation in those days.[1]

Almost a century later, in the 1920s, the feminist writer and philosopher Simone de Beauvoir ruminated about her changing body. At fifteen she thought she looked simply "awful." She had acne, her clothes no longer fit, and she had to wrap her breasts in bandages because her favorite beige silk party dress pulled so tightly across her new bosom that it looked "obscene." Later in life, de Beauvoir described adolescence as a "difficult patch."[2]

Although Margaret Mead's 1928 classic *Coming of Age in Samoa* suggested that there are cultures where girls do not experience self-consciousness in adolescence or discomfort with their changing bodies, in the United States and in Western Europe they clearly have experienced both for at least a century.[3] A matronly queen, a popular poet, and a mature feminist—each left indications that she felt self-conscious in adolescence, as most girls do.

In the nineteenth century, the "growing pains" of adolescence were diminished by society's emphasis on spiritual rather than physical matters. There were rigid standards of decorum that made discussion of the body "impolite." Yet among girls in the middle and upper classes, there was concern about the size of certain body parts, such as the hands, feet, and waist. To be too large or too robust was a sign of indelicacy that suggested lower-class origins and a rough way of life. Even the exalted Victoria and her mother, the Duchess of Kent, worried about body size. Victoria's feet were admirable because they were tiny; yet she was warned periodically by her mother against becoming too stout, and she was chided for eating too much. A future queen, after all, was not supposed to look like a husky milkmaid or mill girl, and her body must never imply that she did demanding physical labor.[4]

Still, there is an important difference between the past and the present when it comes to the level of social support for the adolescent girl's preoccupation with her body. Beauty imperatives for girls in the nineteenth century were kept in check by consideration of moral character and by culturally mandated patterns of emotional denial and repression.[5] Nineteenth-century girls often noted in their diaries when they acquired an exciting personal embellishment, such as a hair ribbon or a new dress, but these were not linked to self-worth or personhood in quite the ways they are today. In fact, girls who were preoccupied with their looks were likely to be accused of vanity or self-indulgence. Many parents tried to limit their daughters' interest in superficial things, such as hairdos, dresses, or the size of their waists, because character was considered more important than beauty by both parents and the community. And character was built on attention to self-control, service to others, and belief in God—not on attention to one's own, highly individualistic body project.

Good Works Versus Good Looks

The traditional emphasis on "good works" as opposed to "good looks" meant that the lives of young women in the nineteenth century had a very different orientation from those of girls today. This difference is reflected in the tone of their personal diaries, a source I use extensively to tell the story of how the American girl's relationship to her body has changed over the past century. Before World War I, girls rarely mentioned their bodies in terms of strategies for self-improvement or struggles for personal identity. Becoming a better person meant paying *less* attention to the self, giving more assistance to others, and putting more effort into instructive reading or lessons at school. When girls in the nineteenth century thought about ways to improve themselves, they almost always focused on their internal character and how it was reflected in outward behavior. In 1892, the personal agenda of an adolescent diarist read: "Resolved, not to talk about myself or feelings. To think before speaking. To work seriously. To be self restrained in conversation and actions. Not to let my thoughts wander. To be dignified. Interest myself more in others."[6]

A century later, in the 1990s, American girls think very differently. In a New Year's resolution written in 1982, a girl wrote: "I will try to make myself better in any way I possibly can with the help of my budget and baby-sitting money. I will lose weight, get new lenses, already got new haircut, good makeup, new clothes and accessories."[7] This concise declaration clearly captures how girls feel about themselves in the contemporary world. Like many adults in American society, girls today are concerned with the shape and appearance of their bodies as a primary expression of their individual identity.

At the end of the twentieth century, the body is regarded as something to be managed and maintained, usually through expenditures on clothes and personal grooming items, with special attention to exterior surfaces—skin, hair, and contours. In adolescent girls' private diaries and journals, the body is a consistent preoccupation, second only to peer relationships. "I'm so fat. [Hence] I'm so ugly," is as common a comment today as are classic adolescent ruminations about whether Jennifer is a true friend, or if Scott likes Amy.

In my role as a teacher of women's history and women's studies at Cornell University, I have heard variations of this kind of "body talk" for almost two decades. It usually takes the form of offhand comments, but it recently surfaced in a seminar discussion about the health of women and girls in the nineteenth century. Clad in a variety of comfortable clothes, ranging from leggings and jeans to baggy sweaters and dresses, my students deplored the corset and lamented the constraints Victorian society imposed on women. Clearly, they considered themselves much better off than the young women who had braved public criticism to study at Cornell a century earlier.

Then the conversation drifted to the present, and somehow we ended up talking about a current body project that I had known little about. My students told me how they remove pubic hair in order to wear the newest, most minimal bikinis. As we talked, a few uttered a disapproving "No way" or "Ouch," but others felt compelled to offer a rationale for this delicate procedure. "It's necessary," they said, "so you can feel confident at the beach." Although they admitted that male ogling made them nervous, they also regarded the ability to display their bodies as a sign of women's liberation, a mark of progress, and a basic American right. Madonna was mentioned as a model: she keeps her body absolutely hairless, my students assured me, and she retains a highly paid, personal cosmetologist to do the job.

These young women were bright enough to gain admission to an Ivy League university, and they enjoyed educational opportunities unknown to earlier generations. But they also felt a need to strictly police their bodies. I was intrigued by both their discreet euphemism for genitalia—"bikini-line area"—and their willingness to add yet another body concern to the already substantial litany of adolescent anxieties: hair, pimples, thighs. We talked some more, and I offered my perspective as a historian and feminist, but also as a grandmother. Life in the world of the microbikini is obviously different from life in the world of the corset, I argued, but there are still constraints and difficulties, perhaps even greater ones. Today, unlike in the Victorian era, commercial interests play directly to the body angst of young girls, a marketing strategy that results in enormous revenues for manufacturers of skin and hair products as well as diet foods.[8] Although elevated body angst is a great boost to corporate profits, it saps the creativity of girls and threatens their mental and physical health. Progress for women is obviously filled with ambiguities.

What makes the situation today especially urgent, however, is that the problem begins so early in life, when the female body first begins to gear up for reproduction. Puberty begins earlier today, which means that girls must cope with menstruation and other aspects of physical maturation at a younger age, when they are really still children emotionally. Until puberty, girls really are the stronger sex in terms of standard measures of physical and mental health: they are hardier, less likely to injure themselves, and more competent in social relations. But as soon as the body begins to change, a girl's advantage starts to evaporate. At that point, more and more girls begin to suffer bouts of clinical depression. The explanation of this sex difference lies in the frustrations girls feel about the divergence between their dreams for the future and the conventional sex roles implied by their emerging breasts and hips.[9]

In addition to an increasing risk of depression and suicide attempts, adolescent girls today are more vulnerable than boys of the same age to eating disorders, substance abuse, and dropping out of school. And of course, early childbearing has a greater impact on a girl's life than it has on that of her male sexual partner. The well-known work of Harvard psychologist Carol Gilligan is premised on the notion that adolescence is a time of crisis for contemporary girls; so is *Reviving Ophelia,* a recent best-seller by clinical psychologist Mary Pipher. Gilligan's sensitive studies reveal that between the ages of eleven and sixteen young women lose their confidence and become insecure and self-doubting; Pipher sees adolescence as the time when a girl's self-esteem crumbles.[10]

The body is at the heart of the crisis of confidence that Gilligan, Pipher, and others describe. By age thirteen, 53 percent of American girls are unhappy with their bodies; by age seventeen, 78 percent are dissatisfied. Although there are some differences across race and class lines, talk about the body and learning how to improve it is a central motif in publications and media aimed at adolescent girls. *Seventeen* magazine tapped into this well of angst when it ran a headline on a story in the July 1995 issue: "Do You Hate Your Body? How to Stop." The article itself proposed ways to stop the agonizing, but the author also admitted that it was awfully hard to do so in a world where "your body is very, very important."[11]

Adolescent girls today face the issues girls have always faced—Who am I? Who do I want to be?—but their answers, more than ever before, revolve around the body. The increase in anorexia nervosa and bulimia in the past thirty years suggests that in some cases the body becomes an obsession, leading to recalcitrant eating behaviors that can result in death. But even among girls who never develop full-blown eating disorders, the body is so central to definitions of the self that psychologists sometimes use numerical scores of "body esteem" and "body dissatisfaction" to evaluate a girl's mental health. In the 1990s, tests that ask respondents to indicate levels of satisfaction or dissatisfaction with their own thighs or buttocks have become a useful key for unlocking the inner life of many American girls.[12]

Why is the body still a girl's nemesis? Shouldn't today's sexually liberated girls feel better about themselves than their corseted sisters of a century ago? The historical evidence I present in this book, based on research that includes diaries written by American girls in the years between the 1830s and the 1990s, suggests that although young women today enjoy greater freedom and more options than their counterparts of a century ago, they are also under more pressure, and at greater risk, because of a unique combination of biological and cultural forces that have made the adolescent female body into a template for much of the social change of the twentieth century. I use the body as evidence to show how the mother-daughter connection has loosened, especially with regard to the experience of menstruation and sexuality; how doctors and marketers took over important educational functions that were once the special domain of female relatives and mentors; how scientific medicine, movies, and advertising created a new, more exacting ideal of physical perfection; and how changing standards of intimacy turned virginity into an outmoded ideal. The fact that American girls now make the body their central project is not an accident or a curiosity: it is a symptom of historical changes that are only now beginning to be understood.

Because the body is central to the experience of female adolescence, I also use it as an organizational framework. *The Body Project* begins with a biological event, menarche, or first menstruation, and moves through a series of chapters that explore the changing experience of female maturation. Ultimately, this is a story about what it means to grow up in a female body, and the ways in which girlhood in America has changed since the nineteenth century. But it also explains how the pressures on young women have accumulated, making girls at the close of the twentieth century more anxious than ever before about their bodies and, therefore, about themselves.

DEAR DIARY

What was it like to develop breasts or begin your periods a century ago? Did these biological events occur at the same age in the Victorian era? Have American girls always regarded the body as their most important project? In pursuit of answers to questions like these, I culled girls' diaries, particularly old ones, which are remarkably similar to the diaries many of us have written and stored away at the bottom of dresser drawers or in attic trunks. Unfortunately, I threw my own diary away in my early twenties, in a moment of "emotional housekeeping," but I still remember the way that red leatherette volume—with its tiny lock and key—harbored my innermost secrets and private obsessions.

I found girls' diaries everywhere. I found them in libraries and archives, but I also acquired them from friends, from students, and from lecture audiences—people who were more than willing to dig them out and dust them off. When I advertised my research interest in girls' diaries in *The New York Times* in 1982, I received many useful and fascinating responses, including one from a New York City sanitation worker who sent me a diary he had rescued from a garbage can.[13] Although many people regard the literary remains of ordinary girls as silly or worthless, this man intuited that a small beat-up diary might contain private ruminations with a great deal to say about the experience of life as a female adolescent.

Throughout this book I intermingle my own voice as a historian with girls' voices drawn from their personal diaries. And because diaries reveal so much about the heart of being a girl, I use them whenever possible to provide entry into the hidden history of female adolescents' experience, especially the experience of the body. Unlike samplers, which died out with the decline of young women's sewing and embroidering, adolescent diaries persist, providing generations of girls with a way to express and explore their lives and feelings. Old diaries are a national treasure, providing a window into the day-to-day routines of family, school, and community. They also recapture the familiar cadences of adolescent emotional life, and they provide authentic testimony to what girls in the past considered noteworthy, amusing, and sad, and what they could or would not talk about.[14]

As emotionally intimate as diaries can be, more often than not girl diarists have been silent on the subject of their own changing bodies. A century ago, menarche was a private affair, and girls handled the first sign of menstrual blood with enormous reserve. Some Victorian adolescents made brief comments in their diaries about being "unwell," or they repeated a pattern of cryptic marks, such as X's, every twenty-eight or thirty days; but most said nothing at all. In the early 1890s, Lou Henry, a fifteen-year-old high school girl in Pasadena, California, who would later become Mrs. Herbert Hoover, noted in her diary that her mother made her stay home on the lounge all day, and that she was excused from gym "for reasons best known to myself."[15] This sparse commentary suggested that Mrs. Henry limited Lou's activities during her periods, and that her school made allowances for girls on those special days. But this was all that nice middle-class girls, the kind who kept diaries, ever really said about their physical transition into womanhood.

Similarly, little was said about intimacies with young men. Consider Antha Warren, a young woman who taught school in St. Albans, Vermont, in the late 1860s. When she was in her late teens, Antha "kept company" with Henry Munsell, who fought in the Civil War when he was only eighteen and brought back dental skills learned in a military hospital. Whenever the couple kissed, Antha put an asterisk (*) in her diary, and since Henry came to call at least four or five nights a week, these symbols mounted up. "Too many * to count," she wrote one evening with some satisfaction. Antha's tone suggested that she took pleasure from her growing intimacy with the young dentist (whom she married in 1870), and that the couple may have done more than just kiss. Yet she always wrote about these interactions in a coded way, either because she feared that her diary might be read by others or—more likely—because she did not have the vocabulary to describe what happened: "After tea H[enry] and I went into the parlor, shut the door, and had a visit; he tried to sleep in my lap but couldn't. Had such a good time—[here she drew some squiggles] buttons."[16]

Antha's squiggly lines and her reference to buttons certainly piqued my curiosity. Did Henry simply play with her buttons and pine for the time when they would be married? Or did he unbutton Antha's dress and engage in what would come to be called, in the 1920s, petting? Until the twentieth century, most adolescent diarists were as reticent as Antha Warren and Lou Henry. Sexuality was generally restrained (if not secretive) among the middle-class girls who kept diaries. And even if they had the inclination to write about their changing bodies, it was hard to find the right words to express what was happening.

Even in more recent times, most diarists are not as forthright as Anne Frank, who, you may remember, called menstruation a "sweet secret"—despite its "pain and unpleasantness." In 1956, when I first read Anne's account of menstruation, I was twelve years old and I was thrilled by her honesty. What I did not know then was that her father, Otto Frank, a man born in the nineteenth century, was so uncomfortable with her commentary on the body that he had those lines edited out of the 1947 Dutch version of the diary. Otto Frank and his editors thought it was unnecessary, if not unseemly, to speak of such things.[17]

From a historical perspective, the great deluge of explicit "girl talk" about the body and sexuality is a relatively recent American phenomenon. As language about sex and the body has changed, so have the body projects of different generations of American girls. As you will see in the chapters ahead, by the 1920s young women were mentioning (with some delight) intimate interactions with boys at parties, in cars, and at the movies. They also began to write about their efforts to develop sexual allure through clothing and cosmetics, and, for the first time, they tried "slimming," a new body project tied to the scientific discovery of the calorie. The dieters and sexual players of the 1920s were generally girls in middle to late adolescence who were finishing high school or heading off to college and jobs in the business world—not young teenagers, as they are today.

By the 1950s, younger girls—those who filled the hallways and classrooms of postwar junior high schools—regularly mentioned their changing bodies and initial sexual adventures. At school and in scout troops, girls in early adolescence were now prepared systematically for menstruation, and this education meant that they knew the anatomical names of their own body parts. "Robin put a wetted piece of toilet paper in Cathy's vagina," a twelve-year-old reported with authority in her description of playing "doctor" at a weekend pajama party in Queens. Because full, pointed breasts were the beauty ideal in the 1950s, girls of this generation wrote wistfully about classmates with larger chests, and their envy led to a rash of commercial breast-development projects that now seem hilarious. Most of all, postwar diarists obsessed about particular boys, and they filled endless pages with the logistics of their first kiss, cast in melodramatic language picked up from films and romance magazines. "His lips were on mine, hard and pressing and insistent, making my head fall back," wrote an earnest fourteen-year-old about that special moment when she and her boyfriend waited for a bus after a dance at the Holy Name School in Brookline, Massachusetts. "I never knew a kiss would be like that," she said. "I grew up tonight. Now I am a woman."[18]

By the 1980s, American girls were writing less romantic, but more graphic, accounts of their initiation into heterosexual and lesbian relationships. Although some girls were almost clinical in their reporting, others still used colloquialisms for body parts. "He wanted me to put my hands on his Beewa," wrote a sixteen-year-old who attended Catholic high school in Michigan, and "when I did he told me I made him happy." A new level of frankness in the popular media, plus more exposure of the body itself, had an effect on girls and the nature of their body projects. Dieting became pervasive, exercise became more demanding, and some young women even began to pierce intimate body parts as a way of making dramatic statements about themselves. By the 1990s, adolescent sexuality had become a routine part of public discourse. "My boyfriend and I have been going out for four months, and we've been doing some stuff," a sixteen-year-old wrote candidly to the editor at *Seventeen.* "We kissed and he put his finger inside me." From a historical perspective, this behavior was probably not new, but having young women talk about it in public was revolutionary.[19]

The way different generations talk about their bodies and about sexuality is an important theme in this story. As a society, we certainly are more open about many aspects of our sexual lives than we were fifty or even twenty-five years ago. Today's "shock talk" on radio and television obviously provides a way for many Americans, young and old, to taste a wide range of sexual behaviors that used to be hidden and taboo. Advertising and films also show us body parts—often beyond the "bikini-line area"—that past generations rarely saw and probably never worried about. And yet, despite this national preoccupation with sex and the body, there is still a deeply embedded cultural reluctance, even in supposedly "enlightened" circles, to talk honestly or openly about certain aspects of the female body. My own blushing face and halting speech whenever a professional colleague asked me about the subject of my research symbolized the problem: it is hard to talk out loud about menstruation, pimples, or hymens without feeling just a twinge of embarrassment, much like a fourteen-year-old. In the course of writing this book, I came to understand that, in talking about their bodies, women still struggle to find a vocabulary that does not rely on Victorian euphemisms, medical nomenclature, or misogynistic slang. Ironically, we live with a legacy of reticence even in this time of disclosure.

For this reason, I have an ambitious goal for this book: *The Body Project* is intended to provoke the kind of intergenerational conversation about female bodies that most adult women like myself have wished for but never really had. The chapters ahead were designed to ignite memories about those awkward years and to foster conversation among mothers and daughters, women teachers and students, friends and colleagues. These memories will stimulate laughter as well as concern, but both reactions are appropriate. Adolescence is a time of volatility and exuberance, but it is also a time when many young people make forays into dangerous social and personal territory. As you read about the maturational experiences of young women in the past, I am sure that you will recognize yourself and the ways in which "girls will be girls." You will also see that something critical has happened to girls and their bodies that requires us to confront the differences between the world we have lost and the one we now inhabit.

Over a century ago, in the 1870s, Elizabeth Cady Stanton—a tireless crusader for the rights of women—began talking about the importance of girls' bodies, in a lecture entitled "Our Girls." She gave this lecture in cities on the East Coast and in the Midwest, but also in small towns throughout Ohio, Iowa, Nebraska, and Missouri. By this time, Stanton was a matronly, gray-haired grandmother in her sixties who felt comfortable speaking out against corsets, cosmetics, and tight, high-heeled boots because of the dangers they represented for the physical development of young girls. Although Stanton was clearly interested in improving the overall health of American women, robust, energetic bodies were never an end in themselves for her. "God has given you minds, dear girls, as well as bodies," she reminded her audiences, which often included mothers with adolescent daughters in tow. Instead of pandering to fashion, Stanton advocated loose clothes in adolescence, vigorous exercise, and real intellectual challenges. "I would have girls regard themselves not as adjectives but as nouns," she pronounced pointedly, in a manner characteristic of her lifelong struggle to make women independent, rational actors rather than decorative objects tied to the whims and fortunes of men.[20]

The book that you are about to read echoes themes in Elizabeth Cady Stanton's popular lecture, and it is rooted in her idea that girls' bodies mirror American cultural values. *The Body Project* is both a story of the Victorian past and a guide to the future. As history, it argues that the body projects now absorbing our girls are a symptom of deep changes in twentieth-century life, changes that have taken a toll on American girls in ways no one could have anticipated in 1900. Understanding what has happened historically to girls' bodies and to their relationships with those who surround them—especially their mothers, teachers, and physicians—provides the first step in crafting an effective, progressive response to a predicament that already threatens the prospects of young women who will come of age in the twenty-first century.

CHAPTER ONE

The Body's New Timetable

How the Life Course of American Girls Has Changed

Photos on p. I: *(left)* Permission of the author; *(right)* permission of Jane DeWalt Jones.

In 1808, when eleven-year-old Susanna Adams began to menstruate, it was a shock, and a matter of deep concern, because of her age. At the time, Susanna lived in Quincy, Massachusetts, with her paternal grandparents, John and Abigail Adams, the former president and his wife. "She may properly be called an out-siz'd girl," Abigail Adams told Susanna's mother, who was far away in Utica, New York. "She is already as tall as her cousin Louisa, and almost as large *and a woman* tho not yet 12 years old [emphasis in original]. All these things are a disadvantage to her," the anxious grandmother observed, because she lacks "maturity and discretion" despite her mature appearance.[1]

When Abigail Adams expressed her concern about the gap between her granddaughter's biological development and her intellectual development, menstruating eleven-year-olds were extremely unusual. In the early nineteenth century, menarche—first menstruation—typically occurred at fifteen or sixteen, a pattern that explains the former First Lady's surprise. Today, however, the average age is just over twelve.

As a result, contemporary girls have very different expectations for their bodies than did girls who grew up in Susanna Adams's day. "I got my period today! I'm so happy," Sarah Compton wrote in her diary in 1982. "It's weird to be bleeding," she reported, "[and] it seems like it took forever. Carla said I was a late bloomer. *Thirteen is kinda late,* I admit [emphasis added]."[2]

Menarche's new timetable demonstrates the power of the socioeconomic environment to shape something as "fixed" as the human body. In certain environments—including many societies in the past and some poor countries today—malnutrition and disease inhibit menarche and regular menstrual periods. Young women begin to menstruate early only where living conditions generate better diets and a decline in infectious diseases. Both of these factors contribute to making larger, healthier girls, a process that was already in motion by 1900. American girls today are appreciably larger than they were eighty or even thirty years ago. Size is important because a young woman must have a certain level of stored, easily metabolized energy in the form of body fat in order to start menstruation, and she also needs to attain a certain degree of skeletal growth, especially in pelvic size.[3]

Although most people think of the biology of the human body as relatively static from one generation to the next, the young female body has in fact changed over time. Today, girls follow a new biological timetable as well as a new social timetable. Not only do they menstruate earlier than they did a century ago, but they also have sexual intercourse at a younger age. The average age at first intercourse today is just under sixteen, a fact that suggests how changing values have also transformed the experience of female adolescence. At the end of the last century, in the 1890s, a middle-class American girl was likely to menstruate at fifteen or sixteen and be a blushing virgin when she married in her early twenties. But by the 1990s, a girl of the same social class is likely to be sexually active before the age at which her great-great-grandmother had even begun to menstruate.[4]

Menarche's new timetable is problematic on two levels. Although girls are healthier and mature earlier, there has been no parallel acceleration in their emotional and cognitive skills, such as the capacity to think abstractly, make judgments, or move beyond egocentric—that is, self-centered—thinking. Many young women today may look mature at age twelve or thirteen, but they still think in ways that are essentially childlike. In addition, our society makes no special effort to help girls deal with the lag between their biological and their intellectual development. Although early maturation is known to increase vulnerability to all kinds of psychological and social problems, such as depression and association with older age groups (a tendency that leads to early sexual activity as well as to drug and alcohol abuse), young women are less protected and less nurtured than they were a century ago.[5]

The way girls negotiate menarche is determined by cultural values as well as biology. A hundred years ago, thinking about menarche and menstruation was muddled by inadequate knowledge, rigid ideas about the proper roles of men and women, and a dash of ethnocentrism. Because menarche seemed to announce suddenly both sexuality and reproduction, it was considered a threat to the virtue of young girls. This sense of danger motivated all kinds of protective responses—some of which seem harsh and repressive today. Yet however prudish and "uptight" the Victorians were, our ancestors had a deep commitment to girls that we need to revisit as we look for ways to deal with the implications of the new timetable that is remaking the life course of American girls.

An Ovulatory Revolution

By 1900, a dramatic rise in the standard of living in the United States had had an impact on the bodies of girls, particularly those born into the expanding middle class. In the past, women menstruated infrequently because of repeated pregnancies, breast-feeding, malnourishment, and disease. But by the mid-nineteenth century, affluent American women began to experience more ovulatory cycles during a lifetime. The formula now seems fairly simple: families became more affluent; their children were better nourished and healthier, which meant their bodies developed earlier; young people could afford to attend high school or college, so they married later; thus women gave birth to fewer children—and had more periods.[6]

This "ovulatory revolution" occurred in tandem with an equally important American economic and social revolution. After the Civil War, adolescent girls were not as essential to the household economy as they had been before the war, when they were still needed to tend younger siblings and assist in household manufacturing. By the 1870s and 1880s, there was a dramatic increase in goods produced outside the home, opportunities for women in higher education expanded greatly, and some women began to enter professions that challenged the status quo in terms of relations between the sexes. These changes, plus the fact that there were more single women between the ages of fifteen and twenty-four than ever before, precipitated a national crisis over the issue of what girls should do.[7] Many physicians and middle-class parents worried about the consequences of the new opportunities, and they asked some questions that seem ridiculous today: Can young women do intellectual work, menstruate, and also remain healthy? Can the brain and the ovaries work simultaneously? Their concerns about the health consequences of female education mirrored what the Victorians knew, or didn't know, about female biology.

Victorian Ideas About Menarche: Ovarian Determinism

Even among educated medical men, menstruation was a mystery. In the 1870s, Dr. Albert F. King, a professor of medicine at Columbian University in Washington, D.C., actually claimed that menstrual bleeding was something "new." According to King, women's natural state was pregnancy, and menstruation became regularized—what he called a "fixed habit"—only as a result of higher education, later marriage, and deliberate family limitation, all things he considered "cultural interference" connected to modern life. King was correct about the link between improved material conditions and menstrual regularity, but his peculiar proposition that menstruation was new—and pathological—set off a hot debate: Were periods a sign of disease, as King claimed, or a function as natural as urination and defecation?[8]

As late as 1904, G. Stanley Hall, the Clark University psychologist who is considered the architect of modern adolescence, admitted: "Precisely what menstruation is, is not very well known." Hall confessed that he was uncertain whether the monthly period was analogous to estrus—what we call "heat" in animals. Menstruation remained an enigmatic internal process until at least the 1920s, when Edgar Allen, a professor at Washington University in St. Louis, first demonstrated the existence and the effects of estrogen through studies of mice. Over the next fifteen years, the role of hormonal stimuli in the menstrual cycle was finally established.[9] Until then, most doctors adhered to the idea that menstruation was normal, not pathological, and that "nerve stimulation" provoked activity in the ovaries and uterus. The same physicians who regarded "monthlies" as natural also considered the reproductive organs the primary determinant of female health and well-being. According to Victorian medicine, the ovaries—not the brain—were the most important organ in a woman's body.[10]

The most persuasive spokesperson for this point of view was Dr. Edward Clarke, a highly regarded professor at Harvard Medical School, whose popular book *Sex in Education; Or, A Fair Chance for the Girls* (1873) was a powerful statement of the ideology of "ovarian determinism." In a series of case studies drawn from his clinical practice, Clarke described adolescent women whose menstrual cycles, reproductive capacity, and general health were all ruined, in his opinion, by inattention to their special monthly demands, which he called their new "periodicity." Clarke argued against higher education because he believed women's bodies were more complicated than men's; this difference meant that young girls needed time and ease to develop, free from the drain of intellectual activity. Clarke's frightening portraits of girls whose lives went wrong in adolescence all pointed to menarche as the critical moment when a female life could easily be shipwrecked on the shoals of either too much learning or learning of the wrong kind.[11]

Today we know that most girls do not immediately develop a regular cycle, and that there is considerable individual variation, but Victorian doctors, like Edward Clarke, revered menstrual regularity, expecting it to appear from the start. Regular monthlies were taken to be the consummate sign of good health and a predictor of future motherhood; late or deficient periods were regarded as a symptom of potential disease, such as tuberculosis. Clarke used these medical ideas to justify his conservative point of view about higher education for women. Developing girls, he said, were physically and emotionally damaged by any educational challenge that drew energy to the brain and away from the ovaries. Instead of attending high school or college, the time between menarche and marriage should be spent at home learning domestic skills, such as making beds and sewing, which encouraged the essential "rhythmic periodicity" of women. Clarke advised parents of girls to make the establishment of regular periods the highest priority in the adolescent years, and female advice writers absorbed and repeated his words: "One rule should be absolute in every home. The mother should keep her daughter with her, and near her, until the turning point between childhood and girlhood is safely passed and regularity of habits is established."[12]

This kind of thinking elevated the importance of menarche as a life event. If a girl's reproductive life did not start correctly, it was believed that she was doomed to ill health and debility. Therefore, the age at which menarche occurred began to assume a great deal of importance. Most people, even the authoritative Dr. Clarke, were uncertain about what accounted for individual differences in timing of the onset of menarche. In their professional journals, nineteenth-century physicians explored these issues: Why is it that some girls menstruate before others? Is there an ideal age?

In order to answer these questions, doctors collected and published all kinds of information about the natural history of women, drawn from Western Europe, the Middle East, Africa, the Orient, and the Caribbean.[13] These reports were evaluated for what they revealed about the relative influence on menarche of factors such as race, climate, latitude, social conditions, season of the year, and even hair color. Some people claimed that city girls entered puberty before country girls, that young women were more likely to get their period for the first time in summer than in winter, and that brunettes menstruated before blondes. And many subscribed to the view that both "Negro" girls and "Jewesses" menstruated early because they hailed originally from warm climes where sexuality was likely to be more primitive and precocious. (White southern belles in the United States were somehow excluded from this formulation.)

In the Victorian mind, age at menarche came to be regarded as a marker of the moral quality of a civilization rather than as a sign of economic conditions. Instead of viewing lowered age as an outgrowth of material well-being, as we know it to be, nineteenth-century Americans developed a very different idea: the lower the age, the more libidinous or sexually licentious the society, nation, or race; the higher the age, the more "civilized." As a result, middle-class Victorians were not happy to have menarche appear too early in their own daughters, and they did what they could to put it off. Fearful of what early menarche symbolized, some parents, and even doctors, tried to stop the process by restricting a girl's intake of foods that were considered sexually "stimulating," such as cloves, pickles, and meat.[14]

After 1870, the women's foreign missionary crusade became a powerful vehicle for the idea that in "heathen" lands, menarche led immediately to marriage. In thousands of church-related groups, women and their daughters read and discussed reports from the field about "girlless villages," where the practice of child marriage allegedly forced very young girls into harsh relationships with unfeeling husbands and their kin. These simplistic, and sometimes lurid, ethnographic reports were designed to stimulate charitable donations to the foreign missions, but they also fired up the resolve of American women on the subject of keeping their own daughters innocent and safe as long as possible. Doctors supported this as a worthy goal, arguing that early marriage was a mistake because pelvic development was incomplete until age twenty—a view many physicians still hold. Influential men, such as Edward William Bok, editor of the *Ladies' Home Journal,* said that sexual initiation "at the dawn of sex consciousness"—meaning menarche—was a "primitive" practice.[15]

As a result of these ideas and discussions, most Americans came to believe that a hallmark of Christian civilization was its ability to nurture and protect girlhood innocence: in effect, to guarantee a safe time between menarche and marriage, when girls would be sexually inactive. This principle influenced Victorian mothers in their dealings with developing daughters, and it animated countless community efforts to monitor and supervise young women in single-sex groups designed to promote innocence and purity.

Reaching for Mother—But Not Always Getting Her Help

When adult women recall their sexual maturation, their memories are almost always conveyed in a common language—in terms of reaching for Mother. Emma Goldman, a well-known nineteenth-century socialist and anarchist, "called for her mother" when the pain of her first period struck. At age thirteen, Simone de Beauvoir, the founder of modern feminism, shyly took her mother "into her confidence" when she spoiled her nightdress unexpectedly. And late-blooming Audre Lorde, the prolific African-American poet and lesbian activist, was pleased to "break the news to mother" when she finally saw blood on her underwear the summer she was fifteen.[16]

Yet despite the need to connect with the female parent at the moment of menarche, there is historical evidence that American mothers have not always provided the emotional support girls wanted or the sound practical information they needed. The notion of a lack of communication between the generations began to appear in the mid- to late nineteenth century, at about the same time young women lost their central role in the domestic economy and began to spend more time outside the home, either in classrooms as students or in factories as workers.

Earlier, in the eighteenth century, young women learned about the coming of their menstrual "flowers" from their mothers, sisters, female relatives, and neighbors, all of whom were bound together by a common biology. In this single-sex community of family and kin, developing girls learned about their bodies and about the trials they faced as women in pregnancy and delivery. Childbirth then was predominantly a female experience, orchestrated by women in a social atmosphere that allowed skilled midwives, as well as the pregnant woman, to determine the pace of the delivery. In the Colonial era, most young women had probably seen births—both animal and human—and they often were nearby when someone they knew had a baby.[17]

But in the nineteenth century, most Americans, not just women, became more repressed—or "uptight"—about bodily functions, including sex. In the eighteenth century, for example, Americans accepted their own sexuality: frequent "congress" between husband and wife was considered healthy, and large families were the norm. But by the time of the Civil War, Americans worried that too much sex—even marital sex—was unhealthy for husband as well as wife. Smaller families became economically and emotionally desirable, and higher standards of personal decorum required control over bodily functions and sounds (such as belching and flatulence) that had been acceptable in earlier eras.[18]

In this environment, women had a harder time talking with their daughters about what happens to the female body. In 1852, Edward John Tilt, a physician known for his pioneering work in the field of obstetrics and gynecology, reported that out of every one thousand American girls, approximately 25 percent were totally unprepared for menarche. Many were frightened, he said, and thought they were wounded.[19] For at least a hundred years after Tilt, all kinds of observers—physicians, educators, and women themselves—lamented the fact that so many adolescents did not know what was happening to them because their mothers failed to provide adequate information. While we know from modern psychological studies that children do not always absorb everything they hear, particularly if it is unconnected to their own experience, "My Mother Never Told Me" is too pervasive a story in American culture to be ignored.[20]

So long as young women stayed at home in the bosom of their own families, their lack of preparation for menarche really did not show. But in the last two decades of the nineteenth century, when significant numbers of girls entered high schools and colleges, it became apparent that many were proceeding through adolescence without information about their own bodies. At Cornell, one of the new coeducational universities founded after the Civil War, Professor Burt Wilder, a zoologist and author of books for young people, marveled that parents could send young women of sixteen or seventeen away to a university without telling them about menstruation and the "generative function." (In this era, it was not uncommon to begin to menstruate in mid- to late adolescence.) Wilder cried out for more parental instruction, claiming that many college girls thought the first menses was a hemorrhage.[21]

In one of the best-selling advice books of this era, *Eve's Daughters; Or Common Sense for Maid, Wife, and Mother,* author Marion Harland decried the "criminal reserve" and "pseudo-delicacy" that kept mothers from preparing their girls for menstruation. Harland was no radical or sexual progressive; in "real" life she was Mary Virginia Hawes Terhune, the wife of a Presbyterian minister, mother of six, and a stalwart in terms of charitable parish duties. (One of her sons was Albert Payson Terhune, who became the author of popular dog stories.) Yet this proper Christian matron was critical of the ways in which generations of American women had practiced "mistaken modesty" about the body. In her popular 1882 book, she told a personal story about the way in which her own maternal grandmother and mother, then an adolescent, used to read together from romantic novels "thick with seduction," such as the late-eighteenth-century favorites *Clarissa* and *Pamela.* But as her youthful mother listened, keeping her hands busy making lace and tambour bed hangings, her grandmother said nothing to her own daughter about the physical transformation that was nearly at hand. Despite the suggestive nature of the stories, she apparently "never lisped to the growing girl a word relative to the perils of her sex and age." And when the inevitable "crisis arrived," Harland explained disapprovingly, her beloved grandmother alluded to it only distantly, as one of those things that are "not convenient to be spoken of."[22]

Reports like this were everywhere at the end of the nineteenth century. "I have met numbers of women and some of them young who knew nothing of their coming 'course' until they were upon them," explained Mrs. E. R. Shepherd, another late-nineteenth-century advice writer. One girl in particular told her: "It has taken me nearly a lifetime to forgive my mother for sending me away to boarding school without telling me about it." But the problem existed even among girls who lived at home in close proximity to their mothers. Helen Kennedy's 1895 study of Boston high school girls revealed that 60 percent were ignorant at the time of menarche. Over 25 percent of the college women surveyed by Dr. Clelia Mosher at Stanford University between 1892 and 1920 were totally unprepared; another 50 percent had some slight knowledge, meaning that they had been alerted to the prospect of bleeding and knew the names of some of the reproductive organs.

The words of one Stanford woman said it all: "[Although] my mother was a physician, [she] refused to instruct me when I asked questions. I remember well the first time I asked a question. She told me I would read books about it when I was older and I never asked again." Another responded that her mother told her about the facts of menstruation but simultaneously "taught her that such things were not talked about [and] also not thought of." By all accounts, the mother-daughter dialogue was a painful process characterized by great awkwardness and pervasive maternal reserve.[23]

Today, the "buttoned lips" of these earlier American mothers seem like a sad abdication of maternal responsibility and a clear indication of Victorian sexual repression. But this may be just another form of "mother blaming" that does not recognize how women in the past thought about their maternal role. In late-nineteenth-century America, many well-meaning middle-class mothers thought they were protecting their daughters' virtue by saying little about sex and the body until they absolutely had to. Their reticence was related to the fact that many daughters were menstruating earlier and marrying later than ever before. And most young women were beginning to choose their own spouses, in the name of romantic love, rather than defer to parental wishes or family priorities as girls had done in the past.[24]

From the perspective of a middle-class parent, then, prolonging the time between menarche and marriage increased the prospect of sexual danger. Thus, *suppression* of sexuality was considered absolutely necessary to the healthy development of both the mind and the body of the adolescent girl.[25] (This is in stark contrast to our contemporary view, informed by the theories of Sigmund Freud, that expression of sexuality is both natural and necessary for a healthy adolescence.) By the late nineteenth century, few middle-class mothers were reading seduction novels with their daughters, the way Mrs. Terhune's grandmother did. In fact, they were increasingly vigilant about all kinds of books, or any form of stimulation, that encouraged girls to experience their sexuality. Because knowledge about menstruation was considered the first step on the slippery slope to loss of innocence, many Victorian mothers simply avoided the subject altogether, believing it was in the best interest of their daughters.

The Protective Umbrella: The Support of Single-Sex Groups

If one way to prolong innocence was to say nothing that might stimulate thoughts or feelings about the body, another was to actively promote character development through wholesome reading, charitable works, and social activities, all under the supervision of responsible women of appropriate class and religious background. In the late nineteenth century, this impulse to support and nurture the character of female adolescents led to a vast organizational complex of single-sex groups all devoted to the common mission of keeping girlhood wholesome and chaste.

In the heyday of the protective system, between the 1880s and the 1920s, thousands of middle-class girls between the ages of ten and eighteen spent a portion of each week in organizations whose names many of us still recognize: the Girl Scouts, the Camp Fire Girls, and the Young Women's Christian (or Hebrew) Association. There were also many other organizations that are now extinct: the Girls' Friendly Society, the Life Saving Guards of the World, the Junior Daughters of the King, the Girl Reserves, the Order of the Rainbow, and the Federation of Girls' Leagues, which together served tens of thousands of girls, drawn from both the middle and the working classes.[26]

In the late nineteenth century, most of these groups offered a heavy dose of religious morality, and many were more interested in soliciting young women to do church work than anything else. Yet many organizations, such as the popular Girls' Friendly Society, sponsored by the Episcopal church, worked across class lines and developed goals that suited both privileged and working-class girls; according to its constitution, the purpose of the organization was "to uphold the Christian standard of honor and morality, and to encourage purity of life, dutifulness to parents, faithfulness to employers, and thrift."[27]

Then, beginning in the 1880s, the massive Woman's Christian Temperance Union took an activist, reform position on the issue of protecting adolescent girls, launching a nationwide effort to raise the age of consent for sexual relations (which was as low as ten in some states). The statutory rape laws that emerged from this campaign were heralded by women and reformers as a way of protecting innocent young girls from the vices of adult men. All of this concern—on the local and state levels—about preserving the sexual innocence of younger women resulted in a great deal of community supervision of the physical and social development of girls. Some of it was undoubtedly repressive and unkind; some of it was not. Most of all, this "protective umbrella" meant that girls had many projects—other than their own bodies—to keep them busy and engaged.[28]

Girls found camaraderie and cooperation under the protective umbrella as often as they found control or coercion. In addition to providing opportunities to experiment with dramatics, handicrafts, nature study, literature, and music, these groups forged a sense of community with girls of similar social classes and religious denominations. In adolescence, girls typically want a group identity, so their sense of belonging was enhanced with club paraphernalia, such as pins, badges, and banners, all of which were worn proudly and used to decorate bedrooms and school notebooks. Members also profited from getting to know their leaders, usually adult or young adult women who were not their own relatives. Even when the leaders were decidedly moralistic, or overly concerned about decorum, the attention girls received from these older women helped them feel special, valued, and safe.

Intergenerational Mentoring

The success of the protective umbrella had to do with intergenerational mentoring. Many of the women who worked with adolescent girls in the 1890s were not very old themselves. Typically, young female teachers, ranging from their late teens through their twenties, served as leaders and advisers for chapters of all kinds of organizations, including Bible study groups, the YWCA, and literary societies. This system led to widespread social interaction between girls in adolescence and young women in their twenties, a pattern which both sides seem to have profited from and also enjoyed.

In their diaries, Victorian girls wrote repeatedly about the informal mentoring they received from young women teachers who were different from their mothers yet more mature than themselves and, often, independent. These young teachers, who were usually graduates of normal schools and women's colleges, were always referred to as "Miss," but that formality did not preclude meaningful interaction and also a great deal of fun. In a diary written while she was in high school in Pasadena, Lou Henry (Hoover) mentioned her young women teachers more often than her mother, father, or sister. In some cases, a specific teacher encouraged an intellectual interest, such as "Miss Monks and I had quite a zoological conversation during my vacant hour, and I am going to learn to 'analyze' birds." In another case, a well-liked young woman teacher acted as a sounding board and confidante for Lou and her close friends: "After music, Edith, Marion, Miss Gardner and I staid in the Assembly Hall for an hour and discussed everything (and everybody) thoroughly. After that [we] had an impromptu banquet on the front balcony."[29]

Adult women were the most important part of the protective umbrella that spread over school as well as extracurricular activities. Whether Christian or Jew, black or white, volunteer or professional, most women in this era shared the ethic that older women had a special responsibility to the young of their sex. This kind of mentoring was based on the need to protect all girls, not just one's own daughters, from premature sexuality and manipulation at the hands of men. Although the ethic generated all kinds of censorious directives about sexual behavior and its consequences, much of which was directed at girls from "the other side of the tracks," it also gave a cooperative and expansive tone to American community life. In towns and cities across the United States, middle-class matrons and young adult women, in the time before they married, performed countless mundane acts of guidance and supervision, such as showing girls how to sew, embroider, or arrange flowers, or helping them to organize collections of food and clothing for impoverished families. In all of these settings, there were chattering girls along with concerned adults, bound together by both gender and common projects. Of course, not all girls were kept from stepping off the "path of righteousness," yet there was still a consensus that adolescent girls deserved special attention and consideration because of their biology.[30]

The American Girl: Energetic or Enfeebled?

In the Victorian scheme of things, women were believed to be most lovely in adolescence, so long as they were not tainted or debased by loss of innocence. And American girls were supposed to be the loveliest of all, precisely because of the protections that Christian, as opposed to "heathen," civilization afforded them. In parlors across the land, young women and their families gathered around pianos to sing popular songs that reinforced the connection alleged to exist between the superior condition of life in the United States and the fine appearance of American girls:

O! The Maids of dear Columbia,
So beautiful and fair,
With eyes likes diamonds sparkling,
And richly flowing hair,
Their hearts are light and cheerful,
And their spirits ever gay,
The Maids of dear Columbia,
How beautiful are they!

By the turn of the twentieth century, there was a veritable industry in songs, poems, books, and popular illustrations that extolled the beauty, virtue, and vitality of the American girl. Drawings by Charles Dana Gibson, Howard Chandler Christy, and Harrison Fisher, along with poetry by James Whitcomb Riley, all contributed to making the adolescent girl an icon representing American exceptionalism and material progress.[31]

But underlying this romantic imagery was a different picture, one of a sickly American girl, painted in elaborate detail by American medicine. At the very moment that the ideal "Gibson girl" reigned supreme, many physicians claimed that female adolescents were pallid, nervous, weak, lethargic, and enfeebled. "Instead of the beautiful, blooming creature that she should be by nature," explained George Whythe Cook in an address to a Washington, D.C., medical society, "she is pale, wan, an anemic weakling, poorly prepared for the great change that is to transform her into a procreating woman." In a widely quoted 1900 presidential address to the American Gynecological Society, George Engelmann concluded that "the condition of the American girl at the present day is not what it should be under the unusually favorable conditions of her life."[32]

Which view was correct? Were American girls generally energetic or enfeebled? By 1900, most physicians were reporting that

American girls were menstruating earlier than their mothers—a clear sign of improved general health. Yet this was a reality doctors were often reluctant to admit. In their professional journals and lectures, they now acknowledged that nurture was more important than nature in determining how girls made the critical transition from puberty into womanhood. And this meant they could link almost everything that was wrong with adolescent girls to "the predominating influence of [their] milieu."

Just like Dr. King and Dr. Clarke before him, George Engelmann, in an address at the turn of the century, zeroed in on institutions of higher learning, blaming them for anemia, constipation, menstrual problems, and even earlier menarche. Engelmann even had his own version of a "college guide." He claimed that young women who attended the best private schools—such as those that came to be known as the Seven Sisters—menstruated earlier than those who went only to high school or training schools for nursing or teaching. The difference was due not only to greater affluence among the students but also to the select school's capacity to generate mental and social stimulation that "reverberated in the genital plexus."[33]

Victorian theories like these were obviously shaped by a lack of enthusiasm for women's entrance into higher education and the professions. They were also crafted in response to an important demographic reality: the proportion of childless couples in the United States was on the rise after 1870. Physicians did not want to believe that childlessness could be voluntary; instead, they linked it to menstrual pathology in schoolgirls, pathology caused by careless inattention to "rhythmic periodicity." Despite their socially conservative intent, these Victorian theories about menstruation did reflect some understanding of the role of socioeconomic factors in determining age at menarche. What most people failed to see, however, was the way in which the United States—because of its heterogeneous population and varied geography—was a natural laboratory for investigating the declining age of menarche and its cause.[34]

We now know, on the basis of historical records kept by public health officials and physicians, that the age at which menstruation begins has declined over the past 150 years in both the United States and Western Europe.[35] In the twentieth century, it has become increasingly rare for girls in these countries to begin menstruation at seventeen or eighteen, but the lower limit of the range—nine or ten—still holds. This means that there is no need to worry about precocious menstruators of seven or eight: there seems to be a biological floor that limits the decline in age, and authorities confirm that the downward progression actually came to a halt about thirty years ago.[36]

Although the Victorians liked to think that young women remained "girls" longer in America than anywhere else, this was not, in fact, the case. Young women actually mature physiologically more quickly on American soil. After over a century of immigration, it is clear that within a given ethnic group, daughters menstruate earlier in the United States than in the "old country." Moreover, when they are raised under similar living conditions, girls of Jewish, Gentile, African, Italian, and Japanese descent all begin to menstruate at essentially the same early age.[37] This "leveling influence" is an important feature of our multicultural society, and it gives a new twist to any discussion of what it means to come of age in the 1990s. Regardless of class or race, our girls come to biological maturity earlier than their grandmothers, and they do so in a way that is vastly different from that of earlier generations.

Ironically, the Victorians understood early menarche to be a problem, but they were wrong in their analysis of its cause. The historical trend to earlier sexual maturation is not a sign of immorality; it is a marker of economic progress and of an environment where young women can develop free from the ravages of disease. But this "good news" carries with it some responsibilities that need to be understood: early biological maturity is not accompanied by a parallel increase in intellectual maturity, and that means that supervision and support in early adolescence become even more critical.

In the Victorian era, most middle-class people believed that adolescent girls deserved special attention and support because of their biology. Yet they failed to talk to their daughters openly about sex or the body. Today, Victorian strategies for coping with adolescence seem old-fashioned and sexist because they cast young women solely in terms of their reproductive potential, and they left girls ignorant of and unprepared for sexual maturation. Yet we need to acknowledge that our ancestors' pervasive (if largely unspoken) concern about the bodies of adolescent girls was an impetus for a powerful network of social support that was a functional hallmark of American life well into the twentieth century. Although that structure is not entirely gone—I still buy Girl Scout cookies from shy girls of nine or ten—the older model of single-sex community groups for women and girls has lost its salience for most Americans. And so has our commitment to statutory rape laws, which once established clear, explicit prohibitions against sex with young girls.[38] We are more accepting of the influence of peers now; we have less time to spend with girls; and we no longer regard chastity as a moral absolute, even for the young. For all of these reasons, the Victorian protective umbrella has been folded.

In 1900, Americans claimed, with some justification, that girls in the United States were better off than girls anywhere else in the world. Today, such a claim seems empty, given our well-known problems with girls of all social classes, and comparative data show that adolescent girls actually fare better in Germany, Sweden, and the Netherlands, where youthful sexuality is less problematic because of more open, honest programs of sex education.[39] The umbrella of protection created by the Victorians to shelter sexually maturing girls had many problems, to be sure, but it eased the rite of passage in ways that adolescents today greatly need—and only rarely receive. Instead of beginning an interlude of special guidance and support from other women, menarche today is just another step that moves girls deeper into a consumer culture that seduces them into thinking that the body and sexual expression are their most important projects.

CHAPTER TWO

Sanitizing Puberty: The American Way to Menstruate

Photos on p. 27: *(left)* Permission of National Japanese American Historical Society; *(right)* permission of Peggy Poon and Robert Barker, Cornell University Photography.

In the twentieth century, American girls learned to menstruate in a clean, modern way that was vastly different from the experience of their Victorian counterparts. Instead of spending days on a couch with hot flatirons to ease their cramps, contemporary girls are generally active and energetic during their periods. When they start menstruating, modern girls routinely reach for a sanitary napkin even before they reach for their mothers. Although the shift from inactivity to activity and the change from homemade to commercial products generally meant greater freedom for women, there has been an unintended consequence for American girls and their development. At the moment when they begin to menstruate, American girls and their mothers typically think first about the external body—what shows and what doesn't—rather than about the emotional and social meaning of the maturational process.

The contemporary response to menstruation actually follows

a culturally constructed script with a particular history. Over the course of the past century, there has been a shift in the way menstruation is viewed and handled—a shift that has certainly made domestic life easier for women but has also contributed to the difficulties adolescent girls at the end of the twentieth century have with their bodies and sexuality. Instead of seeing menarche as a marker of an important internal change in a girl—specifically, her new capacity for reproduction—modern mothers typically stress the importance of outside appearances for their daughters: keeping clean, avoiding soiled clothes, and purchasing the right "equipment." Hygiene, not sexuality, is the focus of most maternal discussions with girls who have just started their periods.

The script that we follow in late-twentieth-century America involves mothers, doctors, and the producers of new technologies, all of whom have collaborated over the past hundred years to produce a distinctly American menstrual experience that stresses personal hygiene over information about adult womanhood or female sexuality. In the 1990s, the sanitary products industry is a more-than-$2 billion-a-year business, built on scientific and popular beliefs about personal cleanliness as well as changes in contemporary women's lives: earlier menarche, fewer pregnancies, and later menopause—all of which foster more periods and more sales. The way we menstruate in America today not only affects the economy, it also contributes to the way in which adolescent girls make the body into an intense project requiring careful scrutiny and constant personal control.[1]

A Hygienic Crisis Rather Than a Maturational Event

In the 1870s, fourteen-year-old Alice Stone Blackwell noted the onset of a menstrual period—"M.P. number 3," she wrote—but then she rested for the day and drank soothing tansy tea while she "read and ached." Alice was the daughter of feminist Lucy Stone, who insisted on keeping her own name despite her marriage to Alice's father, social reformer Henry Blackwell. Although Alice was exposed to many liberal, progressive ideas, she never said a word in her diary about how she coped with the problem of personal hygiene during her periods.[2]

By the 1950s, the "menstrual talk" of American girls was laced with concerns about personal hygiene. Unlike young women in the Victorian era, girls of this generation were routinely prepared for menstruation in a number of ways that became commonplace after World War II—conversations with mothers and peers, as well as reading materials and corporate-sponsored films provided at home and at school. These experiences provided instruction in female anatomy and information about the availability of commercial, mass-produced sanitary napkins, but not about the emotions or sensations that were part of a girl's new sexuality. As a result, when twelve-year-old Ruth Teischman got her period in 1959, she immediately "put on a napkin and told her mother," in exactly that order.

In the months ahead, Ruth Teischman continued a normal round of school activities, phone conversations with her friends, disagreements with her mother, and earnest ruminations about death, boys, and blackheads. But she also watched the calendar carefully and made notations about her flow and the number of sanitary napkins that she used: "Today I got my period for the fourth time. It is very light and black. But I think it is light because it's just begun and will get heavier later. I hope so. Not that I like it. I don't like it at all. I just want to have it a long time and heavy so I can have something good to talk about."[3] Among Ruth's girlfriends in suburban Queens, New York, heavy periods had a certain cachet because they required many napkins; this was alleged to be a sure sign of maturity.

Ruth Teischman's reaction to menstruation says a great deal about the direction of change in the American girl's experience of her sexually maturing body. Because she had been coached on the logistics of what came to be called sanitary protection, Ruth knew exactly what to do. Menarche had a certain drama for her: it occurred suddenly; it involved a display of blood; and it required, above all else, an immediate and reliable response in order to protect against public disclosure. In this respect, Ruth really was typical: clinical studies demonstrate that in the United States today both pre- and postmenarcheal girls regard menarche as a hygienic crisis rather than as a maturational event.[4]

For contemporary girls, menstruation implies new concerns about hygiene, but it does not imply fertility or reproduction as it did in the Victorian era. Ruth Teischman's attention was riveted on what her body was doing at the moment, not on being an adult woman or becoming a mother. In the modern world, the adolescent's normal concerns about spotting, staining, and smelling during menstruation routinely translate into purchases of sanitary products—purchases so ordinary that most of us never even question them. Girls who grow up in the modern world of sanitary protection learn early how to keep a menstruating body under control.

In contemporary American society, menarche has become more of an economic ritual than a social one. The Asante of

Ghana place a menarcheal girl beneath an umbrella and then sing and dance in her honor; the Yuork Indians of California expect her to isolate herself from her family. Americans, by contrast, generally have no community rituals of initiation or exclusion. And yet this intimate biological event is marked in our own, distinctly American way. A century ago, mothers lengthened their daughters' skirts, or allowed them to put up their hair; today, American girls and their mothers characteristically head for the mall, where coming-of-age is acted out in purchases—such as bras, lipsticks, and high heels, or "grown-up" privileges such as ear piercing. We also know, from the reports of market researchers, that when American girls begin to menstruate, their mothers usually introduce them to their favorite brand of sanitary protection and that girls remain loyal to that brand, generally without much experimentation. At menarche, then, contemporary American girls establish a firm bond with the marketplace, facilitated by their mothers.[5]

The Medicalization of Menarche

The modern American menstrual script originated at the end of the nineteenth century, when attitudes about women's bodies began to change as a result of an important ideological seesaw: as the power of spiritual belief declined, the authority of medicine rose.

Although the menstrual process was still characterized by many religious people as one of the great wonders of nature, among the educated middle class, menarche and menstruation were less and less likely to be regarded simply as events ordained by God. There was an increasing realization that "monthly courses" were more than the punishment of Eve, and that there was some actual physiology involved, physiology that medical experts could teach laypeople—especially the mothers of adolescent girls.

American mothers had been told by influential Victorian doctors, such as Edward Clarke and George Engelmann, that there were multiple medical risks in store for girls whose mothers did not supervise them properly. The threat of having a beloved daughter become an invalid (or infertile) motivated the respect of many women for medical authority. Because most mothers did not understand the relevant biology and stammered over what to call their own (or their daughters') body parts, they were willing to turn to physicians for explanations of normal life experiences, including the growth and sexual development of their daughters.

The medicalization of menarche meant that, in the twentieth century, doctors shared with women the important job of socializing adolescent girls about their bodies. What physicians did not acknowledge, of course, was their own self-interest: by establishing themselves as experts in the management of menarche and menstruation, they enlarged the constituency for their services and filled their waiting rooms with women of a wider age range than ever before. Victorian physicians justified their intervention in this embarrassing, formerly female domain on the grounds that American mothers did not do their job. Convinced that many mothers did not tell their daughters about menstruation because they did not know how, doctors took an increased role in defining and treating menstruation at the same time middle-class women were more than willing to accept their expert help.[6]

Reading Her Way into Adulthood

In the Victorian era—when mothers feared "vulgar" information and felt inadequate about how to explain menstruation—many families relied on health and hygiene guides to teach their daughters what they could not say out loud. Many experts considered good books, monitored at home by sensitive middle-class mothers, the best way to teach girls about changes in their bodies. "I learned everything I knew from good sources and in a pure and sacred way," explained a young woman who came of age between 1890 and World War I. Apparently, this experience was typical: over half of the respondents in a survey at Stanford University learned about menstruation and reproduction through health and hygiene manuals that were given to them by their mothers, or via medical books read surreptitiously in libraries.[7] (Most women today recall educational pamphlets such as "You're a Young Lady Now" or "Very Personally Yours," which usually accompanied a box of sanitary napkins and were hidden in dresser drawers.)

But in the late nineteenth and early twentieth centuries, adults still worried about how to keep these menstrual discussions from moving on to graphic descriptions of intercourse, particularly among adolescent girls. "[We] would like to put books treating of these topics in the hands of [our] girls," said Mrs. Shepherd, a popular author of advice books for women. "There are plenty of medical works which present them well enough, but there are so many other themes introduced that [we] hesitate to give them the book at all."[8] Still, reading was always regarded as a better option than learning from peers, because "girl talk"—informal, social learning among peers—implied a coarser, rougher way of life associated with the working class and the poor.

By the turn of the twentieth century, learning about menstruation was still private and highly moralistic, but it was also more systematic and scientific. Middle-class girls were expected to acquire a basic anatomical vocabulary to describe their bodies and the menstrual process. As a result, their parents provided popular health books, usually written by doctors, that told the narrative story of how eggs are produced in the ovaries, released every twenty-eight to thirty days, and so on. There were also rules about how to behave at that "special time of the month," menstruation. This new "hygiene of puberty" was presented in a mix of scientific and romanticized language. Although doctors tried to teach the correct anatomical words, some authors continued to refer to the uterus, for example, as the "mother-room." These popular guides were also used to establish what was normal and what could go wrong, such as too much pain (dysmenorrhea), too much blood (menorrhagia), or no blood at all (amenorrhea). This catalog of pathology always had an implicit message: menstruation required medical as well as maternal management.[9]

In the work of bringing girls successfully into womanhood, the doctor (typically male) assumed the role of biomedical strategist, and the mother was his chief assistant. He applied scientific knowledge to the mysteries of the female body; her role was to monitor habits and behaviors that would affect blood flow and reproductive capacity, such as bathing, dress, and exercise. A good mother announced a litany of things to be avoided during menstruation: excessive exercise, hot and cold baths, wet feet. (The ever-popular "gym excuse" is a remnant of this idea that a girl has to be especially careful during menstruation.) These directives, which were repeated millions of times to millions of girls, encouraged American mothers to fixate on external matters of habit and behavior, such as cleanliness and school attendance, which were outside the day-to-day supervision of physicians, rather than on their daughter's most important internal changes—that is, what really happens to a girl as both her body and her mind grow into womanhood.

Mothers with a Sanitary Sensibility

Although doctors were considered "experts" about the physiology of menstruation, they left the dirty work to mothers. Mothers—not doctors—taught adolescent girls how to "fix themselves" in order to prevent displays of blood and soiled clothes. Most women at this time knew how to make something absorbent out of superfluous pieces of cotton or chambray, the kind found in the ever-present "rag bag." The best napkins were supposedly made from folded linen, as opposed to cotton, and they were "worn between the limbs." When they were soiled, they were left to soak for a few hours before washing, so that the same rags could be used again. Hygiene books were generally so polite that they avoided any mention of these intimate but essential matters.[10]

By the 1890s, however, homemade equipment was on the way out, at least among women with a certain "sanitary" sensibility and the pocketbook to go with it. Many middle-class women began to purchase gauze and cheesecloth to assemble their own pads, or they ordered mass-produced napkins through the Sears, Roebuck catalog. This behavioral change was stimulated by new scientific ideas about the sources of disease that had developed a few decades earlier. In the 1870s, Americans became conversant with Joseph Lister's concept of antisepsis and the idea that human waste, and even air and water, contained something alive and dangerous. In the 1880s, public health officials, motivated by the new germ theory, began to advocate antiseptic cleanliness of the house and the person. As a result, feminine washing and menstrual discharge were subjected to new hygienic standards. "Every part of the body [should be] as clean as the face," wrote Dr. Joseph H. Greer in his guide *The Wholesome Woman* (1902). At menstruation time, this meant that "the napkins should be changed at least every morning upon dressing and at night upon retiring." Greer's recommendation was based on the idea that absorption of blood was not wholesome, and that soiled napkins generated unpleasant odors, a sure sign of "noxious effluvia" and breeding bacteria.[11]

Menstrual blood, which had long been taboo, was now suspect on scientific grounds as a potential contaminant. Menstrual rags were considered dangerous, precisely because they facilitated a dangerous mixing of germs and gases in a warm place. Consequently, many middle-class women and their daughters began to use disposable napkins made of gauze and surgical cotton. Advertisers claimed that doctors endorsed them because of their antiseptic and absorbent properties, and they suggested that this new product would revolutionize the menstrual experience by eliminating heat and chafing. In a growing number of middle-class homes, American mothers were teaching their daughters that these commercially produced napkins were a personal necessity.[12]

In 1913, the American Medical Association (AMA) presented its formula for the correct mix of maternal nurturance and sanitary hygiene in "Daughter, Mother, and Father: A Story for Girls." This widely circulated pamphlet stands as a model of middle-class sensibilities in the early twentieth century and the *ideal* of preparedness.[13] I stress the word *ideal* precisely because there are so many indications that middle-class mothers, even in the twentieth century, did not talk with their daughters in the ways suggested by the AMA.

In an episode entitled "Life Problems," an imaginary family named Dawson began to prepare for the physical maturation of their thirteen-year-old daughter, Margaret. In this enlightened, middle-class household, both parents anticipated their daughter's need for preparation and spoke to each other about it. Mr. Dawson, conveniently, was a physician who had educated Margaret as a young girl about female anatomy and the function of the ovaries, but it was Mrs. Dawson who initiated the subject "which every girl should know, preferably from her own mother's lips."

In the cozy serenity of her sewing room, on a beautiful April day, Mrs. Dawson used the example of the lilacs outside her window to talk with Margaret about blooming and fading foliage. Borrowing from Edward Clarke, Mrs. Dawson spoke about cycles in nature and how they echoed the natural "periodicity" of women. Because she was concerned about her daughter's reaction to this heady information, the pace of the conversation was slow and deliberate; there was no maternal unease. Mrs. Dawson warned Margaret that "the sight of a stain on her garment" was the sign that she had "crossed the threshold from girlhood to womanhood." But she pointed out, in a reassuring manner, that staining was perfectly natural and that it happens to "all women in all lands." When Margaret asked nervously how much blood she could expect to lose, her mother assured her that it was only a few spoonfuls and, though periods may seem difficult at first, "they are your Creator's preparation of you for future motherhood." Margaret responded enthusiastically to this linkage to motherhood, proclaiming happily: "Oh, that's different. It isn't really a sickness at all then." (There was no mention of intercourse.) Three weeks later, when Margaret noticed a stain on her bedsheets, she immediately sought out her understanding and prescient mother. Mrs. Dawson put her arm around her daughter's waist and then showed her how the lower drawer of the dresser in her bedroom already held a plain canvas package containing two or three dozen disposable napkins. In the privacy of Margaret's bedroom, Margaret's mother offered instruction in the latest methods. "Here is the whole outfit," she explained. "Some girls wear little folded napkins made from old linen or cotton, but such napkins have to be washed. As a rule, the girl washes them herself. But by using thoroughly laundered cheesecloth and absorbent cotton, materials which a girl may get in any department store at a reasonable price, she is able to make for herself these little 'sanitary napkins' as we call them. They need not be washed; after they are soiled they are rolled up in paper and thrown into the furnace." In an appeal to her daughter's generational identity, she pointed out that these products were the wave of the future: they were used by smart high school and college girls, as well as young adult women in the business world.

Mrs. Dawson was right. American middle-class women were developing a heightened sensibility about issues of feminine hygiene. They found the new disposable napkins extremely desirable because they promised less work, more comfort, greater mobility, and a germ-free environment. The new hygiene also provided middle-class mothers with a safe script for their private conversations with their daughters. Instead of talking about the "curse of Eve" or "nerve stimulation" (which one could not see), they focused on the logistics of "sanitary protection."

In the twentieth century, intimate maternal conversations with daughters were more often than not about the use of a particular technology or product, rather than about sexuality or reproduction. For example, a striking 1927 ad for Lysol featured a concerned mother offering her brooding teenage daughter advice about sexuality—but in the form of a pamphlet. (At that time, Lysol was used for personal hygiene and not as a household cleaner, as it is today.) Maternal advice about the purchase and use of sanitary napkins, as well as other hygiene products, was certainly well intentioned and extremely useful, but it did have an unintended effect: it encouraged the idea that menarche was a matter of consumer decision making, and that coming-of-age was a process to be worked out in the marketplace rather than at home.

Badges of Status

Among working-class girls, especially those from immigrant families, sanitary napkins became a badge of Americanization. Before World War I, most working-class mothers did not have the money or the inclination to adopt commercially made products of the kind recommended by Mrs. Dawson. In immigrant homes, many young women wanted to adopt the new ways because they were easier, less cumbersome, and clearly the modern, scientific thing to do. But limited family budgets, as well as some old-world ideas, made the purchase of commercial products extremely difficult.

Because working-class mothers and daughters lived in such close proximity to one another, female biology announced itself around common washbasins and metal tubs. "Every once in a while when the washing would come up, you would see rags soaking. So after a while you would ask what that was all about," explained a woman who came of age in an immigrant family in Pittsburgh in the early twentieth century.[14] Watchful mothers sometimes monitored the family wash to see if a young daughter's "change" had come, or if an older daughter with a beau had regular cycles—a clear sign that she was not pregnant. Many mothers simply waited until they saw proof of menarche before they ventured any explanation or offered words of advice. One fourteen-year-old who knew nothing of menstruation and thought she was "hurt" treated her genitals with Mercurochrome and cotton until her stained underwear divulged her secret. Unlike Margaret Dawson, her menarche stimulated no special coddling, no lengthy scientific explanation, and no introduction to special "sanitary" products. Instead, she was provided with a rag to wrap around her bottom and sent directly to school.[15]

Instead of books, which were costly, working-class mothers left their daughters to pick up the information they needed at school or on the street. This was the case with Kate Simon, the popular writer, whose memoir of growing up in a polyglot ethnic neighborhood before World War I included a vivid description of how she learned about the mysteries of the female body. When she was only ten or eleven, Kate became chummy with some older girls who "knew everything." One of them, a twelve-year-old named Debby, told her about "shooting scum" (male ejaculation) and the way women used rags to catch the blood that allegedly came each month from having "the thighs separate from the lower belly." (At ten, Simon wondered how anyone who was butchered that way could survive more than one period.) Similarly, in rural Minnesota, Malvis Helmi learned about the female body from the whispers of older girls in the lavatory at her school. Fifty years later she could still recall the atmosphere of that particular, girl-dominated space: "[They always talked] just loud enough so we younger ones could hear them complaining—and bragging—about 'the monthlies' and 'Grandma coming to visit.' "[16]

Learning about womanhood probably was less private and more social among the working class because poor girls had more of an opportunity to mix with women of different ages at work, in the kitchen, or in a shared bedroom. Girls who developed early initiated others into the mysteries of womanhood. Irene, the daughter of Jewish immigrants in Pittsburgh, menstruated for the first time in 1912 at age thirteen. Although her Romanian-born mother told her nothing, she garnered information from a girlfriend at the Irene Kaufmann Settlement House: "[My friend] was mature, she was like a woman and she would tell me things that would just go over my head." When her periods came, Irene was able to take it "as a matter of course" because of what this friend had told her. "We didn't learn about [menstruation] at home," confirmed the daughter of an Austro-Hungarian coal miner. "We just had to learn it from each other."[17]

In every ethnic group, mothers seemed reluctant to talk, although the reasons differed. "We ashamed people. We don't tell mother nothing, mother no tell us," explained Mika, a Yugoslavian immigrant daughter, as she recalled her first menstruation at age fourteen. When her mother finally did talk, she offered a common religious explanation: "God made a woman that way. That's why we, every month, going to be sick, till you go into trouble."[18] Although Orthodox Judaism required special practices for menstruating women, such as the *mikvah* (a ritual bath to which Orthodox women go after a menstrual period), Jewish girls generally experienced the same lack of communication, and many, such as Emma Goldman and Kate Simon, remembered feeling shocked, or even insulted, by their mother's sudden ritualistic slap on the face at menarche, a gesture intended to protect against the difficulties of life as a woman.[19] Among African-Americans, silence also prevailed. According to Onnie Lee Logan, a midwife who grew up in rural Alabama: "Nobody told me one thing. Mother thought she was right in her own way for not lettin me know that. She put that outa my sight."[20]

In the Italian community, the high value put on female innocence and chastity meant that mothers tended to say very little to their daughters. Rose, born in Petilia, Italy, in 1892, came to Pittsburgh at age fourteen and married at age sixteen in 1908. Her first menstruation, however, occurred one week after her marriage: "I just got blood, that was it," she remembered many years later. Rose had been totally unprepared for both menstruation and sexual intercourse, but when she complained later in life, her mother justified her silence: "They say [we] weren't supposed to tell you."[21] Italian immigrants also resisted middle-class efforts to sanitize the menstrual experience. In fact, they worried about any intervention that would divert or interfere with menstrual blood. To the chagrin of physicians and health educators of the Progressive era, Italian mothers did not encourage their daughters to change their menstrual rags often. In their minds, a heavily stained napkin was a good sign, because it signified fertility and stimulated the blood flow.[22]

Although ideas from the Old World lingered, the immigrants' American-born daughters wanted New World bodies. In the process of assimilating to American mores and values, young women in many ethnic groups became disdainful of the menstrual practices of their mothers and grandmothers. They wanted to be like the young working women and college girls who made up the first mass market for disposable sanitary napkins—sold as Kotex and made from cellucotton by Kimberly-Clark.[23] However, because of the cost, some girls could not adopt modern sanitary protection. Well into the 1930s and 1940s, there were some American girls who had to make do with homemade protection. In 1945, when Lillian Petrillo got her first period, she was totally unprepared and her mother immediately supplied her with the kind of handmade "diapers" she and her three elder daughters always used. But after three cycles it was clear that homemade napkins gave Lillian a nasty rash, which caused Mrs. Petrillo to capitulate to her daughter's request for Kotex. Fifty years later, Lillian still felt triumphant: "[My mother] figured that was one expense she was going to have."[24]

For immigrants' daughters, it was extremely important to be "scientific" and "up-to-date" in menstruation as well as appearance. Girls born on American soil learned about modern hygiene at school, where sanitary napkins had become an article of faith. Because daughters were the primary conduit for bringing techniques of feminine hygiene into the immigrant home, public school teachers created situations that fostered a dialogue led by the daughter rather than by the mother. In 1911, after learning the physiology and hygiene of the pelvic organs from a papier-mâché female body, girls at Cleveland's Technical High School were required to take home and read out loud with their mothers nine typewritten sheets containing "the essential facts."[25] Of course, these "facts" included descriptions of commercial products that many immigrant mothers still regarded as luxuries. Daughters of immigrants understood, before their grandmothers and mothers did, that there was an American way to menstruate, and that it required participation in the larger consumer society.

Going Public

In the twentieth century, talk about menstruation became acceptable in certain public school settings, in girls' groups, and in magazines for women and girls. As a result of experience in World War I with venereal disease, physicians, social workers, and teachers embarked on a crusade to promote the moral health of American youth, a crusade in which many aspects of sexuality, including menarche and menstruation, were sanitized and openly discussed. Although there were conservative critics who worried about "decency" and feared that teachers were trying to usurp the mother's role, the men and women who made up the "social hygiene" movement agreed that "better a year too early than an hour too late," as far as sex information was concerned. As they argued over where menstruation should be taught—in high school biology, physiology, physical education, or home economics classes—they admitted that maternal initiation was now just a faded ideal. "No one can quite take the place of the mother in instructing her daughter in the simple and beautiful truths of reproductive life," physician Emil Novak wrote with nostalgia, but he also called sex education a "legitimate" enterprise, badly needed among American youth.[26]

The Girl Scouts of America (GSA) was one of the first groups to systematically teach menstruation to girls. By the 1920s, a scout in pursuit of the Health Winner Badge had to learn about the physiology of menstruation and also have a private talk with her troop leader about it. She was also required to tell her leader when she was menstruating, on the grounds that the older woman could help her avoid "overdoing it" and determine an appropriate level of activity. The leadership of the Girl Scouts recognized the difficulty of asking volunteer troop leaders to position themselves between the natural authority (the mother) and the professional expert (the physician, biology teacher, or nurse), but they also knew that some girls had no one else to turn to for information. As a result, GSA training materials highlighted information about the hygiene of the female body and utilized the most enlightened strategies for talking to girls about menstruation.[27]

In the effort to sell products, menstruation finally burst out of the closet in the 1920s when popular magazines, such as the *Ladies' Home Journal* and *Good Housekeeping*, began to run ads for Kotex.

These advertisements constituted the first real public acknowledgment of menstruation. In the earliest ads, Kimberly-Clark targeted mothers and their well-known difficulties preparing their daughters. The illustrations typically showed either the idealized mother-daughter conversation, or a pensive young woman with unanswered questions. The ad was given authority by the personal signature of a professional nurse, who was available to answer letters and send free samples in a plain, unmarked wrapper. A generation of mothers who had suffered the indignities of unhealthy, unhygienic makeshifts were now urged to tell their daughters: "This new way is Kotex, widely urged by doctors and nurses. Kotex is used by eight women in ten in the better walks of life."[28] Across the country, in large cities as well as in small towns, these ads were accompanied by thousands of drugstore displays that made Kotex familiar and accessible even to young girls.

In the 1930s and 1940s, newly established educational divisions within the personal products industry (i.e., Kimberly-Clark, Personal Products, Tampax, Inc., and Campana Corporation) began to supply mothers, teachers, parent-teacher associations, and also the Girl Scouts with free, ready-made programs of instruction on "menstrual health." Oral history interviews done in Pittsburgh reveal that these programs were extremely effective. Beginning in the 1930s, but especially in the 1940s, almost all the daughters of Slovak, Italian, and Jewish families in that city were given corporate-sponsored pamphlets, such as "Marjorie May's Twelfth Birthday" (1932), either at school or by their mothers. In 1946, in conjunction with Walt Disney, the industry also developed the first corporate-sponsored film on the subject, *The Story of Menstruation,* an animated cartoon that has been seen by approximately 93 million American women either at school or in some single-sex setting. Other films followed, along with famous brochures, such as "Very Personally Yours," "As One Girl to Another," and "You're a Young Lady Now."[29]

These are the experiences that produced girls like Ruth Teischman, who were comfortable thinking, writing, and talking about menstruation. In recognition of earlier maturation, menstruation began to be taught as early as the fifth or sixth grade, at age nine or ten. All the attention paid to menstruation untied many tongues and stimulated a great deal of talk about which girls had their periods and which did not. This kind of girl talk was not invented in the years after World War II, although it did become more frequent and more audible in those years. In 1952, a Chicago girl wrote to the editors of *Seventeen:* "I am fourteen and have not as yet begun to menstruate, which worries me considerably. Since I am nearly fifteen, I often wonder if I am abnormal." (The young letter writer was told to see a gynecologist.)[30]

The late 1940s and 1950s were absolutely critical in forging the modern teenage girl's relationship to her sexually maturing body. After World War II, mothers were deleted from advertisements and testimonials for sanitary napkins in order to encourage autonomous consumption by teenage girls. Yet independent buying was embarrassing so long as sanitary products were kept behind drugstore counters and sold by male clerks. Most girls still needed their mothers to help them acquire the feminine paraphernalia they needed. After she went to see a "menstruation movie" with her mother at a Cleveland junior high school in 1950, Sandra Rubin wanted a sanitary belt like the one she saw in the film, but her mother was not convinced it was necessary: "I am afraid Mom doesn't understand me and laughs when I ask for a sanitary belt."[31] Readers who have reached menarche since the 1960s may not realize that feminine napkins were once much bulkier and that before the invention of panty hose and press-on paper tape, they were usually pinned to either suspension belts or underpants. Panty hose, which facilitated very short skirts, also helped to hold sanitary napkins in place.

Although the postwar sanitary products industry encouraged autonomy in teens, it also stimulated angst. Advertisements for sanitary protection consistently played to adolescent awkwardness, concern about peers, and the embarrassing specter of soiled clothes. For young girls who were already self-conscious and uncertain about their maturing bodies, the right sanitary product, used correctly, was promoted as the most important form of social insurance. *Seventeen* featured both articles and advertisements about how to cope with the stress of "special" days and how to handle a heavy flow while remaining active, attractive, and dainty. "Above all, don't retire from the human race during your period," advised a postwar physician. "Menstruation is not a 'sick time.' It's as natural and normal as breathing. It should be viewed with a healthy, matter-of-fact attitude."[32] This was clearly an improvement over the fear tactics of the "ovarian determinists," but girls still had to be extremely wary—not so much about health but about showing, smelling, offending. In effect, they had to get their bodies under control.

Marketing strategists understood that sales to the baby-boom generation—soon to be the largest cohort of adolescents in American history—could turn menstrual blood into gold.[33] As a result, they elaborated even more exacting standards of feminine hygiene. Girls growing up in postwar America (like Ruth Teischman and myself) were taught that napkins had to be changed as often as six times a day. Women born in those decades, many of whom are still menstruating, routinely select from at least three types of sanitary protection—napkins, tampons, and panty liners—each with different absorbent capacities. And some use tampons and napkins simultaneously and panty liners almost continuously, throughout the month. Foreign visitors often stare in wonder at the size and diversity of the sanitary products aisle in a contemporary American supermarket.

Despite our long-standing and vigilant attention to feminine hygiene, tolerance for "menstrual talk" is still relatively new. Although people today refer casually (and loosely) to something called PMS (premenstrual syndrome), this was not true thirty years ago. In fact, in 1965, the publication of a novel by Louise Fitzhugh, entitled *The Long Secret,* prompted debate about the appropriateness of even mentioning menstruation in fiction for girls. Fitzhugh was the author of *Harriet the Spy,* a popular adventure story; *The Long Secret* was a sequel that focused on Harriet's efforts to solve a local mystery by being brash and ingenious. Reviewers, however, focused on the fact that Harriet's friend Beth got her period, and that Fitzhugh allowed the girls to talk about it. Although the entire discussion was upbeat and healthy—"[Menstruation] happens to every woman in the world, even Madame Curie," Harriet said—some critics were disquieted because they thought it inappropriate to include the subject in juvenile books. A reviewer in *The Washington Post* reported that there were some "startling scenes," such as the girls' "clinical discussion of the physical changes of maidenhood, that will make squeamish parents blanch."[34]

Both the times and girls have changed. In 1995, when I asked a group of Cornell women students to construct a list of favorite books from their adolescence, Judy Blume's *Are You There, God? It's Me, Margaret* (1970) was number one, well ahead of both Anne Frank's *Diary of a Young Girl* and Louisa May Alcott's *Little Women.* I had known Blume as the successful author of "problem books" for young people, novels about such topics as divorce and death, but I was unaware that she also wrote a coming-of-age classic that put menarche and menstruation at its center. (By 1996, the book had sold over six million copies.)[35]

Blume's story about growing up in New Jersey clearly tapped into the contemporary menstrual script. The central character is twelve-year-old Margaret, who repeatedly asks God for two biological favors: bigger breasts and periods. At her new school, Margaret makes friends with a group of equally undeveloped girls who share her preoccupations. In secret club meetings, they exercise together in order to develop their chests, and they are ever vigilant (and sometimes dishonest) about who does or does not have periods yet. The story is told with a great deal of humor and includes a parody of the experience of watching a movie about menstruation in sixth grade. After listening to the stilted language of a representative from "Private Lady" personal products, Margaret mocks her pronunciation ("menstroo-ation") and vows never to buy Private Lady napkins even if she needs them.

My students realized that this was not sophisticated literature, but they were more than willing to suspend that kind of aesthetic judgment because the subject—how a girl adjusts to her sexually maturing body—was treated so realistically and hit so close to home. Just like the fictional Margaret, they had all worried about the pace of their own development and giggled their way nervously through "the movie." In contrast, when I taught *Little Women,* a student complained that she had real difficulty relating to the women in that famous story of nineteenth-century family life. There was something "unnatural," she said, about Alcott's depiction of the March girls because "you never know when they [Meg, Jo, Beth, and Amy] get their periods."

According to our contemporary script, girls should talk about menstruation. And, in fact, they do, and that talk is increasingly graphic, just like the television and movies we watch. In a 1989 issue of *Sassy*, a lively and sometimes irreverent magazine for adolescent girls, the editors (all women in their twenties) shared personal stories about menarche and menstruation.[36] As if they were sitting in a private bedroom sipping diet sodas, they swapped "menstrual nightmares" about what it was like to leave a puddle of blood on a chair, or to struggle to find the right opening for a tampon. These stories of embarrassing personal moments were honest and funny, but they all focused on issues of personal hygiene because that is the language we use in America for talking about such things.

Keeping Clean Is Not Enough

In the course of the past century, menstruation has been demystified by medicine, by marketers, and by mothers. Each group had a particular interest in the bodies of adolescent girls; each group helped to shape the experience of menarche and menstruation into the hygienic, essentially commercial ritual it is today. The long-term consequences of demystifying the process of menstruation, however, are not entirely benign. On the one hand, American girls are more knowledgeable about their bodies than girls were in the Victorian era. More than at any other time in human history, young girls are equipped with a clinical vocabulary and medical information learned from parents, from lessons at school, and from discussions in magazines. In some liberal families, parents have even stopped using euphemisms for genitalia and encourage children as young as three or four to talk openly about the vagina and penis. Children who grow up in an environment without shame are better prepared in adolescence for changes in their own bodies and for making distinctions among the barrage of sexual stimuli that popular culture directs at adolescents.

Unfortunately, though, more information does not always translate into a real understanding of one's own body. Before she left for a Cape Cod vacation in 1982, a sophomore at a select New York City high school wrote in her diary: "I would get my period tonight. It's just like my eggs to reach ovulation tonight." This young woman sounded sophisticated, but she obviously misunderstood the relationship between ovulation and her monthly period. Others diagnose themselves on the basis of medical models provided in popular periodicals: "I was reading an article in *Seventeen* about PMS and I'm *almost* positive that's what I have now. I have all the classic symptoms except cramps—I'm moody, irritable, bloated and have low self-esteem. I really want to get some Midol PMS and see if it works."[37]

Although information is always better than silence, we need to think about how girls learn about their bodies and whose interests inform the presentation of this critical information. Unfortunately, many American girls grow up equating the experience of menarche and menstruation with a hygiene product. A woman who grew up in the 1940s recalled that before any of her friends had gotten their periods, one of her fellow fifth-graders suddenly declared one day that she would not slide down a snowy hill. When asked why, this prepubertal girl said laughingly, "I can't. I'm practicing Kotex."[38] This childish remark captures the extent to which the sanitary products industry dominates the experience of sexual maturation in America. The comment was also a perceptive piece of cultural logic on the part of a young girl coming of age in a society where female identity is so closely linked to purchases in the marketplace. By creating a profit-making enterprise from adolescent self-consciousness, the postwar sanitary products industry paved the way for the commercialization of other areas of the body, such as skin, hair, and breasts—all of great concern to developing girls.

The surrender of a life event such as menarche to the sanitary products industry probably contributed in some measure to the difficulties we face today with female adolescent sexuality. As the industry became an ever-present "third party" in mother-daughter, doctor-patient, and teacher-student discussions, personal experience and testimony from older women became even less authoritative or important. Although there was more information available, it was increasingly abstracted from real-life experience, and it was also made less (rather than more) personal in the hope of reducing embarrassment. In the case of the Disney film, menstruation was reduced to an animated cartoon, which mothers and daughters could watch together without ever engaging in the kind of frank, intimate talk about sexuality or reproduction that modern adolescents need. (Neither sexuality nor reproduction is mentioned in that influential film.) Instead, the availability of so much free, corporate-sponsored teaching material meant that many mothers and teachers simply gave out pamphlets and samples rather than provide individual advice and counsel about growing up female.

In preparing girls for menarche, we still tend to emphasize selecting a sanitary product rather than the meaning or the responsibility that menstruation implies. However, we know from the experience of generations of American women—and from the success of Judy Blume's insightful parody of school instruction about menstruation—that being handed a pamphlet or shown a movie is not very satisfying, and that young women want meaningful exchanges about female sexuality as well as the best techniques for coping with the vagaries of menstrual blood. In a world where the female body is sexualized so early and the stakes are so high, it now seems obvious that it is not enough to teach girls how to be clean and dainty.

When contemporary American girls begin to menstruate, they think of hygiene, not fertility. That is the American way, and it is taken for granted—as if it were part of the "natural order." But the historical "disconnect" between menstruation and reproduction is actually quite modern, and it has important psychological implications for how girls think about themselves and what kind of women they become. It was strategically helpful for our grandmothers and mothers to cast menstruation as "only" a matter of hygiene, in order to offset Victorian myths about its debilitating effects. In today's world, however, that dismissiveness means something else. In fact, it sets the stage for obsessive overattention to other aspects of the changing body, such as size and shape. In an environment like ours, where looks mean so much, this turning away from the hidden aspects of female biology has put excruciating pressure on those body parts that the world can see. For girls in the twentieth century, this reorientation toward the visual, or the outside of the body, has only intensified the difficulties of being an adolescent.

CHAPTER THREE

Perfect Skin

Photos on p. 57: *(left)* Permission of the author; *(right)* permission of Bronwen Densmore.

In 1899, a Philadelphia pediatrician was called to the home of a seventeen-year-old patient who was having "an hysterical attack." Dr. Edwin Rosenthal had seen "Miss E.L." before, because she suffered from headaches and irregular periods. But this time the young woman, who was studying to be a teacher, was agitated and sobbing about her skin. She had acne on each cheek and claimed that "pimples [were] the bane of [her] life."

Dr. Rosenthal's patient was obviously preoccupied with how she looked. Like many adolescent girls, past and present, she was sufficiently self-conscious that a crop of pimples brought her to tears. In order to defuse her anxiety, Rosenthal fashioned a therapy suited to both her medical and emotional needs: he treated her with purgatives and Gude's Pepto-Mangan, an iron supplement. (These were standard, minimally effective fare at the time for handling gastric and menstrual disorders, believed to cause adolescent acne.) Because he knew that "E.L." would do almost anything to rid herself of the embarrassing blemishes, Rosenthal was confident that she would take her medicine. "Vanity came to my assistance," he noted, in describing how he had handled this unhappy daughter of the Victorian middle class.[1]

Pimples are a natural part of biological maturation, but the meaning we give to them is derived from the culture in which we live. According to G. Stanley Hall, young people at the turn of the twentieth century already had a highly developed "dermal consciousness." In his massive study in 1904, Hall reported that adolescents of both sexes had a "strong desire" to remove pimples and sometimes "picked" their skin for hours. But Hall also noted a gender difference in the intensity of adolescent self-scrutiny. It was girls, not boys, who displayed a "new sense of toilet" marked by zealous concern about their hair and skin.[2]

From a historical perspective, adolescent acne was very much a girls' disease until the mid-twentieth century. The reason was simple: girls demonstrated more urgency than boys about pimples. As early as 1885, in the first professional monograph devoted exclusively to acne, L. Duncan Bulkley, a physician at New York Hospital, noted that girls were more likely than boys to seek medical help for the inflammatory form of pustules and blackheads so common in adolescence. Of the nearly three hundred patients he saw in private practice, 78 percent were young women between the ages of ten and twenty-five.[3]

"Acne in all its forms" is "undoubtedly more common in females than in males," Dr. Bulkley concluded, and he provided an insightful explanation: "The very great difference is in part accounted for by the less attention given to the eruption by males." Although most Victorian doctors thought that girls had more acne than boys because of physical weaknesses such as digestive problems, menstrual disorders, and anemia—all believed to be inherent in the female sex—Bulkley understood that it was social and cultural pressures, as much as biological vulnerability, that filled his waiting room with young women rather than young men. Although boys surely suffer from the stigma of acne, girls' pimples get more cultural attention. Because of cultural mandates that link femininity to flawless skin, the burden of maintaining a clear complexion has devolved disproportionately upon women and girls.[4]

In the battle against acne, girls have not fought alone. In fact, skin care was really the first of many body projects endorsed and supported by middle-class parents for their adolescent children. Maternal influence over menarche and menstruation declined in the twentieth century, but parental intervention in cases of acne increased. This exchange says a great deal about the cultural priorities of middle-class mothers, who increasingly invested themselves and their money in external aspects of their daughters' bodies: aspects, like skin, which were as public as clothes.[5]

American parents cooperated with a body project like skin care because they understood that good looks were an important vehicle of social success for their daughters. Twentieth-century medicine made clear skin in adolescence a priority and also a possibility. Until then, medical treatment for acne was considered either a luxury or unimportant, because acne was never life-threatening. In the nineteenth century, many Americans still had skin that was scarred as a result of smallpox (which left pitting) or tuberculosis (which stimulated acne). In contrast to those who suffered with "real" diseases like these, unhappy adolescent girls like Miss E.L. seemed shallow and less than deserving.

But attitudes began to change in the twentieth century, when modern dermatology and pediatrics began to take adolescents and their blemishes seriously. Attention to acne was justified by the new idea that pimples could be destructive to the mental health of young people. For the field of dermatology, recognition of the emotional anguish of adolescent acne was good news: acne now promised to be a lucrative staple of the trade, one that would exist as long as girls and families cared deeply about their looks. Medical intervention was also important for girls, however, because it stimulated new drugs and treatment strategies that effectively reduced both acne and scarring from it. As concerns about beauty and disease merged, the pursuit of perfect skin—one of the most common adolescent body projects—was transformed into a legitimate health strategy deserving of adult support, and generating enormous profits for both the cosmetic and the drug industries.

Complexion: A Window on the Soul

When Margaret Fuller—who would later make her name as a writer and feminist—was growing up in Cambridge, Massachusetts, in the 1820s, she was intellectually gifted, and she also suffered from adolescent acne. The "ugly flush" on Fuller's fifteen-year-old face was a source of concern to her and to her family. "Both [my parents] were very much mortified to see the fineness of my complexion destroyed," she later wrote, "[and] my own vanity was for a time severely wounded but I recovered and made up my mind to be bright and ugly." Few girls in the early nineteenth century had the opportunity to put brains over beauty the way Fuller did.[6]

In the nineteenth century, young women were commonly taught that the face was a "window on the soul" and that facial blemishes indicated a life that was out of balance. Many people actually believed that blemishes were telltale signs of masturbation. (Allegedly, the nervous excitement produced by the "solitary vice" led to eruptions on the skin.) This connection, of course, made ordinary adolescent pimples mortifying, and it prompted some overanxious Victorian parents to speculate about the "hidden" lives of their adolescent children.[7] In addition, physicians regarded skin eruptions as an indication of a serious disturbance within the body such as smallpox, tuberculosis, or, worst of all, syphilis, a dreaded venereal disease that announced itself with sores and rashes. Because most people in this era believed that these diseases could be transmitted through casual contact with an infected person, no one was considered really immune to tuberculosis or syphilis. Thus, skin was a critical marker of both moral and physical health.

The connection between skin and sexuality was institutionalized in the practice of medicine. Dermatology, the modern science of skin diseases, actually grew out of the field of syphilology, the study of venereal diseases. Beginning in 1870, a journal called *The Archives of Dermatology and Syphilology* published clinical findings in what was then a joint field. Throughout the nineteenth century, there was a continuous movement of physicians back and forth between syphilology and dermatology.[8] Many of the same doctors who handled the shame of syphilis and gonorrhea also dealt with the ordinary problems of adolescent acne. Dr. Bulkley, for example, was "physician for skin and venereal diseases" in the outpatient department at New York Hospital; another New York City doctor, Prince Morrow, actually called himself a "dermatovenereologist."

Because of the connection between sexual disease and skin lesions, sexual behavior was implicated as a cause of adolescent acne—known clinically as *acne vulgaris,* but also as *acne adolescentium.* (Acne was a corruption of the Greek *aknē,* signifying the point or bloom of life; *vulgaris* simply meant that the eruptions were of an ordinary inflammatory type involving pustules and comedones, known colloquially as blackheads.) In some cases, adolescent acne was thought to be the result of "sexual derangement" such as masturbation or promiscuity; in others, pimples were attributed simply to impure or lascivious thoughts. In either scenario, each agonizing new blemish was read as a sign of moral failure, a situation that created deep anxiety in respectable middle-class homes with adolescent sons and daughters. Because of the alleged connection between sexual desire and pimples, many people in this era believed that marriage—the only acceptable outlet for sexual expression—cured acne.

Sophisticated physicians were generally circumspect, however, about advising marriage or charging young people with "sexual derangement." They certainly did not want to insult parents who paid for their services, and they also believed that premature marriage was disastrous for girls. Yet in influential textbooks, physicians were advised to consider immorality as a cause if acne did not respond to the usual clinical ministrations. Although "statistical proof of masturbation is extremely difficult to obtain," Bulkley wrote, "the fact is thoroughly established by many reliable observations, and should always be borne in mind in intractable cases."[9] By the last decades of the nineteenth century, most doctors felt that this approach to acne was outmoded and tried to discredit the old association between pimples and moral perversion. But the idea still lingered in the minds of many, and it probably caused some discomfort to polite young people whose facial eruptions were intense. For that reason, Dr. W. A. Haraway felt compelled to assert in his *Manual of Skin Diseases* (1892): "There is no proof beyond mere surmise that excessive venery [sexual intercourse], any more than continence, is responsible for acne."[10] Fifty years later, the Victorian connection between skin and sexual deviance still persisted. When asked why she avoided salesmen with acne, a middle-aged woman in the 1930s whispered that men with acne were probably "pansies" who engaged in "questionable" sexual practices; similarly, a respected dermatologist told me while I was writing this book that in the 1950s, his own blemished teenage face prompted comments that he was probably "jerking off."[11]

Because the cause of acne was imprecise, treatment was variable and eclectic. Those Victorian physicians who assumed a constitutional cause—such as constipation, poor circulation, headaches, nervousness, and anemia—administered tonics such as cod liver oil, mixtures of iron and arsenic, mineral waters and salts, gelatin-coated sulphide of calcium, glycerin, quinine, and plain old hot water. Yet despite this wide range of constitutional treatments, most doctors at the end of the century still concurred with Ferdinand Ritter von Hebra, a widely respected Austrian expert on skin diseases, that "the uselessness of internal remedies against acne compels us to resort to local applications." By local applications Hebra meant soap and water applied directly to the skin. But his advice was vague as to whether soap of potash, glycerin, or sulphur was most effective or whether mineral water actually was more successful than anything else. What ultimately seemed most important was the method used to apply soap. "Whatever kind of soap is used," said Hebra, "it must be thoroughly rubbed into the skin" in order to achieve a complexion that was smooth, soft, and unblemished.[12]

In pursuit of a fine complexion, Victorian girls rubbed their skin with strips of soaped flannel, and they rubbed it hard, the way physicians advised. In severe cases they sometimes left the soapsuds on overnight, even though, as we now know, this practice could exacerbate facial irritation. Many bought special salves, such as Kosmeo, a popular skin cream advertised in the Sears, Roebuck catalog. "When a man marries, nine times out of ten he chooses a girl with a pretty complexion," advised the product's spokesperson, Mrs. Cervais Graham, whom Sears called the "greatest beauty doctor" in the country: "You can't blame men for not being attracted to women whose faces are disfigured with pimples, blotches, blackheads and other unnecessary blemishes." In order to avoid an unhappy future as a spinster, thousands of American girls ordered Kosmeo, and then rubbed earnestly with camel's hair brushes and Turkish towels in order to increase friction and improve blood circulation to the face.[13]

Mirrors: A New Kind of Self-reflection

Mirrors play a critical role in the way American girls have assessed their own faces and figures. In the early nineteenth century, when a reflective mirror or "looking glass" was a luxury of the rich, humble girls still managed to find mirrors in order to study their faces. In her autobiographical account of coming of age in New England in the 1830s, Lucy Larcom recalled that she did not like to look at her own face in the mirror because "it was so unlike" the ethereal faces of the heroines in the romantic novels she read. Those fictional young women had "high white foreheads" and "perfect oval" cheeks—both a distinct contrast to Lucy's round, ruddy, homespun appearance.[14]

When the mirror became a staple of the American middle-class home at the end of the nineteenth century, attention to adolescent acne escalated, as did sales of products for the face. Until then, pimples were primarily a tactile experience, at least for the girl who had them. But all that changed in the late 1880s with the widespread adoption in middle-class homes of a bathroom sink with running water and a mirror hung above it. (At the same time, city girls used department store mirrors and shiny windows to look at their faces.) This set the stage for the kind of dermal consciousness displayed by "E.L." and promoted by marketers like Kosmeo.[15]

Mirrors made pimples more accessible, but they also stimulated greater concern about the face. Although diaries in this era almost never mention such an indelicate issue as pimples, they do contain traces of the Victorian adolescent's "new sense of toilet." In the 1890s, American girls displayed a notable enthusiasm for a particular hairdo that was linked to their anxiety about blemishes on the face. "Bangs," or a ruffle of hair on the forehead, became popular among adolescent girls in public high schools at the end of the century. (This was the same class of girls whose homes were equipped with modern bathrooms.) In an era when proper young women did not use makeup, a crop of pimples had to be covered in some discreet way, particularly if it had been rubbed red in the morning and evening with soaped flannels or brushes.

In the 1890s, fifteen-year-old Lou Henry noted her own efforts, and those of her friends at her high school in Pasadena, to maintain this popular hairstyle. "I went downtown after school with Nellie St. Claire to have her bangs cut," Lou wrote. A year later, bangs were still a major preoccupation: Lou spent evenings curling her own and sometimes worked on those of her friends. All this mutual grooming was facilitated by the presence of mirrors and the fact that Lou's school, like high schools all over the country in that era, had a disproportionate number of middle-class girls. (Adolescent boys in the middle class were employable without advanced education, and they could learn important skills on the job; in contrast, middle-class girls needed a high school education for the teaching jobs they wanted.) In high schools, self-scrutiny intensified as adolescents watched and mimicked each other in the care of their skin and the arrangement of their hair. The advice writer Marion Harland confirmed that adolescent girls in the 1890s used "banging" to hide "unsightly clusters" of pimples, and that they also covered them with "artful dots" of something called court plaster, a fabric coated on one side with an adhesive, much like a modern Band-Aid.[16]

Whenever I see contemporary girls adjusting their hairstyles to the demands of bumpy foreheads, I think about Lou Henry and the amount of time she spent "banging" with her Victorian friends. The familiar parental refrain "Keep the hair off your face" probably originated in that bygone era when American girls began to use bangs as a cover for blemishes that were still considered a telltale sign of immorality. Although the pimples and the bangs remain, our thinking about what is being disguised, and how to disguise it, has surely changed. As the twentieth century progressed, scientific medicine and new cultural forms, such as the movies, reinforced the American girl's interest in the person she saw in her mirror.

Beauty Is Skin-Deep

In the early twentieth century, adolescent acne was seen less as a sign of moral perversity than as a marker of "dirtiness" and low social class. With the rapid popularization in the late 1870s and 1880s of the idea that diseases were linked to particular germs, Americans began to look everywhere for invisible agents of disease. By 1900, a bacteriologically based public health movement solidified the idea that microorganisms caused ill health and suffering. Most people came to believe that dirt and squalor generated disease, and this equation led to an increased emphasis on the hygiene of homes, bodies, and faces among the American middle class. "You can't be healthy, or pretty, or even good, unless you are clean" was the slogan used to sell Hand Sapolio, a popular soap, at the turn of the century.

In a world where germs were so important, adolescent acne was attributed to specific bacteria: staphylococci or corynebacteria.[17] Although dermatologists were uncertain about how the bacillus actually worked, each adolescent was now personally responsible for maintaining proper habits of hygiene and self-discipline that made for a germ-free environment on the face. Dirt was a problem for both sexes, but there was always more advice about complexions for girls because grooming—that is, careful attention to the body's surfaces, such as skin and hair—was such an important part of the middle-class feminine ideal.

In the pages of the popular *Ladies' Home Journal*, physician Emma Walker explained that the crusade against acne had to be waged with washcloths in the privacy of one's own home: "When you see and smell the condition of some girls' washcloths you wonder that there are not more pimples and unwholesome skins than there are. Have your washcloths boiled and sunned at least once a week."[18] In the middle-class war against germs and pimples, well-trained domestic servants were important, as well as the right equipment. In addition to a sterile washcloth, the hairbrush loomed large because of the increased importance of an absolutely clean scalp. According to Joseph Grindon, a St. Louis doctor, adolescent acne was caused by a "microbian invasion" that usually got its "foothold" in the scalp. As a result, he considered a clean hairbrush "as sacred as the toothbrush."[19]

The association between adolescent acne, germs, and dirt made personal cleanliness a critical imperative for middle-class mothers and their daughters. But there were other factors at work by the 1920s that heightened female attention to pimples and their meaning. In the Victorian era, beauty was thought to derive primarily from internal qualities such as moral character, spirituality, and health. However, in the first two decades of the twentieth century, women began to think about beauty and the self in ways that were more external than internal. Because of the introduction of many new kinds of cultural mirrors, in motion pictures and popular photography, in mass-market advertising in the women's magazines, as well as on department store counters and in dressing rooms, most women and girls began to subject their face and figure to more consistent scrutiny. This focus on the visual rather than the spiritual self put enormous importance on the face, and stimulated even respectable women and girls to experiment with their appearance in ways that had once been considered disgraceful.[20]

In the effort to look like the attractive women they saw in movies and magazines, American women in the 1920s put aside long-established objections to face makeup and began to purchase and use a wide range of cosmetics. At first, face powders were the most popular; eventually, rouge, lipstick, and eyebrow pencil were added to the list of acceptable beauty aids. Gadgets for curling eyelashes were also marketed in drugstores for the first time in the 1920s. By the middle of the decade, the American cosmetics industry was flourishing and its growth was unrelenting, largely because teenage girls, as well as mature women, were making up in a way that was associated with the "flapper" ideal. Sales of compacts (small, handheld mirrors with a compartment for powder) soared because they allowed women to scrutinize and "reconstruct" the face almost anywhere, at a moment's notice.[21]

Cosmetics probably exacerbated adolescent acne. While makeup camouflaged some skin flaws, it did not alleviate the pimple problem. Instead, girls who used makeup became even more preoccupied with their skin as they confronted pores, pustules, and blackheads every day, close-up. The strategies girls used to cope with pimples in the 1920s and 1930s depended on where they lived, as well as on family aspirations and resources. Those who lived in small towns or on isolated family farms continued to rely on self-medication, such as soap and water combined with creams, lotions, and tonics available for purchase by mail or at the nearest drugstore. Popular products, such as Pond's Extract and White Lily Face Wash, had been around since the nineteenth century; personal blackhead extractors were available at the local druggist or through Sears, Roebuck. Many young women also followed "acne diets," which put foods like cake, ice cream, chocolate, and carbonated drinks off-limits, despite the fact that the research was unclear as to the role of sugar metabolism in generating pimples. Still others experimented in the 1920s and 1930s with controversial remedies, such as eating ordinary Fleishmann's yeast cakes three times a day. Dermatologists painted self-medication as a dangerous craze because *acne vulgaris,* they said, might "in reality be tuberculosis or syphilis." And they always insisted that picking and squeezing should never be done by anyone but a professional, not even a girl's own mother.[22]

But there was another way for girls to rid themselves of the dreaded blackhead, particularly if they lived in the city and had some money to spare. In the ordinary beauty shops of the 1920s and 1930s, female cosmetologists offered facials that included procedures to stimulate the skin, remove blackheads, open pustules, and peel away unattractive roughness or bumps. Because their youthful clients wanted it, and because there were as yet no laws against it, operators in these establishments were willing to incise the skin and smooth it, a practice that drove dermatologists wild. According to Dr. Howard Fox, president of the American Dermatological Association, in 1925 there were nearly two thousand beauty parlors in the boroughs of Manhattan and the Bronx that "practice[d] medicine illegally." Cosmetology clearly attracted enough teenage acne sufferers to constitute a persistent thorn in the side of professional medicine.[23]

For girls with severe acne, professional dermatology probably did offer the most effective therapy, but it was always more costly than any other treatment, and it was not always available. In the 1920s, dermatology was still not a board-certified medical specialty; expert skin doctors were clustered in urban centers such as New York, Boston, Philadelphia, and St. Louis.[24] For that reason, when Eleanore Crehore went off to Smith College in Northampton, Massachusetts, there was some doubt about whether she could continue the skin therapy she had been receiving at home. She wrote to her mother: "My face has been decidedly breaking out again the way it was before and although it is decidedly not as bad as it was, I am afraid if I don't go on with the stuff that it will be soon." The "stuff" Eleanor was talking about consisted of injections of iron and a vaccine made from acne flora found on her own face and cultured in the doctor's office. After she found someone in Northampton to make the vaccine, she wrote again: "Do you think I should go to some other doctor here so that I can go right on with the Hypos?"[25]

After the discovery of sex hormones in the 1930s, dermatologists offered girls another treatment: oral and subcutaneous doses of commercially made estrogen. (This was based on the idea that acne was connected to an estrogen deficiency.) But the most popular therapy of all was a localized but unfiltered X ray known as a "Roentgen treatment," named for the physicist Wilhelm Conrad Roentgen, who had demonstrated the penetrating properties of X rays back in the 1890s. Guidelines for use of Roentgen rays in *acne vulgaris* were provided by Philadelphia dermatologist G. M. MacKee, whose widely read *X Ray and Radium in the Treatment of Diseases of the Skin* (1921) became the clinical handbook for thousands of doctors. For dermatologists, X ray was the therapy of choice because it was effective in many cases, it linked professional skin care to modern scientific technology, and it could not be done at home. For girls, however, there was a risk of scarring, and we know now that excessive X rays can have a carcinogenic effect. Yet American dermatologists and their adolescent patients were willing then, as now, to experiment in the dogged national effort to have perfect skin.[26]

Two Nice Jewish Girls

Most American girls wanted to be free of pimples, but in certain ethnic communities there was a heightened sensitivity to them because of what they suggested about the quality of the home environment. Diaries, oral histories, magazines, and fiction all suggest that skin was loaded with meaning for girls who wanted to assimilate and wanted to dispel the idea that their particular group was somehow unclean or degenerate. Among Jews and African-Americans, whose social acceptance was precarious, faces were monitored with a particularly critical eye. And when they were able, girls in both groups invested considerable resources and energy in achieving the "good" skin that was necessary for middle-class status.

The pattern of critical self-scrutiny is evident in the life histories of two Jewish girls who came of age in the 1920s, an era when anti-Semitism was overt and institutionalized. Early in the decade, when Harvard University announced publicly its intention to impose a Jewish quota, the policy was justified on the grounds that the university did after all accept good Jews; it simply had no responsibility for the others: "No one objects to the best Jews coming but the others make such trouble especially in the Library."[27] Popular distinctions between "good" and "bad" Jews gave the identity struggles of Jewish girls—as well as their worries about pimples—a painful edge.

Helen Laprovitz, who grew up in Amherst, Massachusetts, a small college town, was the daughter of Russian Jewish immigrants who changed the family name to Landis in order to appear more American, and also to improve the chances of their six children for educational and economic success. In Amherst, the Landis family worked hard and lived above their clothing store; until sometime after World War I, they were the only Jewish family in town. Helen's girlhood diary revealed that she was accustomed to being singled out, if not picked on, by some of her schoolmates. One day a local boy rode by on a bike and yelled at her with derision, "You Jewess!" On another occasion she told her diary: "The girls [at school] do not like me because I am a Jew."

As she moved through adolescence in this Yankee stronghold, Helen and her family took pride in her petite, blond good looks, a valuable asset in a society where Jews were still suspect because they were "dark and swarthy." Helen knew she was pretty by American standards; she was also a good student with hopes of attending nearby Smith and becoming a real collegian. At fifteen, she understood that blemished or pitted skin—just like an unpronounceable family name—would handicap her because it was a sign of poverty and uncleanliness, both of which were associated with lower-class status and newly arrived immigrants.

In an effort to put distance between herself and these "greenhorns," Helen collected advice about skin care from columns in popular women's magazines; from her older sister, who studied hygiene in the College of Home Economics at Cornell; and from the family doctor, a general practitioner. And in her diary she sometimes made notes about her complexion, notes that revealed a trace of the old idea that sin manifested itself on the skin. "How terrible I am," she wrote, after a fight with her sister. "For that I got another pimple." Throughout her high school years, before she entered Goucher College in 1923, Helen kept count of her blemishes and watched her skin almost as carefully as she assessed the young college men who bought clothing in her father's haberdashery.[28]

Helen's watchfulness was not unique, as the story of my own mother and grandmother reveals. My mother, Frances Storck, also the daughter of Russian Jewish immigrants, grew up in New Rochelle, a suburb of New York City. In 1929, at age seventeen, she began to travel by train once a week to see Dr. Frank Combes, a well-known dermatologist at Bellevue Hospital in Manhattan. Although my mother had only a few pimples on her forehead, my vigilant grandmother sent her to the "specialist" because she did not want anything to darken the future of an attractive daughter soon to graduate from high school with high grades and marketable stenographic skills.[29] My grandfather was a busy tailor who catered to New Rochelle's wealthiest families, but the Storcks felt they did not have the means to send a daughter to college. (A son, however, would go to City College of New York and graduate from Brooklyn Law School.) The family nevertheless found resources to invest in Frances's skin. Instead of college tuition, they paid for three months of the most sophisticated dermatology (i.e., Roentgen rays), which, in 1929, was no small matter.

Jewish immigrant parents were not the only ones to make this kind of investment in their teenage girls. In Buffalo, New York, in 1932—the worst year of the Depression—the Mitranos, an Italian immigrant couple, managed to send their fifteen-year-old daughter, Helen, to the dentist every week for a number of months to ensure that she would have good, attractive teeth. Although Joseph Mitrano's small business was failing because his customers could not pay, Helen's health and appearance were not compromised.[30] In the minds of aspiring middle-class parents like the Storcks and the Mitranos, perfecting a girl's looks was far more important than developing her mind. An unblemished complexion (and also decent teeth) was as important as a diploma in the modern female "rags to riches" story.

A Double Bind: Race and Racism

In the 1930s, when she was growing up in Chicago, brown-skinned Gwendolyn Brooks—later a Pulitzer Prize–winning poet—learned a hard "truth" about herself at school. "To be socially successful, a little girl must be Bright (of skin)," she realized. As a result, dark or "dusky" young girls, like herself, had little hope of real acceptance or admiration—unless their parents had professional status or sufficient wealth to offset their skin pigmentation.[31]

Gwendolyn Brooks's early recognition of the social and emotional power of skin color echoes an important theme in fiction by African-American women. In *Plum Bun,* one of many novels written about "passing" in the first half of the twentieth century, African-American author Jessie Fauset provided a revealing portrait of the psychology of an adolescent girl who wanted to be white. Her character Angela Murray is a fair-skinned daughter of a middle-class African-American family in Philadelphia in the 1920s; although her father is quite dark, her mother is light enough to "pass" and does so, occasionally, along with Angela, but only as a joke. For adolescent Angela, however, the ambiguity of her skin color is a persistent problem: in high school, she suffers the pain of lost friendships when her real racial identity is disclosed. And as she comes into maturity and begins to consider her life options, it is clear that everything she desires in life—riches, glamour, pleasure, and freedom—is associated with whiteness. "No, I don't think being coloured in America is a beautiful thing," she tells her darker sister and some of their friends. "I think it's nothing short of a curse."[32] Eventually, Fauset's character leaves her home in Philadelphia for New York, where, in order to avoid the constraints of racism, she starts a new life, "passing" for white.

The words of Gwendolyn Brooks and the character Angela Murray symbolize the problem of skin color in the historical experience of many African-American girls. Their relationship to their own skin was complicated not only by institutional racism but by the ways in which light skin has been valued over dark, even within the black community. Historically, light skin was a key to middle-class status within the African-American community; it was also perceived as a determinant of beauty. As a result, light skin was something many African-American women worked hard to achieve, and this created a difficult "double bind" for adolescent girls who had to subdue pigment as well as pimples.

The dermal consciousness of African-American girls has been complicated by the biology of race as well as by racism. In addition to the deep cultural bias against black skin, African-American girls tend to have more problems with dry skin, usually called ashy skin, than do Caucasian girls of the same age. This tendency to dry skin and hair stimulates sales of products intended to lubricate both hair and scalp, but the same oils and greases also lead to a skin condition called pomade acne, seen almost exclusively in African-American girls. Of course, skin follicles blocked by pomades or greases lead to acne in all girls, regardless of race. The special problem for African-Americans is that they are more prone to "postinflammatory hyperpigmentation," or what is commonly called scarring, because of the amount of melanin in their skin. According to dermatological reports, African-American girls complain about these "ugly dark spots" even more than they do about outbreaks of acne.[33]

Well into the 1950s, Negro magazines (as they were then called) mirrored the hierarchy of hue in the African-American community. Although there was no cosmetic cure for blackness, a middle-class magazine such as *Ebony* was filled until quite recently with advertisements that preached the gospel of "lighter and brighter" skin. Skin bleachers such as Nadinola, Covermark, Nevoline, Beauty Star, and Dr. Fred Palmer's Skin Whitener all promised popularity and romance to black women who lightened up. These ads were seductive, particularly for *Ebony*'s adolescent readers who were fighting both racism and pimples. Nadinola, for example, claimed not only to lighten and brighten skin that was "dark and unlovely" but also to loosen, remove, and clear up blackheads and pimples. By contrast, the ads in *Jet,* another popular Negro magazine, featured brown-skinned, darker women, who reflected the magazine's less affluent working-class readership.[34]

Until recent times—probably the 1960s—the color of a girl's skin was central to her sense of self, as well as her place in the community of people of color. Although skin bleachers are still sold today, they generally are not used by the current generation to bleach the entire face, the way older generations did, before the Black Pride movement of the 1960s and 1970s. Today, African-American girls use special "race products," such as skin bleachers like Ambi Fade Cream and Porcelana, to lighten troublesome dark spots on their skin, but they can also purchase a broad range of "crossover" cosmetics that are adapted to the diversity of skin tones found in women of color.

The old notion that "light was right" meant that many African-American girls in the past grew up dissatisfied with their own faces and that they scrutinized themselves (and others) in ways that were hard, unrealistic, and sometimes unkind. Such slurs as "high yella" and "red bone" reflected this special sensitivity to color. And in fiction at least, some were driven to insanity by images of perfection that required white skin. (This was the story of Pecola Breedlove, the anguished black protagonist in Toni Morrison's *The Bluest Eye.*)[35] In addition to the particular problems associated with blemishes on dark skin, African-American girls worried about hue, and that combination of concerns motivated purchases of "race products" designed, ironically, to mask or obliterate the reality of race. The fact that skin bleachers and fade creams sold so well is a painful and compelling reminder of how much class and racial anxiety has been invested in skin in American society, particularly among groups who suffer from exclusion and bigotry.

Boys and the Acne Alert

Although pimples were traditionally a girls' issue, in the 1930s and 1940s boys' acne became a national concern for the first time. Both the Great Depression and World War II directed attention to the skin problems of young men. In 1938, in the first systematic survey on the incidence of acne in the United States, researchers discovered that young men in the Chicago area were paying an economic price for pimples. Apparently, boys with blemished and pitted skin who tried to find work in the bleak labor market of the 1930s were judged undesirable. With so many men looking for jobs, why hire those whose skin suggested that they were morally suspect or unclean? On the basis of this experience, the authors of the survey warned against the possibility of an "acne embittered" generation of young men.

The war in the South Pacific also highlighted the male experience with *acne vulgaris.* The conditions of warfare in that region—heat, mud, and inadequate toilet facilities—led many young men to break out so severely that they reportedly could not do their jobs. Acne lesions on the face, neck, back, and extremities apparently became so infected that sufferers were unable to carry heavy equipment without pain. This made them "almost useless" to their units and "permanently unfit" for further tropical duty. According to navy physicians who saw action in this region, within only a few months young Americans in the South Pacific developed the kinds of scars that took five to ten years to develop stateside.[36] Navy doctors treated these sailors with the same techniques used on young people at home. They also experimented in the last years of the war with the new wonder drug, penicillin, but penicillin was not particularly useful with acne, even though it was highly effective against life-threatening generalized infections.

The experience of boys in the 1930s and 1940s heightened the medical community's interest in *acne vulgaris.* Before the Depression and World War II, acne was regarded as a relatively unimportant disease: it was never life-threatening; it affected more girls than boys; and its primary impact was on beauty. However, as a result of the national experience with unemployment and warfare, acne was linked to blocked economic opportunity and failed performance, issues that were salient to a medical profession that was essentially male. As a result of their new sensitivity to the consequences of acne in their own sex, dermatologists began to take an increasingly activist stance against it and, in that process, they recast it as a life-threatening disease.

Although acne did not kill, it could ruin a young person's life. By undermining self-confidence and creating extreme psychological distress, acne could generate a breakdown in social functioning. Acne was considered dangerous because it could foster an "inferiority complex," an idea that began to achieve wide popularity among educated Americans. (The "inferiority complex" was the creation of Alfred Adler, a Viennese psychiatrist who was associated with Freud and who had published two books that had appeared in English translation by the 1920s.)[37] In advertisements for skin-care products, in advice to parents, and in medical literature, everyone in the 1930s and 1940s talked about the ways in which pimples and blackheads undermined self-confidence and led to unhealthy behaviors in both sexes.

According to *Hygeia*, the American Medical Association's magazine for the lay public, acne put over four million teens at risk for serious emotional disorders. Popular articles pulled no punches about this "adolescent agony." In boys, doctors and parents noted an "acne salute," a kind of persistent chin fondling that supposedly hid blemishes; in girls, they saw a familiar pattern of hiding pimples "under the coiffure" and obsessive self-scrutiny in front of the mirror. In both sexes, pimples caused deep despair and, in extreme cases, "suicidal attempts [and] mental crack-up from being made to feel like a social outcast." No adolescent was immune: "Little subdebs and boys in the most exclusive preparatory schools have it as well as those who live in squalor and dirt."[38]

The Plague of Youth

Acne was now everybody's disease: it struck boys as well as girls, the rich as well as the poor. As a result, the nation went on an acne alert. In the 1930s and 1940s, acne became the "plague of youth," and the realization that pimples were really quite democratic constituted a call to arms. If social status and a clean washcloth were not protectors, then anyone's child could develop a disfiguring skin condition that led to extreme timidity, social ostracism, and personality aberrations—all of which affected life options and marriage choices. In magazines popular with the educated middle class, parents were urged to monitor teenagers' complexions and to take a teenager to a dermatologist as soon as any eruptions appeared: "Even the mildest attack is best dealt with under the guidance of an understanding medical counselor." Those parents who took a more acquiescent view were guilty of neglect: "Ignoring acne or depending upon its being outgrown is foolish, almost wicked."[39]

Mothers, of course, were more important than fathers in the acne alert, since they were generally at home in close daily contact with their children. Mothers, more than fathers, paid attention to new blemishes when they appeared on faces at the breakfast table. And mothers, more than fathers, advised on the important business of selecting soaps, over-the-counter medications, and cosmetics for troubled skin. In the women's magazines, a mother's involvement with the physical care of her daughter was a constant theme. Tending to an adolescent girl's complexion was made to seem as natural and benign as tending a flower garden. "What mother lives who doesn't want her daughter to be good-looking?" asked Jeanette Eaton, beauty editor of *Parents' Magazine.* The answer was obvious. A good mother wanted a beautiful daughter, and if good looks did not come naturally, the mother had critical work to do: "Whether a girl is pretty or plain, there is apt to be a beauty problem to solve. It must be handled with wisdom and requires the best resources of the beauty business."[40]

By the 1930s, mothers were being encouraged to invest their energies in their daughters' appearance in the name of physical and emotional health. Self-scrutiny—perhaps even with a dash of vanity—was now considered healthy and productive. It was also promoted by public school teachers in hygiene classes across the nation. In 1935, the Massachusetts State Department of Health issued a pamphlet entitled "Are You as Attractive as Nature Intended You to Be?" Students were asked to score their own appearance and urged, if they did not like the result, to take action to improve their skin, hair, or figure.[41] This rating exercise failed to suggest that character or personality might compensate for a few blackheads or a cowlick. Instead, it was based solely on what the teenager saw in the mirror.

Because middle-class parents (especially mothers) wanted to protect their children against the social cost of pimples, they used their energy and their checkbooks to fight them off by using a dermatologist, the drugstore, or both. In the late 1940s, Jane DeWalt, a sixteen-year-old growing up in a comfortable Cleveland home, became concerned about acne. "I came right home after school and fussed with my face," she wrote in her diary. "It is broken out awful. I wish I knew what was the matter with it." Jane's mother, with the help of advice from women's magazines, suggested a strategy that she was willing to fund and supervise. Together, mother and daughter bought Tussy Cleansing cream and a "heat lamp," both of which eventually helped to reduce the oiliness on Jane's face, as well as the level of her self-consciousness. Many other middle-class mothers invested in over-the-counter vitamin products that were supposed to produce clear skin and shiny hair, two important cultural symbols of solid nurturance and good health.[42]

Sometimes, however, material and psychic investment in the complexion of a daughter backfired, causing increased unhappiness. In a significant number of cases, pimples continued to erupt, despite scrupulous attention to personal hygiene and diet and despite medical treatment. In certain families, the inability to control this process resulted in emotional flare-ups in the doctor's office. "I have not infrequently been the observer of a scene enacted in my consultation room," recalled Lester Hollander, a Pittsburgh physician, "in which the parent, pointing an accusing finger at an embarrassed, blemish covered, tearful adolescent, recites a legend of beautiful skin in the family, a story of proper cleansing while she, the parent herself, supervised it, of properly balanced diet, vitamins, greens, laxatives and insistence on plenty of rest, only to have this ungrateful offspring take matters into her own hands and bring about this shameful result—acne."[43] It was obvious that some parents were frustrated by their inability to subdue pimples, and they blamed their teenagers for not eating or living correctly. (Today we know that acne is not simply a matter of eating chocolate or fried, fatty foods; acne has to do with hormones.)

Doctors in the 1950s agreed that bad skin was particularly hard on girls, especially if the social effects of blemishes were exaggerated by the "pecking and heckling of a 'complexion-fixed' parent or relative." In professional journals, they warned of the difficulties of working with girls whose mothers were "nagging complexion hounds." In private, some girls did endure a form of maternal intervention that doctors suspected and despised. "Tonight my mother picked two blackheads," a thirteen-year-old wrote in the 1950s. "She said that if I let her do it, she'd get me a red boatneck [sweater]." Despite the problem of the overbearing Mom, most physicians were understanding of the multiple pressures on American girls—particularly what one doctor called "the atrocious cosmeticism that rides American womanhood." In the modern world, where image meant so much, it surprised no one that so many adolescent girls regarded even an occasional blackhead as "a physical and psychic calamity of the first magnitude."[44]

Baby-Boom Blemishes

There was a new intensity about acne in the post–World War II world that escalated the emotional pain of the experience but eventually led to its demise. By "demise" I mean that *acne vulgaris* in its extreme forms is much less common in the 1990s than it was in the 1890s because of general improvements in medical care, as well as the acne alert that made attention to pimples a distinguishing feature of middle-class parenting. Acne has not really disappeared, but in the past fifty years it has been handled differently, earlier, and better.

After World War II, American girls began to talk about pimples in their diaries, and they did so in a nearly formulaic way: "I wish I didn't have all the pimples I now have. I'm steaming my face and all that and I'm putting on Acnomel every night (starting tonight) and still I have pimples. I hope I can get rid of them soon." This excerpt from a diary written in the 1950s suggests that pimple medicines had become a fact of teenage life in America and that young women expected results from the skin care techniques they learned in popular magazines.[45]

An array of nonprescription acne preparations with suggestive names, such as Acnomel, Clearasil, PropaPH, Pro Blem, Teenac, and Ting, was widely advertised and designed for the pocketbooks of girls. In the three decades between 1940 and 1970, the proportion of sixteen-year-old girls who held part-time jobs mushroomed, creating a lucrative market for products that girls could buy with their own money. One obvious way to capture all this new spending money was to exploit the adolescent girl's predictable angst about pimples, and that is exactly what advertisers did.[46]

The early Clearasil campaigns in *Seventeen* demonstrate how marketers spoke to girls. At first, Clearasil did not do much more than tout itself as a "revolutionary, new skin colored miracle medication." At that time the advertisements showed a small line drawing of a worried face, a doctor at a microscope, and a dancing couple. Clearasil's promoters explained how their product was both a medication and a cosmetic: "Clearasil works while it hides pimples amazingly!" A bubble above the head of the happy female dancer proclaimed (ungrammatically): "No more embarrassment of blemishes." In order to entice *Seventeen* readers to try it, the manufacturer promised a money-back guarantee if Clearasil did not "amaze you."[47] When this advertisement first appeared, in 1951, a tube of Clearasil cost fifty-nine cents, which was affordable for girls who had even a small allowance or some weekly baby-sitting money.

Eager to capitalize on the deluge of acne expected to accompany the maturation of the baby-boom generation, Clearasil soon developed a more sophisticated approach geared to the anxiety of girls and their well-known fondness for both mail and samples. For only fifteen cents, *Seventeen* readers could now obtain a two-week supply of Clearasil. They were also encouraged to begin an interactive relationship with the product through exposure to the "Clearasil Personality of the Month." Using close-up photographs and bits of personal biography, *Seventeen* readers were introduced to attractive, wholesome, and (always white) middle-class high school girls who triumphed over pimples and became popular. Not surprisingly, the girls who were chosen reflected the 1950s mainstream ideal of good looks, and their personal stories reinforced traditional values regarding school, church, and community.[48]

Personal testimonials were provided to authenticate the personalities. "Skin blemishes made it impossible for me to really enjoy myself. I was always worrying about the way I looked," wrote Sandra Swanson, a junior at Chandler High School in Arizona. Readers were told that Sandra enjoyed dancing, swimming, tennis, and horseback riding and was also manager of the school's Spanish club. According to her account, life before Clearasil was anguish: "Nothing really worked until I tried Clearasil. Now my friends tell me I have one of the clearest and nicest complexions in our school." The pitch was perfect because it played to the adolescent's concern about what peers were saying. And it suggested that use of the product brought popularity and self-confidence. Moreover, the idea of seeing oneself in the pages of *Seventeen* was nearly irresistible, particularly when participation was couched in the language of female service: "Would your experience help others?" Interested girls were encouraged to send their own story and a good close-up photograph.

Advertisements like these were powerful because they served as a nationwide "support group" that allowed girls to hear about the anxieties of others over pimples. They also reinforced the link between clear skin and social success. Over the years, nonprescription acne creams and lotions became almost as critical as sanitary napkins to adolescent girls. Today, an estimated 66 percent of American girls between the ages of twelve and fifteen purchase over-the-counter medications to eliminate what their generation casually refers to as "zits." (The derivation of this word is still murky; allegedly, the term refers to the squishy "pop" made when puss is squeezed from a pimple or a blackhead.)[49]

By the late 1950s, as baby boomers began to move into puberty, patients with acne accounted for almost 20 percent of the private office practice of American dermatologists. Of these, girls outnumbered boys by two to one.[50] Clearly, middle-class tolerance for facial blemishes was declining, and fewer young women (or young men) experienced the disfigurement that was so common in the nineteenth century.

Postwar dermatologists could not cure acne, but they could control it with a widening arsenal of treatments. By the 1950s, patients with severe cases were subject to a multiphasic approach that combined X rays, prescription drying lotions, antibiotics (such as Aureomycin or tetracycline), topical hormones, and orally administered hormones given premenstrually. Heightened attention was also given to the scarring that resulted from acne. Innovations in this domain, known as dermabrasion or skin planing, were described in *Time* and *Newsweek* as well as in women's magazines. Adolescents with pitted or scarred faces were urged to consider the most up-to-date approach for coping with the unsightly remains of their condition. "Ask your dermatologist about the dry ice treatments (performed only by skin specialists). The ice peels the skin and improves circulation. If properly given it reduces and does away with ugly scarring," explained the beauty editor at the influential *Ladies' Home Journal*.

The "dry ice treatment" was a form of carbon dioxide slush applied by the dermatologist with a high-speed rotary wire brush. (This well-known procedure exemplified medicine's general turn in this era to more invasive, "high-tech" interventions.) In the 1950s, William G. McEvitt, a plastic surgeon from Detroit, promoted the benefits of sanding the skin under anesthetic with surgical sandpaper in the hospital. This procedure was more expensive than the dry ice treatment, and it opened the way to plastic surgery for acne. Apparently there were plenty of affluent acne sufferers willing to pay $300 to $800 for this kind of dermabrasion, even though it was not covered by insurance and the results were not always 100 percent successful. According to Veronica Lucey Conley, secretary of the American Medical Association's Committee on Cosmetics, there were many teenagers who expected miracles from dermabrasion, miracles that never materialized.[51]

In the explosive 1960s, adolescent girls were more likely than ever before to be sexually intimate with boys, and this change in their behavior had unexpected implications for skin care. Most young women were introduced to oral contraception in the office of a gynecologist, but dermatologists became supportive players in the contraceptive revolution, even though many were uneasy with that role. By the 1960s, physicians understood that it was testosterone (not estrogen) that tended to provoke acne, and that both male and female hormones exist in a delicate balance in every individual. Because the early oral contraceptives contained enough estrogen to counteract testosterone, they were often helpful in eliminating *acne vulgaris.* Thus, the Pill turned out to provide protection against unwanted pimples as well as unwanted pregnancy.

This information was no secret. In the *Ladies' Home Journal* in 1967, mothers read: "For girls with acne, it is often helpful to give them the birth control pill that contains hormone-like substances that counteract androgen [a male hormone]." Some dermatologists objected to this therapy on the ground that too much estrogen in young girls deterred normal growth; others simply refused to provide unmarried women with a way to become sexually active. But in college health services, where the pressure was most intense, physicians put aside traditional moral concerns about premarital sexuality and sometimes wrote prescriptions for the Pill in the guise of fighting acne. Others made a nod to the old morality by asking for assurance that the patient was at least engaged to be married before prescribing it.[52]

Retin-A: A Magic Bullet

In the early 1970s, adolescent girls started to anticipate a "magic bullet" in the form of tretinoin, a derivative of vitamin A (retinoic acid), known commercially as Retin-A. Available by prescription in cream, gel, and liquid forms, Retin-A had to be used under medical supervision, in small amounts, and over a period of time. For some users, it caused extreme dryness and even inflammation: "I have stopped using Retin-A on my face," a New Jersey high school senior told her diary, "and I'm starting to see the difference. Personally I like the way I look now better. My skin isn't so dry and not as pink, now it's more orangey and my freckles have come back on my nose." Retin-A was powerful stuff but it did work—especially with the dreaded blackhead. Many acne sufferers regarded Retin-A as a miracle, and one called it dermatology's "most important gift to girls."[53]

When Retin-A's success stories began to filter into the culture of adolescent girls, some young women decided to take matters into their own hands and began daily dosing with vitamin A. Unfortunately, a few overly enthusiastic girls took a great deal more than the recommended daily dosage. In 1972, it took months, and all kinds of neurological tests, before doctors discovered that an eighteen-year-old with headaches, swellings, blurred vision, sleep disturbance, and depression was actually suffering from "hypervitaminosis." This well-meaning eighteen-year-old had been taking 50,000 units of vitamin A—a hundred times the minimum suggested amount—at least two or three times a day, in order to rid herself of mild acne. (Her acne never disappeared entirely, but all the other disturbing symptoms did when she stopped taking such a mammoth quantity of vitamins.)[54]

It has become commonplace for American girls to take extraordinary risks in their quest for perfect skin. In 1982, Accutane, another vitamin A derivative, was licensed for use, despite warnings that it caused birth defects in laboratory animals. By 1988, over one million Americans were using the drug even though the Federal Drug Administration (FDA) linked it to fetal malformation and miscarriage in humans. Hoffman-LaRoche, Accutane's manufacturer, admitted that there was a problem by sending letters to dermatologists and druggists pointing out the risk to unborn babies. Red stickers were affixed to prescriptions with the warning: "You should not take Accutane if you are or may become pregnant during therapy." Yet despite its thalidomide-type consequences, Accutane remains on the market. It continues to be popular among adolescent girls and young adult women—the population most desperate to eliminate pimples but also the least experienced in controlling fertility.[55]

The expectation of perfect skin has made America's female adolescents extremely vulnerable. Filled with insecurity and anxious about their looks, young adolescents constitute a fertile market for almost any drug or cosmetic that promises perfection. The demography of the next two decades has already begun to intensify promotional efforts by the skin care industry. In 1992, the ranks of American adolescents started to grow again, ending a fifteen-year decline in their numbers. When this new bulge of adolescents peaks in 2010, it will be larger in size and duration than the well-known teen explosion of the 1960s and 1970s. In theory, at least, this means more adolescent pimples and more sales of skin care products than ever before.[56]

Wrinkles as Well as Pimples

As we approach a new century, the prospect of so many adolescent faces presents manufacturers with an enticing opportunity to sell more products. However, the progress made in controlling adolescent acne means that the skin care industry must develop new strategies for selling if it wants to keep profits up. With that goal in mind, adolescent girls are now encouraged to be as proactive about aging as they are about acne.[57]

Instead of acne intervention, lifetime skin care is the new strategy for selling to adolescent girls. In addition to pushing the usual pimple creams, Procter & Gamble spent $11 million in 1992 for a market research program (involving two million high school girls) designed to promote Oil of Olay, an anti-aging and moisture-replenishing lotion traditionally associated with mature women. In order to ensure megasales in the next few decades, Procter & Gamble is promoting the virtues of lifetime skin care to adolescent girls and, in the process, establishing brand loyalty to their product. (The strategy obviously follows the model of the sanitary products industry, where corporate profits are tied to purchasing patterns established in girlhood.)

For adolescent girls, this new marketing agenda is less than helpful because it adds yet another pressure to all of the existing ones shaping the experience of growing up in a female body. To be required to develop a personal regimen to keep the skin youthful even before youth has ebbed taxes the normal dermal consciousness of girls in some unfair ways. It certainly requires them to spend more money and time on their own faces at a stage in life when their creative and intellectual development would be better served by looking beyond the physical self. Although it is wise to encourage young women to protect themselves from the ultraviolet rays of the sun, responsible adults should not encourage precocious primping, or the idea that a lifelong battle against the "ravages" of age is a prerequisite of good womanhood.

Girls suffer enough with the vagaries of adolescent acne. In the 1980s and 1990s, even the smallest blemish looms large in their struggle against self-consciousness. A fourteen-year-old told her diary: "I have three pimples. Yuck! I look like I have chicken pox!" A seventeen-year-old, who was considerably more mature and bound for Mount Holyoke College, still felt the same intense agony: "I could just feel a pimple growing on my chin. It was awful! I put tons of Clearasil on it when I got home so hopefully it will be gone tomorrow."[58] Although this familiar refrain echoes the unhappiness of "Miss. E.L." in the 1890s, girls today have expectations about skin blemishes that their Victorian sisters did not. Both improved nutrition and scientific medicine have made pimples easier to control and, at the same time, middle-class nurturance has made them less and less acceptable.

In the twentieth century, American girls had their dermal consciousness raised—by mirrors and by medicine, by the aspirations of middle-class parents, and by the emergence of a seductive visual culture in which fantasies of perfect female faces and bodies became pervasive and potent. These developments—aided and abetted by dermatology's increasing success in controlling adolescent acne—explain why pimples loom larger than ever in the psyches of contemporary girls. More than any previous generation, they expect to look perfect—just like the models and personalities they see every day in retouched, airbrushed photographs in magazines as well as on television and in the movies.

The social history of acne in this century ultimately demonstrates the power of medicine and middle-class nurturance to refine the adolescent body, in effect bringing one of its well-known physical developments under control. Although acne was never really life-threatening, pimples were considered sufficiently critical in the lives of girls to justify medical intervention. In this way, skin care was the first of many different body investments made by middle-class parents. Orthodontia, weight-loss camps, contact lenses, and plastic surgery all followed, revealing how parental resources have been harnessed in the twentieth century to a new ideal of physical perfection. American girls could not help but internalize this powerful imperative and, in the process, they developed their own, even more compelling, body projects.

1

In the nineteenth century, adolescent girls were self-conscious, but they worried about different body parts than do girls today. Even Victoria, the princess who became queen of England, worried that her hands were too large; in that era, large hands and feet implied a coarse, working-class way of life. She is shown here in a portrait by Sir George Hayter, painted in 1835 when she was sixteen.

2

This sixteen-year-old in the 1860s posed demurely to highlight her good character rather than her physical beauty. She was smaller than today's girls of the same age, and she probably began menstruating later. Over the course of the century, girls of all social classes and ethnic groups became larger and experienced menarche earlier due to improved nutrition and the decline of infectious diseases.

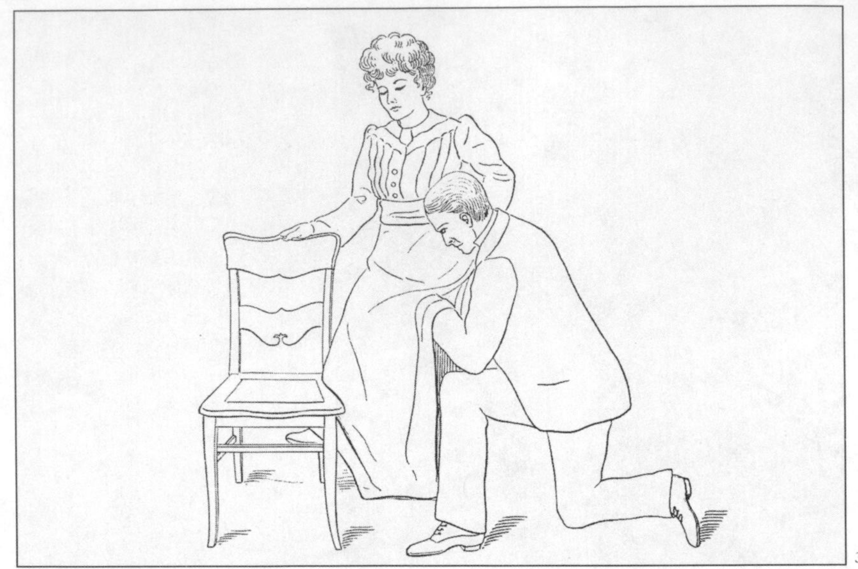

3

Victorian modesty influenced medical practice and ideas about the female body. This illustration from a 1905 medical textbook demonstrates the recommended way to examine women's reproductive organs. The "private parts" of adolescent girls were protected from medical scrutiny (and self-scrutiny) for as long as possible. Mothers accompanied their daughters when and if they had to endure such a repellent and dangerous interaction.

4

By the late nineteenth century, adolescent girls like these from a small town in upstate New York did not look much different from their urban counterparts. Through magazines and books, as well as from their experience in public high schools, girls of this era began to see themselves as part of a larger "girl culture," and they imitated the fashionable clothing, jewelry, and hairstyles of friends.

Photographs of Styles No. 204, 527, 532.

At Every Step

the girl in a Ferris Waist grows in grace, health and beauty. With its support she passes through childhood in safety, blossoms into girlhood with unrestricted development, and arrives at womanhood with a perfect figure.

FERRIS GOOD SENSE WAIST

Fits the form and brings health, comfort and grace to every age

Made in styles adapted to every form and size. Sold by leading retailers everywhere. "Ferris Good Sense" in red letters marks it genuine. **The Model Book** mailed free.

THE FERRIS BROS. COMPANY, 341 Broadway, NEW YORK

5

Among middle-class women—the kind who saw this advertisement in *The Ladies' Home Journal*—the healthy physical development of daughters was a prime concern. As a result, the Ferris company premiered the idea that there was a "right" undergarment for each stage in a young woman's life. Typically, daughters donned corsets only when they were fully developed; until then they wore undershirts and camisoles designed for flat chests.

6

Age 12

7

Age 16

8

Age 18

Harriet (Hattie) Cooper was the daughter of Sarah Cooper, a pioneer in the kindergarten movement in San Francisco. These pictures, taken between 1868 and 1874, show Hattie at ages twelve, sixteen, and eighteen.

"Standard"

Modern Bath Room—Design P 70

THIS room is tiled in 6 x 6-inch white glazed tile and the floor is unglazed ceramic tile. The tints showing on the tile walls are reflections. It is impossible to make a picture do entire justice to the tile treatment.

An important feature of this room is the separate closet enclosure, reached from both the bath room and the hall. This is a style of construction that we predict will become more general in the future.

PRICES

Bath, 5½ ft., Plate P 1980 J	$47.75
Shower, Plate P 2812 . . .	38.00
Foot Bath, Plate P 2580 J .	30.00
Lavatory, Plate P 3096 G . .	47.00
Closet, Plate P 7532 . . .	42.50
Total	$205.25

NOTE:—Bath Tub and Foot Bath as illustrated and priced furnished regularly with one coat of paint on outside.

See page 21 for exterior finish and decorations.

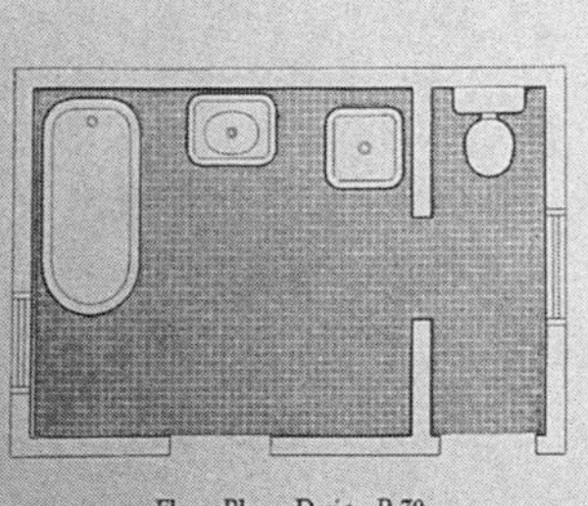

Floor Plan—Design P 70

9

The advent of modern plumbing had a great impact on the adolescent girl's psychological investment in her face and body. By the turn of the century, running water, mirrors, and electric lights provided middle-class girls with vast opportunities for self-scrutiny, especially of their skin and hair. The bathroom was as important as the private bedroom in setting the stage for modern girlhood.

The growing focus on appearance meant that girls spent more time in front of mirrors arranging their hair. In many families, mothers, daughters, and sisters also spent considerable time brushing each other's hair. Typically, girls wore their hair long until their figures began to develop; at that point, they were allowed to wear their hair up, piled on top of the head. In 1898, when this advertisement appeared, weekly hair washing was unusual and daily shampooing would have been considered a health risk.

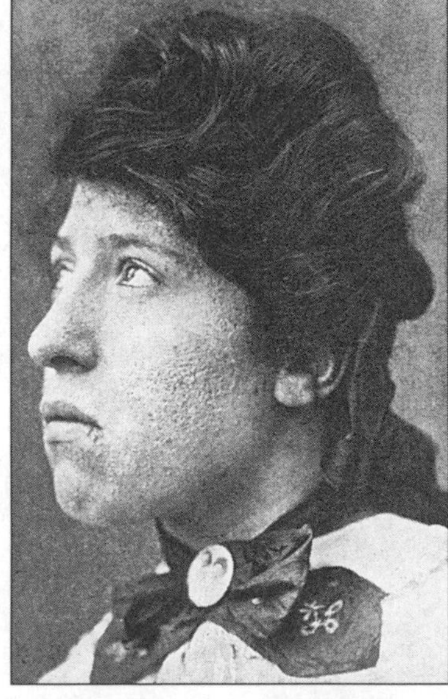

Pimples were a source of great embarrassment to girls in the nineteenth century because they were associated with masturbation, sexual perversion, and venereal diseases such as syphilis. In the twentieth century, middle-class parents and physicians regarded adolescent acne as a psychological as well as a medical problem, so they began to treat it more aggressively.

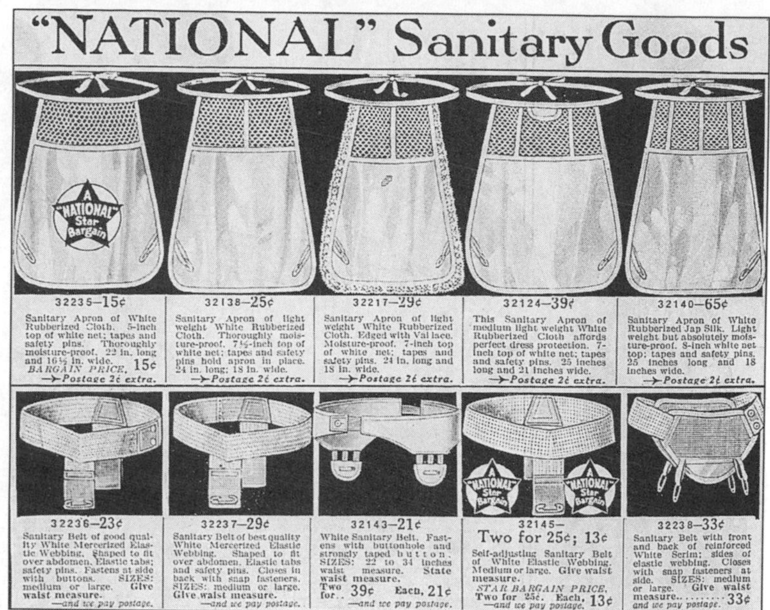

New scientific ideas that created pressure to keep the body free of germs and odor transformed menstruation. By 1900, American women were giving up homemade devices and experimenting with many different kinds of "sanitary" products, including mass-produced belts, aprons, and napkins. This advertisement from the Bellas Hess Company shows the range of options available from one mail-order catalogue in the spring of 1917.

Menstruation was a private topic until the 1920s, when advertisements for disposable sanitary napkins began to appear in women's magazines. The manufacturer of Kotex promised local druggists a lucrative business if they displayed sanitary napkins in their stores. This 1923 advertisement from *Retail Druggist,* a trade magazine, shows how the pursuit of profit helped break the traditional silence about female physiology.

Adolescent girls in the "bloom of youth" were widely admired, and their images were used by painters and popular illustrators as symbols of both promise and expectation. At the turn of the century, popular illustrators such as Charles Dana Gibson, Howard Chandler Christy, Harrison Fisher, and Henry Hutt produced hundreds of images of the American girl in books and magazines as well as on cards and calendars. Although doctors at this time decried the ill health and fragility of America's young women, the girls of the American imagination were always vigorous, graceful, and athletic.

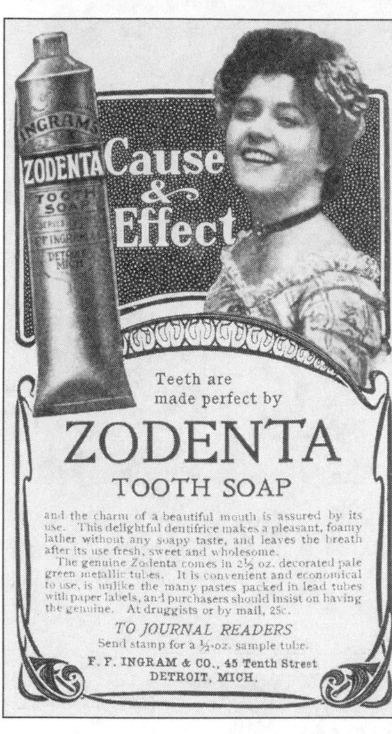

16

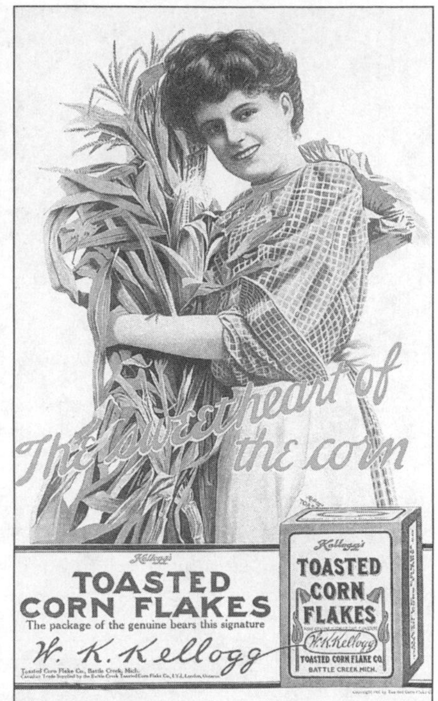

17

18

By the early twentieth century, a girl's face—including her teeth—was expected to be clean and pretty. Advertisements for soaps, lotions, and skin tonics, as well as for some of America's other favorite products, now featured drawings and photographs of healthy young women rather than of older matrons.

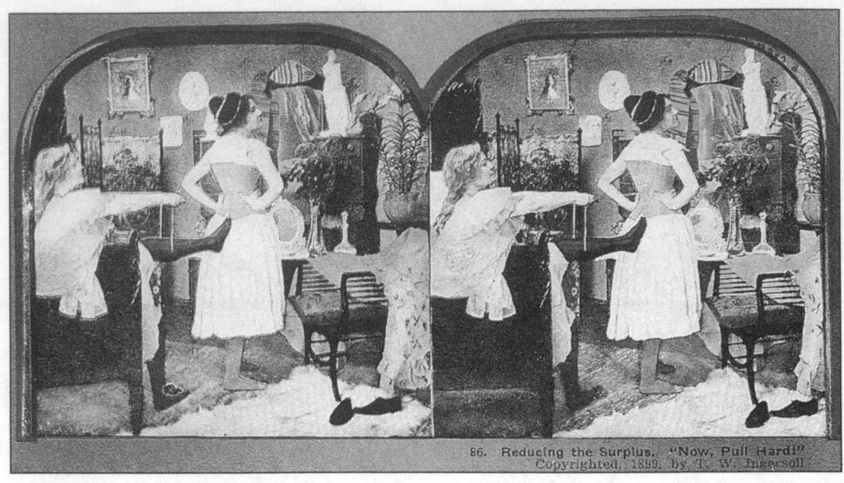

19

Women's bodies began to appear more prominently in many different forms of popular culture, such as this risqué stereopticon slide that purported to provide an intimate view of a young woman being laced into a corset by a friend. The caption—Reducing the Surplus. "Now, pull hard!"—reflects the nineteenth-century emphasis on the small waist.

20

21

By the turn of the century, female legs were increasingly exposed and evaluated. In this 1903 advertisement for Onyx hosiery, ankles were bared seductively but discreetly.

22

23

Many educators, as well as parents, regarded competitive athletics as harmful to young women because it allegedly destroyed their grace and refinement as well as their physical and emotional well-being. As a result, many middle-class girls were steered into light calisthenics that were performed as a group, using dumbbells, wands, or rings in response to verbal commands.

24

Despite the emphasis on recreational rather than competitive exercise, basketball became increasingly popular in high schools. Teams like this one in Ithaca, New York, were often coached by young women who had learned to play the game at the state normal schools for training teachers.

25

Weight was not a critical part of female identity until the 1920s, when home scales and dieting became more common among American women. Until then, drugstores or county fairs were the only places where young women could weigh themselves. This 1905 postcard suggests that guessing an individual's weight was not a particularly sensitive issue and that there was still a premium on young women who were robust.

Thousands of American women and girls had their hair cut short for the first time in the 1920s, either by male barbers or in the new commercial "beauty parlors" operated by women. Bobbed hair was accompanied by a slimmer silhouette, and both served as a sign of new attitudes about sexuality and autonomy.

26

27

Powder, lipstick, and eyebrow pencil were all increasingly common on the faces of young women in the 1920s, as was the act of "making up" in public. This illustration from a 1927 *Ladies' Home Journal* symbolized the wide acceptance of cosmetics, something that earlier generations considered inappropriate among "nice" women.

The stylish "flapper" chemise of the 1920s had straight lines and short skirts, and required a flat chest. Although many corset companies began to produce and market special bandeau bras to bind the breasts for the new, youthful look, control of the body came increasingly from within, through "slimming," what we now call dieting.

28

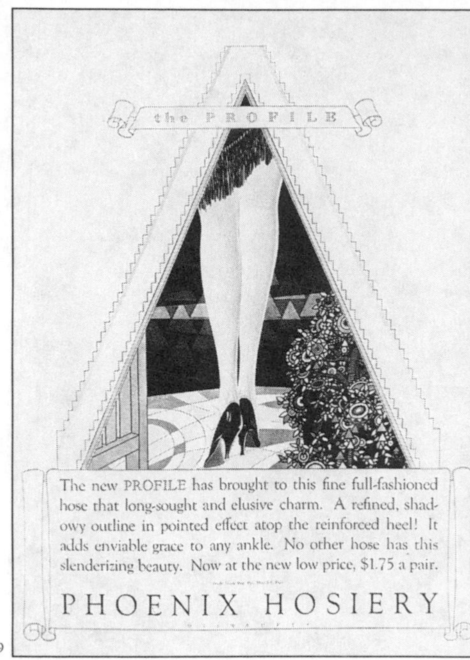

29

30

An elongated calf, a trim ankle, and a glimpse of thigh were the ideal in American fashion in the 1920s. The modern body required hairless legs and underarms, and this 1924 ad from the magazine *Delineator* promoted the benefits of Neet, one of the first depilatories.

Mothers in the twentieth century turned increasingly to books and commercial pamphlets as a way of handling intimate discussions with their daughters about necking, petting, and premarital intercourse—all of which were on the rise. In this ad, from a 1927 *Ladies' Home Journal,* a mother who was concerned about the connection between sexuality and germs counseled her daughter and recommended a hygiene pamphlet, written by a woman doctor and supplied by the makers of Lysol.

31

32

In the 1920s, beauty pageants grew in popularity. They focused attention on the outside of a girl's body rather than on her spirit or her character. Pageants like this one, in 1927 at the Park Ridge Country Club for Colored People near Corona, California, were segregated by race and usually involved adolescent girls.

33

The body itself became the fashion in the 1920s. Girls at the beach in this era exposed more flesh than ever before. These girls used the sun and stencils to put the names of their favorite movie stars directly on their bodies.

In 1945, when this picture was taken, a modest two-piece bathing suit was still considered somewhat provocative. This stylish fifteen-year-old, from James Madison High School in Brooklyn, shopped at Macy's and wore a snood, a haircovering made popular during World War II by movie stars and women's magazines. *Seventeen,* which began publication in 1944, was an important vehicle for promoting the latest teenage styles among middle-class American girls.

In the 1950s, there was an explosion of special clothing designed specifically for adolescent girls. Manufacturers typically used brand names that highlighted teenage identity, and some even claimed to involve girls in the design of the garments.

Teen Chesterfield
Chesterfield coat that's a girl's best chum. It's the three-button, big-button style with a dandy velvet collar and roomy pockets. Tailored as nicely as his coat — of suedy-look KINGORA — that's all warm cuddly wool with a cotton backing. And lined with Earl-Glo. Twelve top-teen colors in sizes 10 to 16. Under $40.00.
KINGORA REG. APP'D. FOR
Exclusive
FASHIONED BY Barbara
At these stores:
NEW YORK CITY .... Arnold Constable
PHILADELPHIA, PA. .... Gimbel Bros.
ST. LOUIS, MO. .... Famous-Barr
CHICAGO, ILL. .... The Hub (Henry C. Lytton & Sons)
CLEVELAND, OHIO .... Higbee Co.
DAYTON, OHIO .... Elder & Johnston
BUFFALO, N. Y. .... Adam, Meldrum & Anderson
PROVIDENCE, R. I. .... Cherry & Webb
For store nearest you, write
Barbara COAT CO.
520 Eighth Ave. • New York 18, N. Y.

36

"Double Feature"
"Coke-ette"
Teens Designed These Prize Winners!
We asked America's teen-age girls what they'd like to wear this Autumn and nearly 50,000 submitted their ideas in the National Teentimer Design-and-Name-it-Contest! Marian Sweet and Diana Rudman carried off top honors with these two designs. Delores Vaccaro and Mildred Erickson cooked up the names. "Coke-ette" has been made up in famous Labtex Jiminy flannel with felt applique trim. Colors: Mexican Melon, Gold, Frostleaf Green, Powder Blue, Aqua and Fuchsia. Priced about $10. "Double Feature" combines a dress of Macomba Crepe with a separate jerkin of Cohama Frostpoint. In Red or Kelly with Black and White jerkin, Pistachio or Gold with Brown and White jerkin. The dress is priced about $9 and the jerkin about $4.50. Teen sizes 8 to 16.
At leading stores everywhere.
Teentimer
OHRIGINALS

37

38

This seventeen-year-old beauty queen from New York City exemplified the ideal of female beauty in the 1950s: full pointed breasts combined with long legs, usually displayed in high heels.

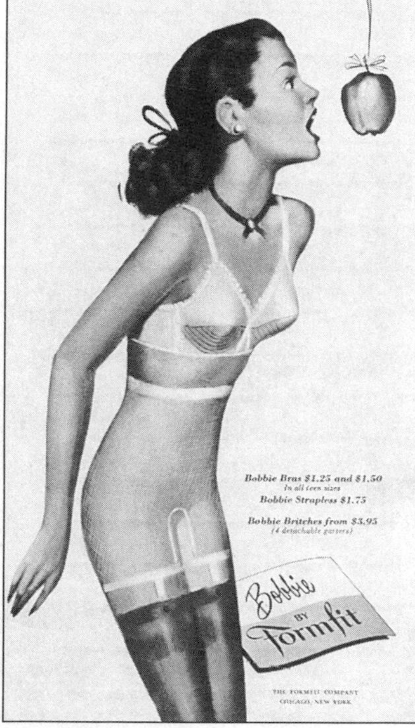

39

In the post–World War II era, when breast size was so important, training bras became a fixture of adolescence. American girls wanted them in order to look mature and pretty; doctors and advertisers recommended them—along with girdles—as the first step on the road to healthy womanhood and a "good figure."

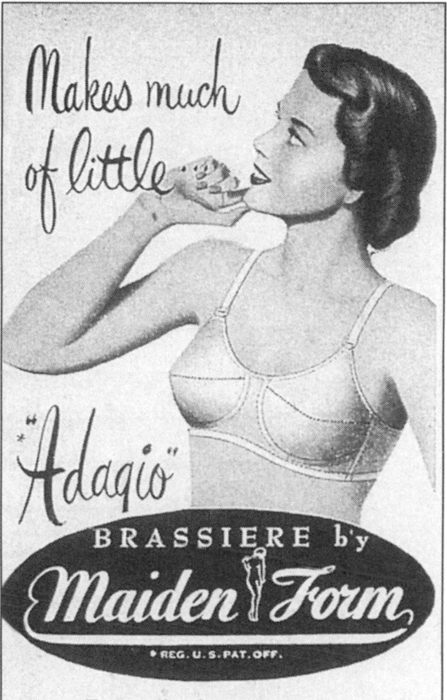

40

41

Many businesses capitalized on adolescent anxieties about appearance, most notably those that sold skin products. The Clearasil Personality of the Month campaign, initiated in 1951, promised acne sufferers both clear skin and popularity if they used the product.

How happy can a chubby girl be?

As happy as a hit with a rollicking beat, or a serenade in a dreamy mood . . . as happy as one whose extra young pounds have been delightfully transformed by the designing magic of

Chubbettes

fashions to make girls 6 to 16 look slimmer

shown above: Sub-Teen Glen plaid sheath, $7.98 — Girls woven gingham plaid, $5.98

FREE! "Pounds and Personality" . . . booklet for parents who want to assure the happiness of their overweight girls. Dr. Gladys Andrews of New York University tells what to do about nicknames, shyness, tactless remarks, diet, etc.

CHUBBETTES, Middlesex, N. J.
Please send me the items checked:
☐ "Pounds and Personality" ☐ Fashion catalog
☐ Name of nearest store selling Chubbettes
Name
Address
City Zone State
(nearest large city)

42

The middle-class audience that saw this 1958 advertisement in *Life* magazine assumed that weight, like acne, was a psychological issue for girls, even for those as young as six. Girls who were overweight were offered "slenderizing" styles, and their parents were provided with expert advice about how to deal with the ridicule that fat girls often received.

43

Cheerleading meant social success in the high schools of the 1950s. It was also the height of female athleticism in an era that gave little encouragement to competitive sports among adolescent girls. Cheerleading squads, like this wholesome junior varsity from Mount Upton, New York, in 1953, typically dressed in heavy sweaters and kneelength skirts that imitated collegiate styles. By the early 1960s, drill teams, such as the Temple City Ramettes in Southern California, were somewhat more provocative.

44

45

Throughout the 1950s, adolescent girls posed next to the cars of boyfriends or parents in imitation of splashy automobile advertisements they saw in popular magazines. When her father and mother brought home a new 1955 Mercury station wagon, this fourteen-year-old posed in the driveway of her Windham, Connecticut, home.

46

The strapless "prom" dress was a national phenomenon in the 1950s and early 1960s, but it was hard to wear without both a developed bosom and a long-line bra. This fourteen-year-old was dressed for a formal sponsored by the Future Homemakers of America in Canyon, Texas, in 1960.

47

Until the 1950s, men, women, and children generally wore the same style eyeglasses, but in the postwar years eyeglass frames were created specifically for women and girls. The notion that eyeglasses were a social liability for women—epitomized by Dorothy Parker's famous quip "Men seldom make passes at girls who wear glasses"—influenced the design and marketing of fashionable frames.

48

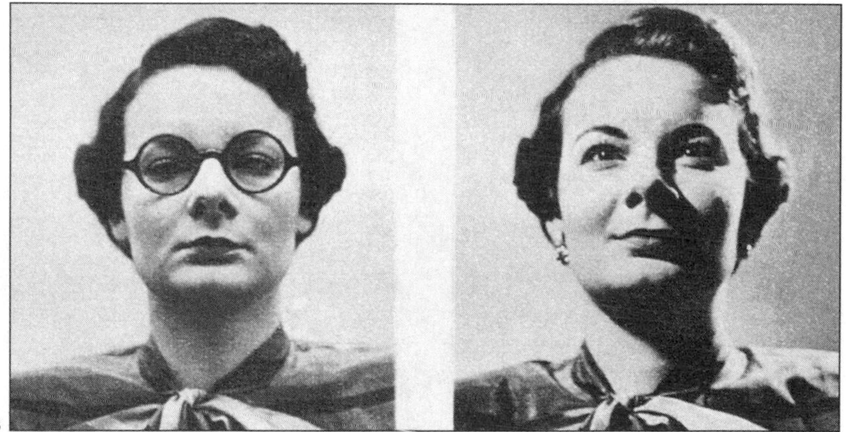

Although contact lenses were available by the 1930s, ordinary adolescent girls did not begin wearing them until the 1950s. This 1954 picture from *Look* shows how the general reading public first learned the cosmetic advantages of contact lenses. By 1959, there were at least one million teenagers wearing lenses, and the majority of those were girls.

By the mid-1960s, when this picture was taken, blue jeans were on their way to becoming a national uniform for the young. Jeans put emphasis on the lower body and were paired increasingly with form-revealing T-shirts rather than traditional blouses. These nineteen-year-olds in Los Angeles also sported sandals and macramé bracelets purchased in a stylish "counterculture" boutique.

49

50

Certain fashions, such as the bra tops and low-slung shorts of the 1970s, require a thin body. This photo, taken in 1972, suggests our increasing tolerance for the display of extremely thin bodies.

Yearbook pictures reflect the shift in emphasis from a girl's face to her entire body. This 1963 senior photograph from Traverse City, Michigan, is typical of an older era when senior photographs showed only the head and shoulders, and every young woman wore the same blouse or sweater with a similar locket, pendant, or pearls. Many girls in the 1990s have made their bodies into projects, and recent yearbook pictures, such as this 1995 senior picture from a Connecticut high school, often imitate contemporary fashion shots.

51

52

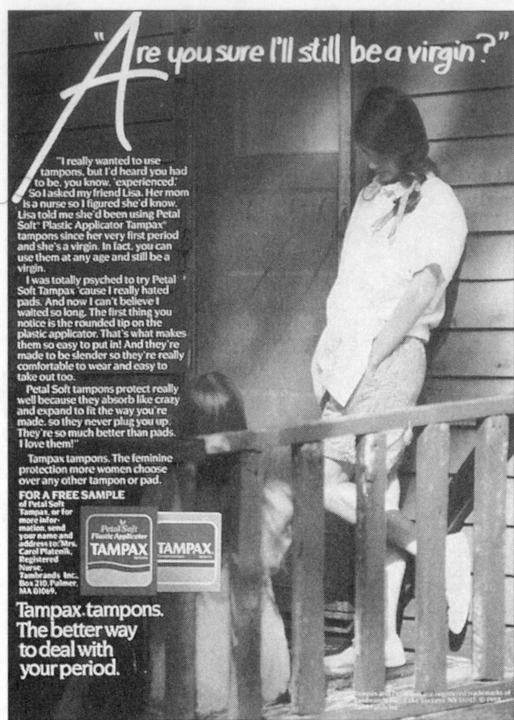

53

Internal sanitary protection is commonplace today even among girls without sexual experience. This 1990 advertisement from *Seventeen* was designed to put to rest traditional fears that tampons threatened a young woman's hymen.

54

As soon as young girls today begin to develop, they are sold underwear and lingerie designed to promote their sexual allure. In contrast to earlier eras, contemporary mothers are not involved in their daughters' choice of undergarments.

Athleticism is admired among girls in the 1990s. As a result of changes wrought by Title IX, a federal ruling that required equity in the support of male and female athletic programs, opportunities for competitive athletics among young women have mushroomed since the 1970s. Today we see girls involved in sports once reserved for men.

This young woman, an all-American swimmer, has the "new shoulders" so much in evidence at the 1996 Olympics in Atlanta. Although her stance is a joking imitation of a traditional male body builder, she is proud of her upper body development because it is crucial to success in her sport.

56

The rugby scrimmage requires that young women abandon the notion that there are "ladylike" positions. When girls play rugby, as they began to do on American college campuses in the 1990s, they must be strong, physically aggressive, and display a fierce competitiveness.

57

Female athleticism is glamorized and idealized in a great deal of contemporary advertising. It it also used to sell new products such as this "sporty clean" deodorant designed, allegedly, for female sweat. In the 1980s, aerobics became the most popular way to combine fitness and femininity, and smart marketers encouraged that connection with pink sport shoes and lavender aerobic equipment.

Although piercing was once considered exotic or deviant, it has become increasingly commonplace as a way of announcing adolescent identity. This eighteen-year-old, who defines herself as a feminist, an environmentalist, and a vegan, pierced her nose in high school with her mother's consent.

59

Young women's normal anxieties about their developing bodies have been at the core of marketing strategies since World War II. This 1990 advertisement from *Sassy,* however, plays on female self-hate in order to sell the product.

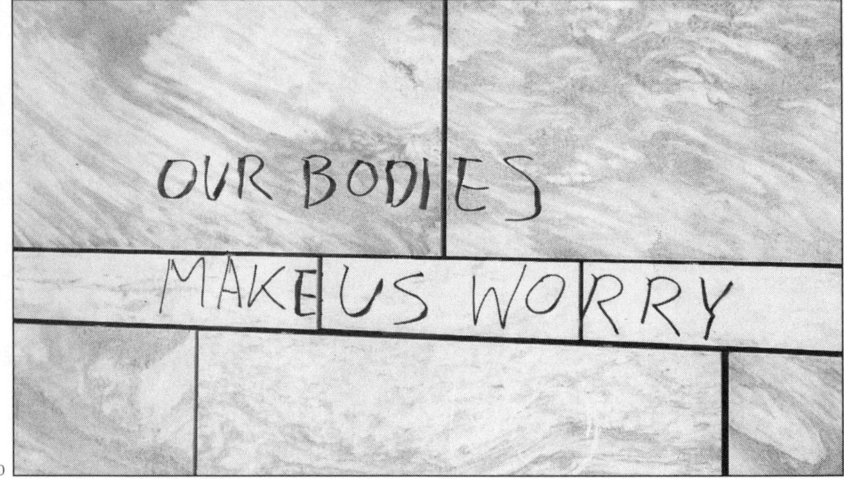

60

Graffiti on the wall of a Cornell University building in 1995 suggests how problematic the body has become for young people in the past twenty years. ("Our Bodies, Ourselves" was the optimistic slogan of an earlier generation.) In addition to the pressure for physical perfection, young women today must navigate a world where sexuality is both an optimum value and also a real and present danger.

CHAPTER FOUR

Body Projects

Photos on p. 95: *(left)* Permission of H. C. Griswold Collection, Photographic Archives, University of Louisville; *(right)* permission of Jessica Fausty.

In the twentieth century, the body has become the central personal project of American girls. This priority makes girls today vastly different from their Victorian counterparts. Although girls in the past and present display many common developmental characteristics—such as self-consciousness, sensitivity to peers, and an interest in establishing an independent identity—before the twentieth century, girls simply did not organize their thinking about themselves around their bodies. Today, many young girls worry about the contours of their bodies—especially shape, size, and muscle tone—because they believe that the body is the ultimate expression of the self.

The body is a consuming project for contemporary girls because it provides an important means of self-definition, a way to visibly announce who you are to the world. From a historical perspective, this particular form of adolescent expression is a relatively recent phenomenon. In the twentieth century, adolescent girls learned from their mothers, as well as from the larger culture, that modern femininity required some degree of exhibitionism.[1] By the 1920s, both fashion and film had encouraged a massive "unveiling" of the female body, which meant that certain body parts—such as arms and legs—were bared and displayed in ways they had never been before. This new freedom to display the body was accompanied, however, by demanding beauty and dietary regimens that involved money as well as self-discipline. Beginning in the 1920s, women's legs and underarms had to be smooth and free of body hair; the torso had to be svelte; and the breasts were supposed to be small and firm. What American women did not realize at the time was that their stunning new freedom actually implied the need for greater internal control of the body, an imperative that would intensify and become even more powerful by the end of the twentieth century.

The seeds of this cultural and psychological change from external to internal control of the body lie in vast societal transformations that characterized the move from agrarian to industrial society, and from a religious to a secular world. But I want to bring the story closer to home and focus on some characteristic "body projects" that have absorbed the attention of adolescent girls since the beginning of the twentieth century. These projects demonstrate how the experience of living in an adolescent body is always shaped by the historical moment. They also show how cultural pressures have accumulated, making American girls today, at the close of the twentieth century, more anxious than ever about the size and shape of their bodies, as well as particular body parts.[2]

The Century of Svelte

In the 1920s, for the first time, teenage girls made systematic efforts to lower their weight by food restriction and exercise. Although advice on "slimming" and "reducing" was usually directed at adult women, college and high school girls also dieted. In 1924, the *Smith College Weekly* printed a letter from students warning about the newest craze on campus: "If preventive measures against strenuous dieting are not taken soon, Smith College will become notorious not for sylph-like forms but for haggard faces and dull listless eyes."[3]

Despite the threat of ill health, college girls in the 1920s worked hard to become slender. Instead of writing home happily about weight gain and abundant eating, as female collegians had done in the 1880s and 1890s, young women at elite schools such as Smith debated the virtues of different diet plans and worried about gaining weight. Popular serial fiction for younger girls, such as Grace Harlow and Nancy Drew, now had a fat character who served as a humorous foil to the well-liked, smart protagonist, who was always slim.[4]

The adolescent girls involved in the first American "slimming craze" were motivated by a new ideal of female beauty that began to evolve around the turn of the century. In 1908, Paul Poiret, a Parisian designer, introduced a new silhouette that replaced the voluptuous Victorian hourglass, with its tiny waist and exaggerated hips. Instead, Poiret's dresses shifted visual interest to the legs. The new, fashionable figure was slender, long-limbed, and relatively flat-chested. American women of all ages donned the short, popular chemise dress that was the uniform of the "flapper" in the 1920s. As they did so, they bade farewell to corsets, stays, and petticoats, and they began to diet, or internalize control of the body. This set the stage for what one writer called "the century of svelte."[5]

The Slimming of Yvonne Blue

The story of Yvonne Blue reveals how the ideal of slenderness was first incorporated into the experience of American girls. Born in 1911, Yvonne was the eldest of three daughters in a Protestant family living in Hyde Park, an intellectual mecca that surrounded the University of Chicago. Her father was an ophthalmologist; her mother was a homemaker with a literary bent. Although the Blues were teetotaling Baptists who enjoyed sedate pleasures such as golf and reading, their daughter tasted the full repertoire of American popular culture: she read everything from comics and women's magazines to best-selling novels, listened to jazz on the radio, and went to the moving pictures regularly. From these sources, as well as from her peers at the University of Chicago High School, Yvonne eventually learned that a slender body was central to female success.

As a girl of twelve and thirteen, Yvonne Blue had been unconcerned about her appearance. She was bookish then, imaginative, and filled with literary ambitions. She wanted to be a famous author or the leader of a pirate gang, or travel the world as Peter Pan. By the time she was fifteen, however, these lively literary and dramatic projects were tempered by a new self-consciousness. Between thirteen and fifteen, Yvonne underwent a growth spurt that increased her height by almost six inches and her weight by over forty pounds, so that she was nearly five feet six inches tall and weighed 150 pounds. This increase in size was natural, but it seemed problematic in the 1920s, when a small, slender female body was considered highly desirable. Yvonne told her diary that she wanted to be "slim and sylph like," like her favorite film stars—or like the sophisticated women she saw in popular magazines and the rotogravure.

The skimpy dresses and frenetic Charleston of the "flapper" may be a cliché, but the flapper image really did capture the new emotional and social possibilities available to Yvonne's generation and to adolescent girls ever since. After World War I, many girls cut loose from traditional moorings to church and community, as well as from ties to their mothers and grandmothers. The adult women who supervised single-sex groups in the 1920s, such as the Girl Scouts, began to note a decline in membership and interest, which they attributed to all of the new entertainment options open to young women.[6] In addition to new experiences with radio and movies, adolescent girls went about unchaperoned, rode in automobiles, and talked on the telephone, all of which increased mobility and autonomy. But as young women became more independent of their mothers and more knowledgeable about the world, their self-esteem began to have more to do with external attributes than with inner qualities, such as strength of character or generosity of spirit. Since movies, magazines, and department stores in the 1920s all gave primacy to a woman's visual image, even young teenagers like Yvonne began to worry about their appearance in ways that required increased attention to their bodies and made the body into a project.[7]

Like most girls of the period, Yvonne's career as a flapper began with a haircut. "Yesterday I went to the barber's and had my hair shingle bobbed cut in a bob just like a boy's only longer," she wrote in 1923, the year she entered high school. For Yvonne and her friends, the bob was an important symbol. In the nineteenth century, hair was considered a woman's crowning glory, and the more the better. Most girls grew their hair long so that it could be piled on top of the head as a declaration of maturity, and they spent long hours with their mothers and sisters reading aloud, sewing, and talking while they dried and brushed their hair. These intimate, intergenerational grooming rituals—like the sewing and reading they accompanied—disappeared once the bob became the order of the day. Short hair did not require the same kind of labor, and it visually separated the young from the old. In addition, it symbolized a new attitude toward the female body—an attitude that proclaimed greater freedom but also required new internal constraints, one of which was controlling food intake.

As Yvonne became more self-absorbed (which is not unusual in an adolescent), she also became more dissatisfied with the way she looked. At fifteen, social events that should have been fun became worrisome because she felt so large and ungainly. When she was invited to a special luncheon for talented young poets in the Chicago area, Yvonne dreaded going because she had to wear a "screaming red dress" that she thought made her look like a "trick elephant." One particularly miserable day, she called herself a "fat, crude, uncouth misunderstood beast" and wallowed in the idea that she was a pariah at school. Like many girls in de Beauvoir's "difficult patch," Yvonne was dramatic and prone to exaggeration: "I wonder if anyone in the world has ever hated herself as I hate myself?"

What was new and modern about Yvonne's adolescent angst was that she focused on weight loss as a solution to her problems. As a result, she began to "slim," in the summer of 1926, when she was fifteen. "I'm so tired of being fat!" she wrote. "I'm going back to school weighing 119 pounds—I swear it. Three months in which to lose thirty pounds—but I'll do it—or die in the attempt." To that end, she sent away for a booklet called "How to Reduce: New Waistlines for Old," written by Antoinette Donnelly, the beauty editor at the *Chicago Tribune,* and she began to count calories, a relatively new concept in the 1920s. Although she had a full-length mirror, the Blues, like most middle-class families in the 1920s, did not own a scale, so Yvonne began taking trips to the drugstore, or the gymnasium at the University of Chicago, to weigh herself.[8]

On some days, Yvonne wrote down everything she ate; on others, she "forgot." Sometimes she noted special temptations, such as ice cream or fried chicken. One summer evening, to avoid eating, she refused to enter a restaurant with her family and sat outside in the car while everyone else went inside. There were a number of unpleasant struggles with her concerned parents, who did not approve of adolescent dieting and thought she looked just fine: "Mother and Daddy make me so mad!" she wrote. "They *make* me eat [emphasis in original]. Last night I dropped most of my meal in my lap, and rolled it in my napkin and fed it to Tar Baby [the dog] later." Although the *Chicago Tribune* reducing plan recommended 1,200–1,500 calories a day, along with a program of exercise, Yvonne was so enthusiastic and impatient that she tried to keep her daily food intake down to 50 calories, allowing herself only lettuce, carrots, celery, tea, and consommé. "No cake or pie or ice cream or cookies or candy or nuts or fruits or bread or potatoes or meats or anything," she wrote unhappily. At one point, she became faint and her mother insisted that she remain at home on the chaise, drinking cocoa and eating fruit to restore her energy.

Yvonne's flamboyant dieting angered her parents, who had little interest in seeing her lose weight. Although they were progressive people for the 1920s, they held to the traditional Victorian idea that weight loss was not particularly healthy or attractive in a growing girl. Yvonne and her friends had a very different idea, however, and they talked incessantly about "slimming." One of Yvonne's best friends, Mattie Van Ness, decided to join Yvonne in her diet even though she herself was not at all large. Together, they made dieting into a game and a competition. Mattie wrote to Yvonne from her family vacation that summer: "I had a dream with you in it. You wore a lumberjack blouse and a checked skirt, and you were so thin I nearly died of envy. I am terribly fat."

Weight was so often a subject of conversation in school that Yvonne developed a savvy response to the familiar question, How much do you weigh?: "I always ask people to guess my weight when they inquire it and I always give them as small a sum as they'll swallow." By watching her sweets and denying herself all carbohydrates and most meat, Yvonne reduced her weight to about 125 pounds, which made her feel triumphant on her return to school for her senior year, in September of 1926.

Image Is Identity

Yvonne Blue's body project feels modern because it reflects a deep faith in the power of personal image, as well as the excitement and potential of a "makeover." By changing the configuration of her body, she hoped to create a new image for herself that would win popularity and status at school. Like many others who grew up in the 1920s, Yvonne was greatly concerned about "image." This was a reflection of the world in which she came to maturity. Even an ordinary girl without Yvonne's literary imagination could re-create herself in a number of different ways. Every time she went to a movie, opened a magazine, entered a department store dressing room, or changed her lipstick, she could try on a new identity. Because it was no longer considered sinful or shallow to care so much about how you looked, girls talked among themselves about how to improve or change their hair, face, and figure. In her bedroom, Yvonne obsessed with Mattie about the ways in which Betty Bronson, a favorite film star, changed her looks in order to play different roles, and that model stayed with both of them as they proceeded through high school.

Yvonne re-created herself in a number of different ways over the course of the next few years. Only a few months before her sixteenth birthday, she did something that is characteristic of modern girls: she deliberately changed her handwriting. This kind of self-conscious transformation of handwriting did not occur in girls' diaries until the 1920s, when girls learned from popular culture how flexible personal image could be. Yvonne's new handwriting was extremely artificial and stylized. It did not slant to the right, according to the Palmer Method taught in grade school; certain letters were executed in clear defiance of the rules of capitalization; and there was an eclectic mixture of cursive writing and printing. By altering her image on the page as well as in the flesh, Yvonne hoped to convey that she was unusual and talented, instead of ordinary and boring. (In the 1950s, I remember changing my handwriting so that I would appear more mature and feminine. Because Joni James was a popular vocalist then, I began spelling my first name the way she did, dotting the *i* with a little circle and making my letters as round as possible.)[9]

Yvonne devoted even more attention to the construction of her image at the University of Chicago, where she became a freshman in 1927. Although she lived at home with her parents, college represented a new social world that was exciting but also frightening. The night before she entered college, she wrote optimistically that tomorrow "will be the most important day of my life so far." But within days Yvonne was feeling ill at ease and inadequate because of the social pressures associated with Freshman Week and rushing a sorority. She feared that she would be unpopular again in college, as she thought she had been in high school. "I am miserable," she wrote, "because Helen [a high school friend] is being rushed for two sororities and I am not. I don't want to go to the events—they're all bridge suppers or dances—[but] it's the principle of the thing. Evidently our high school records precede us. It's not fair and I resent it."

In this difficult moment of transition, Yvonne paid close attention to her figure, her hair, and her clothes. Eventually, she was invited to join the Acoth Club, and she was sufficiently impressed by the behavior of her sorority sisters to write about them in her diary: "[They] talked of nothing but boys, smoked incessantly, and scattered 'O my Gods!' quite liberally through their conversation." Under their tutelage, she took up cigarettes, cut her hair in the most severe bob possible, and began to dress only in black. Two months into her freshman year, Yvonne wrote: "I have lost sincerity and become a cynic. My type is now sophisticated, bored, blasé and it is going over well on campus." But a year later she was cultivating a different persona, and cast herself as a "smart Northshore society girl," the clubby kind, who traveled around in a yellow Whippet roadster.

Over the course of her college career, Yvonne Blue changed her image as regularly as students change classes at the beginning of each term. She also began to demonstrate a lively interest in young men, and spent a good deal of time thinking about ways to attract them. At age eighteen, she chose a familiar form of expression to announce her maturity (and her intentions) to the world. On her own, without the advice of her mother, she went to a downtown Chicago department store and bought a tight, clay-colored, crepe de chine dress that clung to the figure and accentuated her lower torso and breasts. This was an important purchase for a young woman who thought so much about "types" and "images" and also wanted to display "sex appeal," a quality she had read about in women's magazines and popular advice books. (She actually took prolific notes on Doris Langley Moore's *Techniques of the Love Affair.*)[10] Yvonne realized that her new silk dress was revealing. In her diary, she wrote with no embarrassment that it "fit like paper on the wall," and she reported gleefully what the saleswoman said when she came out of the dressing room to model it: "When you are young you should show every bump."

Yvonne's crepe de chine actually revealed more than her slim, grown-up body. The slinky new dress was a symbol of the ways in which culture and fashion in the 1920s had begun to blur the distinction between the private and the public self. Only fifty years before, Yvonne's display of flesh would have been unthinkable for a woman of her class and background, and the words of the saleswoman in Chicago would have made no sense. But by 1930, the year Yvonne purchased the crepe de chine, even nice middle-class girls understood that their bodies were in some ways a public project. In fact, girls like Yvonne intuited that modern femininity required some degree of exhibitionism or, at least, a willingness to display oneself as a decorative object. This sensibility has made girls in the "century of svelte" extremely vulnerable to cultural messages about dieting and particular body parts.

Breast Buds and the "Training" Bra

In every generation, small swellings around the nipples have announced the arrival of puberty. This development, known clinically as "breast buds," occurs before menarche and almost always provokes wonder and self-scrutiny. "I began to examine myself carefully, to search my armpits for hairs and my breasts for signs of swelling," wrote Kate Simon about coming of age in the Bronx at the time of World War I. Although Simon was "horrified" by the rapidity with which her chest developed, many girls, both in literature and real life, long for this important mark of maturity. In Jamaica Kincaid's fictional memoir of growing up in Antigua, *Annie John,* the main character regarded her breasts as "treasured shrubs, needing only the proper combination of water and sunlight to make them flourish." In order to get their breasts to grow, Annie and her best friend, Gwen, lay in a pasture exposing their small bosoms to the moonlight.[11]

Breasts are particularly important to girls in cultures or time periods that give powerful meaning or visual significance to that part of the body. Throughout history, different body parts have been eroticized in art, literature, photography, and film. In some eras, the ankle or upper arm was the ultimate statement of female sexuality.[12] But breasts were the particular preoccupation of Americans in the years after World War II, when voluptuous stars, such as Jayne Mansfield, Jane Russell, and Marilyn Monroe, were popular box-office attractions. The mammary fixation of the 1950s extended beyond movie stars and shaped the experience of adolescents of both genders. In that era, boys seemed to prefer girls who were "busty," and American girls began to worry about breast size as well as about weight. This elaboration of the ideal of beauty raised expectations about what adolescent girls should look like. It also required them to put even more energy and resources into their body projects, beginning at an earlier age.

The story of how this happened is intertwined with the history of the bra, an undergarment that came into its own, as separate from the corset, in the early twentieth century. In 1900, a girl of twelve or thirteen typically wore a one-piece "waist" or camisole that had no cups or darts in front. As her breasts developed, she moved into different styles of the same garment, but these had more construction, such as stitching, tucks, and bones, that would accentuate the smallness of her waist and shape the bosom. In those days, before the arrival of the brassiere, there were no "cups." The bosom was worn low; there was absolutely no interest in uplift, and not a hint of cleavage.[13]

The French word *brassière,* which actually means an infant's undergarment or harness, was used in *Vogue* as early as 1907. In the United States, the first boneless bra to leave the midriff bare was developed in 1913 by Mary Phelps Jacobs, a New York City debutante. Under the name Caresse Crosby, Jacobs marketed a bra made of two French lace handkerchiefs suspended from the shoulders. Many young women in the 1920s, such as Yvonne Blue, bought their first bras in order to achieve the kind of slim, boyish figure that the characteristic chemise (or flapper) dress required. The first bras were designed simply to flatten, but they were superseded by others intended to shape and control the breasts. Our current cup sizes (A, B, C, and D), as well as the idea of circular stitching to enhance the roundness of the breast, emerged in the 1930s.

Adult women, not adolescents, were the first market for bras. Sexually maturing girls simply moved into adult-size bras when they were ready—and if their parents had the money. Many women and girls in the early twentieth century still made their own underwear at home, and some read the advertisements for bras with real longing. When she began to develop breasts in the 1930s, Malvis Helmi, a midwestern farm girl, remembered feeling embarrassed whenever she wore an old summer dimity that pulled and gaped across her expanding chest. As a result, she spoke to her mother, considered the brassieres in the Sears, Roebuck catalog, and decided to purchase two for twenty-five cents. However, when her hardworking father saw the order form, he vetoed the idea and declared, "Our kind of people can't afford to spend money on such nonsense." Although her mother made her a makeshift bra, Malvis vowed that someday she would have store-bought brassieres. Home economics teachers in the interwar years tried to get high school girls to make their own underwear because it saved money, but the idea never caught on once mass-produced bras became widely available.[14]

The transition from homemade to mass-produced bras was critical in how adolescent girls thought about their breasts. In general, mass-produced clothing fostered autonomy in girls because it took matters of style and taste outside the dominion of the mother, who had traditionally made and supervised a girl's wardrobe. But in the case of brassieres, buying probably had another effect. So long as clothing was made at home, the dimensions of the garment could be adjusted to the particular body intended to wear it. But with store-bought clothes, the body had to fit instantaneously into standard sizes that were constructed from a pattern representing a norm. When clothing failed to fit the body, particularly a part as intimate as the breasts, young women were apt to perceive that there was something wrong with their bodies. In this way, mass-produced bras in standard cup sizes probably increased, rather than diminished, adolescent self-consciousness about the breasts.[15]

Until the 1950s, the budding breasts of American girls received no special attention from either bra manufacturers, doctors, or parents. Girls generally wore undershirts until they were sufficiently developed to fill an adult-size bra. Mothers and daughters traditionally handled this transformation in private, at home. But in the gyms and locker rooms of postwar junior high schools, girls began to look around to see who did and did not wear a bra. Many of these girls had begun menstruating and developing earlier than their mothers had, and this visual information was very powerful. In some circles, the ability to wear and fill a bra was central to an adolescent girl's status and sense of self. "I have a figure problem," a fourteen-year-old wrote to *Seventeen* in 1952: "All of my friends are tall and shapely while my figure still remains up-and-down. Can you advise me?"[16]

In an era distinguished by its worship of full-breasted women, interest in adolescent breasts came from all quarters: girls who wanted bras at an earlier age than ever before; mothers who believed that they should help a daughter acquire a "good" figure; doctors who valued maternity over all other female roles; and merchandisers who saw profits in convincing girls and their parents that adolescent breasts needed to be tended in special ways. All of this interest coalesced in the 1950s to make the brassiere as critical as the sanitary napkin in making a girl's transition into adulthood both modern and successful.

The old idea that brassieres were frivolous or unnecessary for young girls was replaced by a national discussion about their medical and psychological benefits. "My daughter who is well developed but not yet twelve wants to wear a bra," wrote a mother in Massachusetts to *Today's Health* in 1951. "I want her to wear an undervest instead because I think it is better not to have anything binding. What do you think about a preadolescent girl wearing a bra?" That same year a reader from Wilmington, Delaware, asked *Seventeen:* "Should a girl of fourteen wear a bra? There are some older women who insist we don't need them." The editor's answer was an unequivocal endorsement of early bras: "Just as soon as your breasts begin to show signs of development, you should start wearing a bra."[17] By the early 1950s, "training" or "beginner" bras were available in AAA and AA sizes for girls whose chests were essentially flat but who wanted a bra nonetheless. Along with acne creams, advertisements for these brassieres were standard fare in magazines for girls.

Physicians provided a medical rationale for purchasing bras early. In 1952, in an article in *Parents' Magazine,* physician Frank H. Crowell endorsed bras for young girls and spelled out a theory and program of teenage breast management. "Unlike other organs such as the stomach and intestines which have ligaments that act as guywires or slings to hold them in place," Crowell claimed, the breast was simply "a growth developed from the skin and held up only by the skin." An adolescent girl needed a bra in order to prevent sagging breasts, stretched blood vessels, and poor circulation, all of which would create problems in nursing her future children. In addition, a "dropped" breast was "not so attractive," Crowell said, so it was important to get adolescents into bras early, before their breasts began to sag.[18] The "training" that a training bra was supposed to accomplish was the first step toward motherhood and a sexually alluring figure, as it was defined in the 1950s.

In the interest of both beauty and health, mothers in the 1950s were encouraged to check their daughters' breasts regularly to see if they were developing properly. This was not just a matter of a quick look and a word of reassurance. Instead, Crowell and others suggested systematic scrutiny as often as every three months to see if the breasts were positioned correctly. One way to chart the geography of the adolescent bustline was to have the girl stand sideways in a darkened room against a wall covered with white paper. By shining a bright light on her and having her throw out her chest at a provocative angle, a mother could trace a silhouette that indicated the actual shape of her daughter's bosom. By placing a pencil under her armpit, and folding the arm that held it across the waist, mothers could also determine if their daughter's nipples were in the right place. On a healthy breast, the nipple was supposed to be at least halfway above the midway point between the location of the pencil and the hollow of the elbow.

Breasts were actually only one part of a larger body project encouraged by the foundation garment industry in postwar America. In this era, both physicians and entrepreneurs promoted a general philosophy of "junior figure control." Companies such as Warners, Maidenform, Formfit, Belle Mode, and Perfect Form (as well as popular magazines like *Good Housekeeping*) all encouraged the idea that young women needed both lightweight girdles and bras to "start the figure off to a beautiful future."[19]

The concept of "support" was aided and abetted by new materials—such as nylon netting and two-way stretch fabrics—developed during the war but applied afterward to women's underwear. By the early 1950s, a reenergized corset and brassiere industry was poised for extraordinary profits. If "junior figure control" became the ideal among the nation's mothers and daughters, it would open up sales of bras and girdles to the largest generation of adolescents in American history, the so-called baby boomers. Once again, as in the case of menstruation and acne, the bodies of adolescent girls had the potential to deliver considerable profit.

There was virtually no resistance to the idea that American girls should wear bras and girdles in adolescence. Regardless of whether a girl was thin or heavy, "junior figure control" was in order, and that phrase became a pervasive sales mantra. "Even slim youthful figures will require foundation assistance," advised *Women's Wear Daily* in 1957. In both *Seventeen* and *Compact,* the two most popular magazines for the age group, high school girls were urged to purchase special foundation garments such as "Bobbie" bras and girdles by Formfit and "Adagio" by Maidenform that were "teen-proportioned" and designed, allegedly, with the help of adolescent consultants. The bras were available in pastel colors in a variety of special sizes, starting with AAA, and they were decorated with lace and ribbon to make them especially feminine. In addition to holding up stockings, girdles were intended to flatten the tummy and also provide light, but firm, control for hips and buttocks. The advertisements for "Bobbie," in particular, suggested good things about girls who controlled their flesh in this way: they were pretty, had lots of friends, and drank Coca-Cola. As adults, they would have good figures and happy futures because they had chosen correct underwear in their youth.[20]

By the mid-1950s, department stores and specialty shops had developed aggressive educational programs designed to spread the gospel of "junior figure control." In order to make young women "foundation conscious," Shillito's, a leading Cincinnati department store, tried to persuade girls and their mothers of the importance of having a professional fitting of the first bra. Through local newspaper advertisements, and also programs in home economics classes, Shillito's buyer, Edith Blincoe, promoted the idea that the purchase of bras and girdles required special expertise, which only department stores could provide. (*Seventeen* echoed her idea and advised a "trained fitter" for girls who wanted a "prettier" bosom and a "smoother" figure.) Blincoe acknowledged that teenage girls were already "100% bra conscious," and she hoped to develop the same level of attention to panty girdles. In order to attract junior customers and get them to try on both items, she had the corset department place advertising cards on the walls of dressing rooms in sections of the store where teenagers and their mothers shopped. Strapless bras were suggested on cards in the dress and formal wear departments; lightweight girdles were suggested in the sportswear and bathing suit sections.[21]

In home economics classes, and also at the local women's club, thousands of American girls saw informational films such as *Figure Forum* and *Facts About Your Figure,* made by the Warner Brassiere Company in the 1950s. Films like these stressed the need for appropriate foundation garments in youth and provided girls with scientific principles for selecting them. They also taught young women how to bend over and lean into their bras, a maneuver that most of us learned early and still do automatically.[22] Most middle-class girls and their mothers embraced the code of "junior figure control" and spent time and money in pursuit of the correct garments. Before a school dance in 1957, Gloria James, a sixteen-year-old African-American girl, wrote in her diary: "Mommy and I rushed to Perth Amboy [New Jersey] to get me some slacks, bras and a girdle. I don't even know how to get it [the girdle] on."[23]

In the postwar world, the budding adolescent body was big business. Trade publications, such as *Women's Wear Daily,* gave special attention to sales strategies and trends in marketing to girls. In their reports from Cincinnati, Atlanta, and Houston, one thing was clear: wherever American girls purchased bras, they wanted to be treated as grown-ups, even if they wore only a AAA or AA cup.[24] In Atlanta, at the Redwood Corset and Lingerie Shop, owner Sally Blye and her staff spoke persuasively to young customers about the importance of "uplift" in order "not to break muscle tissue." And at Houston's popular Teen Age Shop, specially trained salesgirls allowed young customers to look through the brassieres on their own, and then encouraged them to try on items in the dressing room without their mothers. Although many girls were shy at first, by the age of fourteen and fifteen most had lost their initial self-consciousness. "They take the merchandise and go right in [to the dressing room]," Blincoe said about her teenage clientele. Girls who could not be reached by store or school programs could send away to the Belle Mode Brassiere Company for free booklets about "junior figure control" with titles such as "The Modern Miss—Misfit or Miss Fit" and "How to Be Perfectly Charming." In the effort to help girls focus on their figures, Formfit, maker of the popular "Bobbies," offered a free purse-size booklet on calorie counting.[25]

Given all this attention, it's not surprising that bras and breasts were a source of concern in adolescents' diaries written in the 1950s. Sandra Rubin got her first bra in 1951, when she was a twelve-year-old in Cleveland, but she did not try it on in a department store. Instead, her mother bought her a "braziere" while she was away on a trip and sent it home. "It's very fancy," Sandra wrote. "I almost died! I ran right upstairs to put it on." When she moved to New York City that September and entered Roosevelt Junior High School, Sandra got involved with a clique of seven girls who called themselves the "7Bs." Their name was not about their homeroom; it was about the cup size they wanted to be. "Flat, Flat! The air vibrates with that name as my friends and I walk by," Sandra wrote in a humorous but self-deprecating manner. By the time she was sixteen, Sandra had developed amply, so that her breasts became a source of pride. One night she had an intimate conversation with a male friend about the issue of chests: "We talked about flat-chested women (of which, he pointed out, I certainly am not [one])."[26]

Breasts, not weight, were the primary point of comparison among high school girls in the 1950s. Although Sandra Rubin called herself a "fat hog" after eating too much candy, her diary reportage was principally about the bosoms, rather than the waistlines, she saw at school. Those who had ample bosoms seemed to travel through the hallways in a veritable state of grace, at least from the perspective of girls who considered themselves flat-chested. "Busty" girls made desirable friends because they seemed sophisticated, and they attracted boys. In December 1959, when she planned a Friday-night pajama party, thirteen-year-old Ruth Teischman made a courageous move by inviting the "gorgeous" Roslyn, a girl whom she wrote about frequently but usually only worshiped from afar. After a night of giggling and eating with her junior high school friends, Ruth revealed in her diary the source of Roslyn's power and beauty: "Roslyn is very big. (Bust of course.) I am very flat. I wish I would get bigger fast."[27] Many girls in the 1950s perused the ads, usually in the back of women's magazines, for exercise programs and creams guaranteed to make their breasts grow, allegedly in short order.[28]

The lament of the flat-chested girl—"I must, I must, I must develop my bust"—was on many private hit parades in the 1950s. There was a special intensity about breasts because of the attitudes of doctors, mothers, and advertisers, all of whom considered breast development critical to adult female identity and success. Although "junior figure control" increased pressure on the entire body, and many girls wore waist cinchers as well as girdles, it was anxiety about breasts, more than any other body part, that characterized adolescent experience in these years. As a result, thousands, if not millions, of girls in early adolescence jumped the gun and bought "training bras" at the first sight of breast buds, or they bought padded bras to disguise their perceived inadequacy. In the 1950s, the bra was validated as a rite of passage: regardless of whether a girl was voluptuous or flat, she was likely to purchase her first bra at an earlier age than had her mother. This precocity was due, in part, to biology, but it was also a result of entrepreneurial interests aided and abetted by medical concern. By the 1950s, American society was so consumer-oriented that there were hardly any families, even among the poor, who would expect to make bras for their daughters the way earlier generations had made their own sanitary napkins.

Training bras were a boon to the foundation garment industry, but they also meant that girls' bodies were sexualized earlier. In contemporary America, girls of nine or ten are shepherded from undershirts into little underwear sets that come with tops that are proto-brassieres. Although this may seem innocuous and natural, it is not the same as little girls "dressing up" in their mother's clothing. In our culture, traditional distinctions between adult clothing and juvenile clothing have narrowed considerably, so that mature women dress "down," in the garments of kids, just as often as little girls dress "up."[29] While the age homogeneity of the contemporary wardrobe helps adult women feel less matronly, dressing little girls in adult clothing can have an insidious side effect. Because a bra shapes the breasts in accordance with fashion, it acts very much like an interpreter, translating functional anatomy into a sexual or erotic vocabulary. When we dress little girls in brassieres or bikinis, we imply adult behaviors and, unwittingly, we mark them as sexual objects. The training bras of the 1950s loom large in the history of adolescent girls because they foreshadowed the ways in which the nation's entrepreneurs would accommodate, and also encourage, precocious sexuality.

Dieting: The Constant Vigil

As we near the end of the "century of svelte," the body projects of middle-class American girls are more habitual and intense than they were in either the 1920s or the 1950s. Although Yvonne Blue's experience feels familiar, dieting was different in the 1920s from what it is today. In the first place, Yvonne was fifteen years old when she started to diet, instead of nine or ten, the age of many contemporary girls when they begin to monitor their appetite. In addition, Yvonne's efforts to reduce were regarded as inappropriate by her parents, who never made any accommodation to help her, such as purchasing special foods. Yvonne's dieting was confined to a single summer, and her standard of slenderness was not as extreme as today's. In 1995, middle-class white girls define perfection as five feet seven inches tall and 110 pounds, and many work long hours at exercise and body sculpting in order to achieve the body of their dreams. Although some studies suggest that African-American girls are more relaxed about and more accepting of different body types, this may well be a function of economic status rather than cultural differences. *Essence,* a magazine that caters to middle-class African-American women, regularly runs stories on body-size anxiety and eating disorders, a fact which suggests that conventional "white" standards become more relevant among women of color as affluence increases.[30]

In the 1920s, dieting was a fashionable game for Yvonne and her girlfriends; it was not a way of life as it is for middle-class women and girls at the close of the twentieth century. Ever since the 1960s, adolescent diaries repeat, over and over, the same concern: "I've been eating like a pig," "I've got to lose weight," or "I must starve myself." This preoccupation is persistent rather than episodic; it characterizes the teen years of most middle-class girls, regardless of race; and it underlies their struggles with self-identity, peer relationships, and even educational and occupational choices. When seventeen-year-old Heather Ellis was faced with choosing a college in the late 1980s, the New Jersey teenager factored her dieting into that important decision. After she heard that one of her choices, Mount Holyoke, had good food, she wrote, "[That is] a drawback since I want to lose weight not gain any."[31]

American girls are on guard constantly against gaining weight, and, as a result, appetite control is a major feature of their adolescent experience. "I'm too ugly. I'm too fat. I have a crummy personality," wrote Carol Merano, a sixteen-year-old at Westport High School in Connecticut in the late 1960s. Carol was five feet four inches tall and weighed 120 pounds. She had an ample supply of close girlfriends, dates with boys, a good school record, and artistic talent, but her self-esteem was surprisingly dependent on the numbers she saw on the bathroom scale. Before the current cult of fitness and exercise took hold in the 1970s and 1980s, weight was the primary concern, more than a lean, toned body. Carol did not jog with her friends, "work out" at a health club, or do aerobics. Thirty years ago, counting calories and skipping meals were still the primary routes to weight reduction among adolescent girls.

Throughout high school and in her freshman year at George Washington University, Carol weighed herself at least once a day and tried all kinds of diets, including the *Harper's Bazaar* 9-Day Diet, the Doctor's Quick Weight Loss Diet, and the Air Force Salad Diet. Carol's emotional life was grounded in the success or failure of these efforts. When she did not lose weight, she berated herself and her mood plummeted: "I'm very depressed tonight.

Same reason: I'm 120 pounds." A month later, in November 1968, she was on top of the world: "I weigh 112. Everything is great for once." But by the beginning of the New Year, Carol was back to 120 again—unhappy and signing herself "Fatty." Almost everything in Carol's world was conditioned by what she ate, even her relationship to her diary: "I've been hiding from this book because I haven't stuck to my diet."[32]

Like so many other girls in late-twentieth-century America, Carol Merano felt good only when she felt thin. In the hope of getting to 110 pounds, her desired weight, she watched herself like a hawk, restricted calories, and tried to avoid family meals. For a few months, she ate only Carnation Instant Breakfast for supper. Although her mother disliked this kind of behavior because it meant that Carol did not participate in the family's evening meal, she did not make Carol stop. No one in Westport wanted a fat daughter, and dieting seemed to be a normal part of teenage life.

Carol spent a great deal of time thinking about the psychology of eating, as well as the content of different foods and their effects on her body. In her diary she made nutritional pronouncements that reflected dieting wisdom in the late 1960s. "No carbohydrates or fats. That's it. Nothing more, nothing less." One evening, when her weight was up to 117 pounds, she vowed: "No great amount of hunger will drive me to eat until *supper time* [emphasis in original] when I will eat tons and tons of vegetables and whatever else is non-fatty." Despite her low-cal eating, Carol sometimes lost control of her appetite, and this led her to cigarettes, which she considered an effective appetite suppressant. "I've really gone off my diet," she explained, "because I didn't have any cigarettes which is agony." All of this attention to weight and food meant that Carol watched her body very carefully, complaining about constipation and bloating at certain times of the month. Whenever she felt that her stomach was "out a mile," she gave herself an enema, something she considered "gross," but which also made her feel "very thin," and that made her happy.

As a freshman, at a point when her weight hit 120 pounds and she felt like a "stuffed sausage," Carol asked herself: "Why do I want to be thin?" Her initial answer had many layers: "So I will fit in my clothes. To show up Penny [a close friend]. To be the skinniest person in my [dormitory] room. So I will be a changed and better person outwardly—to fit my inner self." But then she stopped to consider her list: "That's bull shit. I just want to be thin so I can stop thinking about it." Yet even when Carol was down to 114 pounds, she was still consumed by the same nagging issue. "All I've been thinking about lately is how I look. That's because I look pretty bad. As soon as I look half-way decent again, I won't have to worry about it so Goddam much," she wrote. Looking "half-way decent" meant losing weight, and the persistence of that perceived need made Carol's appetite control essential to her sense of well-being.

Although weight and dieting were central preoccupations in Carol Merano's adolescence, she did not have either anorexia nervosa or bulimia, two common eating disorders that afflict contemporary girls in increasing numbers. Instead, Carol suffered from what psychologist Judith Rodin, president of the University of Pennsylvania, dubbed the "normative obsession" of American women.[33] Just like millions of other women and girls in the late twentieth century, this suburban Connecticut teenager was sufficiently fearful of fat to become a restrictive eater—that is, someone who habitually monitors food consumption. Because of her vigilance, between the ages of sixteen and nineteen Carol kept her weight within an eight-pound range, but her self-esteem and personal happiness were determined by whether she was at the bottom or the top of that range. By the time she was twenty, the energy this vigilance required began to wear on her. Although Carol did not swear off dieting, she began to think about what a relief it would be if she could only "stop thinking about it." In effect, she admitted her own emotional addiction to weight and appetite control.

Few adolescent girls at the end of the twentieth century are able to stop thinking about "it." Instead of relaxing the imperative to lose weight and be thin, the pressure to control the body has been ratcheted upward by an even more demanding cultural ideal: a lean, taut, female body with visible musculature. This particular feminine icon—epitomized by Jane Fonda, Madonna, and the new Oprah—requires even more attention, work, and control than the thin body desired by Carol Merano. In this aesthetic, the traditional softness of the female body is devalued in favor of toning, muscles, and strength. Instead of poetic tributes to the velvet breast or the silken thigh, we give our highest praise to body parts whose textures suggest metal and building material. At any given time of the day or night in the United States, a sizable number of young women, as well as young men, are working out, trying to achieve "buns" and "abs" of steel, or legs and arms of iron. Companies like Procter & Gamble, maker of Secret deodorant, have developed special "feminine" products to aid young women in the pursuit of a "hard" body. Advertisers portray young women in athletic poses, making a connection between a lean body and their particular product. Today, most adolescent girls control their bodies from within, through diet and exercise, rather than externally, with corsets or girdles. Fashion is a major contributor to this internalization of body controls: if you are going to bare your midriff or your upper thighs, a girdle is not what helps you do it.

Our national infatuation with "hard bodies," combined with the idea that bodies are perfectible, heightens the pressure on adolescents and complicates the business of adjusting to a new, sexually maturing body. On the positive side, the current emphasis on female muscles and strength could translate into less dieting (because of increased exercise) and better nutrition (because of more information about the content of different foods). Girls who go regularly to gyms and exercise studios, and those who participate in organized sports, should be physically stronger than earlier, more demure generations, or peers who "veg out" rather than "work out." But there is a flip side to all this attention to the body that is neither positive nor benign. The fitness craze can aggravate adolescent self-consciousness and make girls desperately unhappy (if not neurotic) about their own bodies, particularly if it is combined with unrealistic expectations drawn from airbrushed and retouched photographs in advertising, and the seductive camera angles and body doubles so common in television and movies. In addition, there are all kinds of regular opportunities—in the fitness room, at the exercise studio, in the shower at the gym—to compare physiques. Although eating disorders, such as anorexia nervosa and bulimia, are not caused by visual images alone, these pathologies thrive in an environment in which so many "normal" people work so hard (and spend so much money) in pursuit of the perfect body.

Hitting Below the Belt

Because we see so many extraordinary, hyperbolic bodies, young women today grow up worrying about specific body parts as well as their weight. At the moment, big breasts are not quite the fashion imperative they were in the 1950s, yet anxiety about them has never really disappeared. A third of the 38,000 girls who replied to a *Sassy* magazine poll in 1989 thought their breasts were too small and 12 percent admitted stuffing their bras.[34] Teenagers in the 1990s continue to wear padded bras, and they also adopt new stylistic innovations in brassieres, such as the recent Wonderbra, whose fame is based on its ability to create seductive cleavage on even the flattest chest. Yet a bosom that is too small (or too large) is fixable in a world where mammoplasty is accepted and accessible. Women between the ages of twelve and twenty-two and between thirty and forty are the most likely to have breast augmentation, although plastic surgeons these days have to deal with much younger girls who are already unhappy with their chests.[35]

In the 1990s, the real heat is on the lower body, especially thighs and buttocks. The current emphasis on the lower body has to do with a commingling of aesthetic, health, and sexual imperatives that make a taut female pelvis, sleek thighs, and a sculptured behind both objects of desire and symbols of success. Our current below-the-waist orientation is reflected in a national discourse about female thighs that has generated new products and procedures, and also increased female insecurity and dissatisfaction with the self.

Americans have talked about glamorous "gams" ever since the Rockettes made good legs a requirement back in the 1930s. But American taste in legs has changed considerably in the past half-century: the Rockettes of yesteryear had shorter, chunkier limbs than today's long-stemmed, lean favorites. Changes in fashion account for the recent emphasis on tight, narrow thighs. In the wake of the 1960s miniskirt, more adult women than ever before began to worry about this particular piece of anatomy. The "jeaning of America" also promoted leaner thighs. As jeans became a national uniform, particularly for adolescents, the upper leg, crotch, and buttocks were all brought into focus. But it was the bikini, and—more recently—bathing suits with legs cut upward toward the pelvic bone, that really made the tone and shape of thighs such a pervasive female concern.[36] When she was asked "What body parts are women most concerned about?," Betsy Brown, founder and president of Great Bodies, Inc., had a succinct and definitive answer based on experience with an exercise studio in Washington, D.C.: "Thighs. And then abdomen. [But] first, thunder thighs."[37]

"Thunder thighs" entered the lexicon in the early 1980s both as shorthand for female anxiety about the body and as a misogynistic slur. In separate, unrelated interviews, Debra Sue Maffet (a Miss California who later became Miss America), Shari Ann Moskau (another Miss California), Cynthia Yantis (Miss Indiana), and Melissa Bradley (Miss Ohio), all complained to reporters about their "thunder thighs." Two of these beauty queens admitted that, because of their thighs, they dreaded the swimsuit competition. The psychology of the modern beauty queen reveals that even the most "gorgeous" women in our society worry about this particular body part, and that they use "fat talk," especially complaints about their thighs, as a way to express their insecurities.[38]

"Thunder thighs" is also used against women in ways that can really sting. In 1982, sixteen-year-old Peggy Ward was dismissed from her high school marching band in Monongahela, Pennsylvania, because she was alleged to be too fat. Peggy was five feet four inches tall and weighed an unremarkable 124 pounds, yet the band director at her school maintained that a majorette of her height should weigh only 120 pounds. (He allowed five pounds for every inch over five feet.) Although Peggy's family physician tried to help by providing medical support for her claim that she was not overweight, the school system justified the requirement on the ground that local fans jeered overweight majorettes. The girls who marched with Peggy Ward did not support her either, and they accepted the litany of slurs that were routinely hurled at heavy girls. In Monongahela, the fans apparently yelled "thunder thighs," as well as some of the old standards: "fatso," "earthquake," "tub of lard," and "beachball." Slurs like these heighten female insecurity about the body, and they contribute to the audience for female self-help books, such as Wendy Stehling's 1982 best-seller *Thin Thighs in Thirty Days,* which sold more than 425,000 copies within seven weeks of its release.[39]

In middle-class America, girls grow up hearing adult women talk about how much they hate their own thighs. In the past two decades, there has been a national crusade against cellulite, the nonmedical term for a kind of dimpled fat that appears on the legs and derrieres of many mature women, not just those who are overweight. As fashion and beauty experts railed against thighs that resemble "orange peel" or "cottage cheese," the research and development divisions of the cosmetic industry put a great deal of energy and resources into developing thigh creams that would melt away this dreaded type of fat. Even the adolescent readers of *Young Miss* were exposed to a "scientifically designed" Firm and Trim Kit guaranteed to "fight the appearance of cellulite in problem areas." By 1995, American women and girls were spending more than $100 million on "cellulite busters," many of which needed to be applied liberally, at least once or twice a day, at a cost of $60 a tube. Although scientific studies have never supported their effectiveness, thigh creams are major business; and liposuction, a procedure that vacuums fat from the thighs and buttocks, has become the most popular kind of cosmetic surgery in the United States.[40]

Our national concern about "thunder thighs" says a lot about what Americans value. In fact, the way we think and talk about the terrain of our bodies is an important determinant of our psychological well-being. Psychological tests, known as "body cathexis scales," confirm that in the contemporary United States there is a deep connection between an individual's sense of self and his or her level of satisfaction with different parts of the body. Not surprisingly, there is more self-hatred among women than men, and women tend to be especially dissatisfied about the lower body—the waist, hips, thighs, and buttocks.[41] To put it another way: when an American woman dislikes her thighs, she is unlikely to like herself. This sad reality needs to be factored into our understanding of girls and the way in which they develop their sense of self.

In the Dressing Room

Because the body is a proxy for the self, selecting clothes for it is always of vital concern. American girls typically evaluate the success or failure of their personal body project in dressing rooms at the local mall or department store. At this stage of life, what a girl wears and how she looks in it determine her level of self-acceptance, as well as her relations with her peers.

Adolescents are incredibly intuitive about the social meaning of clothes, so they understandably invest a great deal of time and energy in selecting and trying on clothing. At home, they may try on an insufferable number of different outfits before choosing one; at the mall, they work conscientiously at making purchases that express what they want to "say" to the world. With the possible exception of shopping for a bathing suit, buying jeans seems to demand the most thought and consideration. In the retail business, the common wisdom is that girls try on approximately fourteen pairs of jeans for every one they eventually purchase.

Why this classic indecision about a pair of pants? And what does it tell us about the contemporary body project? A girl trying on a pair of jeans in the 1990s has many things to consider in addition to cost. Although teens generally look for brand names, market research reveals that fit supersedes brand loyalty when it comes to jeans. Thus, the teenage shopper must first determine her size—which is no small matter, given the way American manufacturers cut and label garments. Because every female clothing company develops its own sizes and proportions, there is no standardized equivalent between body measurements and size. Hips that are thirty-six inches, for example, do not always equal size twelve.

The laissez-faire nature of sizing for American women makes shopping for jeans a physical, as well as a psychological, struggle that is difficult at any age. However, it is particularly torturous for adolescents who regard size, much like weight, as a definitive element of their identity. Some girls assume there is something wrong with their bodies when they cannot fit consistently into the same "standard" size; others will reject a pair of jeans simply because they do not want to wear that size, even though the number has no substantive meaning.[42] (Of course, the connection between size and identity is not limited to adolescence. Plenty of adult women do the same thing throughout their lives.)

In front of a three-way mirror, usually under harsh, uncompromising lights, the adolescent girl assesses herself in terms of the current quest for bodily perfection. Studies indicate that white, middle-class girls tend to strike a series of static poses while trying on clothes; African-Americans are likely to be more fluid, in order to see how "one moves." But almost all girls sit down and bend in their jeans to see if they are comfortable, and they also inspect the cut, color, and details to make sure that a new pair "says" what they want jeans to say.[43] Their real concern is the body inside the pants, so they ask: Do these jeans flatter my body? Do they make my thighs look fat or my butt too big? Is there a "wedgie"—that is, does the garment reveal the crack between the buttocks? As the girl evaluates the aesthetics of her lower body, she imagines how she and her jeans will fare in the world outside the dressing room.

Shopping is a narcissistic pleasure for some young women, but for many others it generates serious emotional anguish because of its symbolic complexities and the insecurities it stirs up about the body and its parts. "I'm afraid my legs are too fat for it," a seventeen-year-old explained about the disappointment she felt when a special outfit did not make her look the way she desired. "I hate my body," wrote another, who, at age twenty, was still trying to come to grips with the dissatisfaction she felt every day and whenever she tried on new clothes. At the end of the twentieth century, fear of fat, anxiety about body parts, and expectations of perfection in the dressing room have all coalesced to make "I hate my body" into a powerful mantra that informs the social and spiritual life of too many American girls.[44]

Pierced Parts

At the moment, there is another body project that is more flamboyant and provocative than either dieting or working out. Body piercing, once regarded as characteristic of "primitive" people, has emerged in the 1990s as the latest form of self-expression among American adolescents.[45] Unlike aboriginal societies, where the part to be pierced is determined by long-standing ritual and tradition, contemporary teens face an array of piercing options, just as they do with food, music, cosmetics, and everything else in American life. Many girls spend long hours pondering what part they ought to pierce and what "piercewear" (i.e., jewelry) they like best. Although multiple ear piercing has been stylish in the United States for at least a decade, the repertoire of pierced parts has recently expanded to include the eyebrow, nose, and navel. There are also some audacious teenagers who pierce their lips, tongues, nipples, and genitals.

Most adolescent "piercees" are ordinary high school and college students who listen to CDs, use computers, and talk openly about why and how they perforated their bodies. (Tattoos are less popular because they are permanent and require expertise; holes, in contrast, can always be allowed to close up if the style passes, and they are also more easily done in the first place.) Because state laws restrict body piercing and tattooing to those who are eighteen and older, many younger adolescents pierce themselves. Others seek out well-known body-piercing studios, such as Gauntlet, which has establishments in New York, San Francisco, and Los Angeles; or they find someone locally, perhaps through a beauty salon or via the Internet. *The Point,* a newsletter published by the Association of Professional Piercers, is available on-line for information and referrals, but there are also countless interactive possibilities, such as: "Hi. I'm making this inquirey (ok, so it's misspelled . . .) on behalf of a thirteen-year-old who is desperate to get her nose pierced. It seems no one will do it for her because of her age. She has her mom's permission—does anyone know a place/person in the Cleveland/Akron/Kent area who can/will do it for her? If so, please e-mail me. You will have the undying gratitude of an eighth grader from the sticks." (Replies came swiftly, such as

"Have you tried bringing the mother along? If the parent/legal guardian signs a consent form then they cannot sue.")

In the 1990s, adolescent body piercing is a provocative symbol of a powerful revolution in sexual mores and behavior that brought gay culture into the mainstream of American life. While previous generations associated body piercing with New Guinea and exotic pictures in *National Geographic,* today's adolescents are apt to learn about piercing from ideas and behaviors emanating from the Castro and Christopher Street, two important homosexual communities in San Francisco and New York. Within the gay community, there is a diverse range of piercing practices, ranging from simply piercing the left ear (in order to announce a homosexual orientation) to bizarre forms of sadomasochism. In 1989, an avant-garde publisher in San Francisco issued a book that unveiled the full range of body piercing in the United States: *Modern Primitives: An Investigation of Contemporary Adornment and Ritual.* The book contained this warning: "Do not attempt any of the body modifications or practices described herein." But it also provided an astonishing array of graphic photographs of extreme forms of piercing, sympathetic interviews with some of piercing's most dedicated devotees, and the names and locations of professional studios that served "piercing needs." Readers also learned about *Piercing Fans International Quarterly* (now *The Piercing Magazine*) and how to mail-order nostril screws, barbells for the tongue, and different kinds of rings for the nipples, penis, labia, and clitoris.[46]

Teenagers today grow up in a world where rigid dichotomies between gay (homosexual) and straight (heterosexual) behavior are disappearing. They also see more people behaving in ways once ascribed to homosexuals. This "homosexualization" of American life, first described by Dennis Altman in the late 1970s, has become a notable feature of current popular culture—particularly in music, sports, and fashion—all "worlds" adolescents value, follow closely, and imitate.[47] In 1991, Madonna's controversial book, *Sex*, featured an array of pierced male and female body parts in a series of sadomasochistic fantasies. Most American teenagers never read this expensive, self-indulgent book, but they did see Madonna flaunt her own navel ring in public, and they knew that she had "lifted" the idea of personal hardware from the gay men and women who were part of her entourage. On MTV other musicians followed her lead: Green Day and the Red Hot Chili Peppers displayed many different kinds of body piercing, and in 1993 an Aerosmith video centered on an innocent schoolgirl who got a tattoo and had her belly button pierced. In professional basketball, Dennis Rodman, the Chicago Bulls' superstar, forcefully moves his pierced and tattooed body around the court, demonstrating that this form of personal decoration has traveled well beyond its gay roots into the world of masculine athletic prowess.

Piercing became even more fashionable among girls when it was introduced in 1994 on the Paris runways by designers Jean Paul Gaultier and Christian Lacroix. Soon afterward, supermodels Christy Turlington and Naomi Campbell decided to pierce their navels. These developments, combined with the popularity of skirts, pants, and shirts designed to display more midriff than ever before, made a bejeweled navel a potent fashion statement, particularly when it was displayed on a flat, tight stomach. According to a poll by *Sassy* in 1994, adolescent boys think belly rings are "sexy" or "cute," and most girls consider them desirable, if you have the right kind of body.[48] By electronic mail, an excited (but concerned) Long Island teenager sent out this message: "I just got my belly button pierced and the guy that did it was pretty nervous, his hand was shaking as he did it. Anyway, I was wondering if it may be too shallow, and how I could tell, cause the ring really sticks out. Is it possible to get a really small ring for it, so that it doesn't stick out?"

Other kinds of piercing, such as the eyebrow, lip, nose, and tongue, are much more controversial. Seventy-five percent of the teenagers in the *Sassy* poll considered this kind of piercing "repulsive" and most middle-class parents dislike facing this kind of adornment across the dinner table. As a result, body piercing can become a contentious family issue. Rather than face her parents' disapproval, one middle-class sixteen-year-old secretly pierced her navel and hid it all winter, until the summer months, when her shorts revealed the truth to her outraged parents. Because of the fierce battles that rage in some homes, talk-show host Jerry Springer devoted an entire program to explaining piercers to parents and vice versa. Young women with rings in their eyebrows and jewels in their nose characteristically report long periods of silent accommodation with mothers who all utter the same, unconvincing refrain: "You looked prettier without it."

For those struggling for autonomy and independence, maternal distaste for the piercing aesthetic is no deterrent. Piercing proves, in a public way, that your body is your own ("I-can-fuck-up-my-own-body-if-I want-to!" seems to be a common refrain). It also signals your personal politics. If you become an "urban aboriginal" at the end of the twentieth century, it is usually a sign of two things: sexual liberalism (because piercing symbolizes opposition to conventional sexual norms) and cultural relativism (because it evokes the primitive and the exotic).

Most young people explain the practice as a way to differentiate themselves from bourgeois society and mainstream youth culture. These are young women who self-consciously reject the "good/pretty girl" ideal presented in *Seventeen* and *Mademoiselle.* But instead of abandoning absurd weight goals, they choose something that their elders and many of their peers regard as mutilative and disgusting. Most of them seem to enjoy the stigma, regarding it as a clear-cut way to separate from those they consider "yuppies" and "princesses." "You don't see JAPS [Jewish American princesses] going around wearing nose rings," a sixteen-year-old with jewels in her face proclaimed with demonstrable pride.

Although piercing acts like a bumper sticker for many young women, there is a smaller group that takes delight in perforating more intimate body parts, such as nipples and genitals. "When people look at you with a nose ring they automatically label you as alternative," said a nineteen-year-old in upstate New York, "but nobody knows about my [clitoral] hood piercing except me and my boyfriend." Although some women—both gay and straight—pierce their nipples and genitals with the expectation that it will increase erotic sensation, the pierced high school and college students I interviewed were heterosexuals and they never offered sexual pleasure as an explanation. Instead, they spoke with girlish enthusiasm about the special "secret" they shared with their boyfriend, and how the genital decoration made them feel "more feminine."

The notion that genital piercing was a "special secret" made me think about the changing nature of intimacy in American society, and the ways in which girls' bodies express these changes. Rather than wear a boyfriend's school ring, the way earlier generations did, these young women tingled at the idea that they had a piece of love jewelry in (or on) the most intimate parts of their body. This was not a token that could be displayed publicly in school hallways, the way you flashed the ring worn on a chain around your neck when you were "going steady" in the 1950s. A ring on the clitoris is a very different kind of marker, intended only for the titillation of the "piercee" and her boyfriend. In an era when the distinction between the public and private has all but disappeared, some teenage girls apparently feel the need to decorate their genitals in order to have *something* intimate—in effect, to claim some degree of privacy in a world where the body has been made public. (What was surprising was the pervasive sense of romance and intimacy that the practice carried, despite the fact that the hole and the jewelry were acquired in a commercial studio, through the intervention of a paid person.)

Most adolescent girls say "Yuck" when they think about piercing such delicate and personal body parts. But the genital-piercing adolescent subculture is not some wild aberration unrelated to broader, more familiar behavioral patterns in late-twentieth-century American society. In a culture that pays such meticulous attention to the body, it is not a fluke that some adolescent girls have become involved in this particular body project. After all, looking good—all over and everywhere—is a national priority, and it explains the economic success of an upscale lingerie chain such as Victoria's Secret, which has a sizable number of adolescent patrons. In the past few years, a mail-order catalog from Delia's LLC has offered teenage girls an opportunity to purchase their own version of the classic—and seductive—black bra and panties.

Adolescent body piercers are representatives of new sexual mores, but they also proclaim the ways in which exhibitionism and commercial culture have come together at the end of the twentieth century. Thirty years ago, sexually titillating underwear and lingerie were, by and large, intended for adults, in the privacy of their bedrooms. Today, we are likely to see it—on both women and girls—at parties or even in the streets. When underwear becomes outerwear, as it has in the past decade, adolescents of both sexes are likely to become confused about the nature of intimacy. At a time in life when sexual activity is beginning, this is no small confusion, yet it is constantly increased by commercial activities—such as the marketing of lingerie or piercewear—that erode the important distinction between the public and the private. Although we may not want to admit it, the current craze for body piercing follows logically from the pared-down, segmented, increasingly exposed, part-by-part orientation toward the female body that has emerged over the course of the twentieth century. In fact, in a culture where everything is "up close and personal," it should not surprise us that some young women today regard the entire body, even its most private parts, as a message board.

CHAPTER FIVE

The Disappearance of Virginity:

Sexual Expression and Sexual Danger

Photos on p. 139: *(left)* Permission of Midge Kerlan and Molly Kennedy; *(right)* permission of Conor Gaffney and Hildi Gerhardt.

In November 1993, Jenelle Roberts, a sixteen-year-old from Union, New Jersey, wrote to a national columnist: "Why isn't there a virgin support group? It seems like there are support groups for every situation in this country except virginity."[1] An articulate young African-American, Jenelle captured the distress of countless contemporary girls who are pressured into premature sexual activity in a world where virginity has become an outmoded concept. Even if a contemporary girl resists intercourse, her eyes and ears have undoubtedly been filled with graphic, sexually explicit information since an early age. In Jenelle's generation, girls may have "virginal" bodies, but they rarely have virginal minds.

At the end of the twentieth century, American girls are far more sophisticated about sex than were their Victorian forebears, or even most of their mothers. Their precocity is driven by earlier sexual maturation, and also by the nature of late-twentieth-century American culture. Well before puberty, contemporary girls learn what earlier generations euphemistically called the "facts of life." The facts that used to be so difficult to tell children, such as the relationship between the arrival of babies and the act of sexual intercourse, seem mild and nonthreatening compared with the information children need to have today.

The "facts of life" are far more extensive now than they were in the past, at least for those willing to acknowledge the full range of sexual behaviors and choices that now exist. Because we live in a world that is less inhibited and more dangerous than it was even fifty years ago, the best sex education books in the 1990s are forthright with children about issues that earlier generations swept under the rug, such as sexual abuse by adults and sexually transmitted diseases. These books also acknowledge sexual behaviors that were once forbidden, such as masturbation, premarital coitus, and homosexuality, all of which are becoming standard fare in enlightened books for girls.[2] As a result, middle-class girls of ten and eleven are socialized into a world where sexuality is regarded as absolutely normal but also rather perilous.

Clearly, our society has come a long way in terms of recognizing that virginity is not the highest value in womanhood, and that modern girls—like adult women—have legitimate sexual desires that need an outlet. This transformation in thinking about female sexuality is one of the most important stories in the history of American women, but it is rarely told in terms of its consequence for young girls, or for how they live. Although there is some historical truth for adolescent girls in the familiar Virginia Slims' slogan "You've come a long way, baby!," the emergence of a right to sexual expression can be as problematic as the right to smoke cigarettes.

At the end of the twentieth century, American girls have to negotiate between their desire for sexual expression and the prospect of sexual danger. Although it is hard to grow up these days without hearing about the hazards of sexual intimacy, the media and popular culture also push the idea that sexuality is the ultimate form of self-expression. In a world where the HIV virus coexists with the imperative to "do your own thing" sexually, adolescent girls need to think about sexuality, and its related body projects, in ways that are healthy and realistic. More than any other generation, and at an earlier age then ever before, they must learn to handle the emotional and physical risks that are involved in being sexually expressive in a postmodern, postvirginal world.

The Meaningful Membrane

In the nineteenth century, virginity was both a biological and a moral state. Few people disagreed that, in women, it was "the largest diamond in the crown of youthful virtue."[3] The body of an adolescent girl was held sacred in the Victorian era because it represented purity, civilized morality, and the future of the race. Reverence for the hymen was part and parcel of the idea of protection, and it translated into a national preoccupation with preserving the virginity and the innocence of American girls. Nice girls were not only chaste but beyond temptation, and their personal behavior upheld the notion that good Christian women were sexually passive as well as pure. The ideal American girl was always naive—attractively so—and she was untarnished by knowledge, or even thoughts, about what the Victorians discreetly called the "sexual connection."

Virginity also had a palpable anatomical marker. According to ancient and common wisdom, a woman remained a virgin until her hymen, a thin mucous membrane at the juncture of the vulva and the vagina, was ruptured by the force of a penis. Although we now understand that hymens tear for a variety of reasons (such as strenuous exercise, excessive menstrual blood flow, douching, tampons, petting, or masturbation), an intact hymen was traditionally regarded as the surest sign and "the best prima facie evidence" of virginity. In some contemporary cultures, such as Kuwait, the bedsheets of newly married couples are still inspected for the bloody remains expected to accompany rupture of this "sacred, God-given seal."[4]

The hymen has been discussed in a variety of different ways, sometimes with reverence but other times as the butt of bad jokes. Historically, the word *hymen* meant both marriage and membrane, a duality that suggests how closely the two were entwined. In the ancient world, Hymen was the God of Marriage, and the word was also applied to a traditional wedding song performed in classical dramas by Aristophanes and Euripides. In much of Shakespeare's work, Hymen was invoked as an anthropomorphic force who encouraged happy marriages, but the word was never used to denote the body part of a virgin. Still, the Bard had an opinion about hymens ("The longer kept the less worth") that had resonance, even among doctors, in the early twentieth century. In an address to the Cincinnati Academy of Medicine in 1906, Dr. E. S. McKee joked that "unlike Kentucky whiskey, [hymens] do not improve with great age."[5] The doctor's quip was an example of a long-standing male interest in the act of defloration, the rupture of the virginal hymen. In ribald, off-color stories and conversations, generations of men have reveled in the erotic pleasure said to be associated with that act. Words such as "maidenhead," "virgin knot," and "cherry" are often used as colloquial stand-ins for the actual anatomical name.[6]

A century ago, the hymen was a meaningful membrane with enormous social and emotional value. Although middle-class Victorian prudery made discussion of sex and genitalia highly offensive, the hymen was nevertheless on people's minds. The typical Victorian counselor told young female readers that they each had a "jewel" or "treasure" worthy of preservation until it was appropriately (and legally) sacrificed at marriage on a sweet "hymeneal altar." Because an intact hymen was a prerequisite to a good middle-class marriage, many mothers and fathers had a vested interest in its preservation. Future husbands were also concerned about it, because a bride who came without a tight hymen was regarded as damaged goods. In this context, a girl's hymen was in effect "jointly owned" by her family and her bridegroom as much as by the girl herself.[7]

Because anatomical virginity was so important, the medical profession became an important arbiter in family and community evaluations of who was chaste and who was not. Doctors were called in to adjudicate debates about the nature of the hymen because it was believed that women lied about men in order to cover up their own sexual lives, and that adolescent girls were unreliable, overly emotional informants. Allegedly, medical science could provide the kind of physical testimony to the "truth" that late-nineteenth-century Americans respected.[8]

Innocent Women and Medical "Operators"

Doctors got involved in the chastity business through the vehicle of the pelvic examination, an intimate intervention in which a female patient exposed her vagina in a nonsexual manner. In the nineteenth century, the propriety of this delicate procedure was questioned, as was the specialty of gynecology, a field of medicine that focused on women's diseases and reproduction.[9]

There was always enormous skepticism about the character of the kind of men who were drawn to a medical specialty that openly avowed its desire to inspect, touch, and look inside the female body. Even Catharine Beecher, a progressive advocate of women's health reform, was uneasy about the central interaction in gynecology. In her 1855 *Letters to the People on Health and Happiness,* Beecher warned that innocent women risked advances by unscrupulous men during examinations performed with "bolted doors and curtained windows, and with no one present but patient and operator."[10] Because so many people were suspicious, nineteenth-century gynecologists had to carefully justify medical interventions that involved scrutiny or manipulation of what were euphemistically called the "private parts." One way they validated their activity was by acting as watchful custodians, conserving the hymen as if it were a piece of valuable commercial or agricultural property owned by someone other than the girl on the examining table.

Because gynecologists have had such an intimate relationship with American girls, they are critical informants about the changing nature of female adolescent sexuality. For over a century, they have been among the first to learn about new sexual mores and the consequences of social change for young women. The history of their experience with young women and pelvic exams provides a convenient window for illuminating what has happened to the hymen, a body part that had far greater cultural power than one would expect, given its minuscule size and natural fragility.

As this chapter shows, the hymen has disappeared—ideologically and physically—as a result of many different social forces, including changes in the behavior of girls themselves. Just about ninety years ago, when virginity was still very much in vogue, an American physician predicted that this might happen, that the hymen would someday become a "vestigial" structure that would "disappear in our remote descendants."[11] This forward-looking doctor imagined an evolutionary or biological process that would make the hymen very much like the appendix. I am arguing something different, however. As the hymen lost its traditional ideological significance in women's lives, there were real, tangible implications for their bodies as well as their social behavior. The history of the hymen confirms that girls' bodies were (and continue to be) a template for the vast social transformations that mark the twentieth century.

Diagnosing Chastity

Until World War II, most American girls never had a pelvic exam because of a deep cultural belief in the sanctity of the hymen. In an era when bodies were hidden rather than exposed, disrobing and undergoing an internal probe of the vagina violated most adult women's modesty and seemed especially horrific for unmarried middle-class girls. Because the doctor was almost always male, there was a great deal of emotion involved. Middle-class mothers were usually present, both as support to the young patient and as a guarantor that the doctor's probe was strictly scientific. A 1910 text warned future doctors that "the habit of 'poking about' with the tips of the fingers is much to be deprecated."[12]

Girls with severe cramps, extreme bleeding, and unusual discharges were the most frequent candidates for a pelvic exam. In 1901, Dr. Herman E. Hayd of Buffalo, New York, told the

American Association of Obstetricians and Gynecology that it was incorrect to think that "womb trouble" existed only in married women.[13] Yet most general practitioners and pediatricians were reluctant to perform the invasive procedure on a middle-class adolescent girl, or even to recommend a specialist in gynecology, unless it was absolutely necessary. This meant that younger patients were likely to be highly symptomatic, uncomfortable, and very frightened by the time they had an internal exam.

Although many adolescents sought professional help for menstrual problems, physicians were loath to do anything but take a medical history, prescribe tonics, give advice about the hygiene of menstruation, and suggest that nature would take its course. In fact, with young girls, some doctors even suggested examination *by the mother,* in order to determine if there were anatomical problems.[14] The reluctance of doctors was a result of their medical education, as well as the reverence for virginity, which they shared with middle-class parents and future husbands, all of whom considered themselves major shareholders in the young woman's body.

In their training, American physicians received a clear, nearly uniform message that reflected the tradition of familial ownership of girls' bodies: "A virgin should but rarely be examined" or "Never make a vaginal examination of a young virgin, if it can be avoided." The prejudice against examination of the genitals of young middle-class girls was pervasive in American medical practice. In 1906, a general practitioner in Liberty, Missouri, told his colleagues about a fellow doctor who bragged that in over forty years of medical practice "he had never examined a girl's pelvic organs before she was married." Pelvic examinations of adolescent girls obviously presented a formidable social and medical problem that many chose to avoid, even if they were specially trained in how to negotiate and execute this particular interaction.[15]

By submitting to a vaginal exam, a young woman allowed the doctor to touch her hymen, an anatomical structure regarded by most laypeople as absolute proof of virginity. In order to hone their diagnostic technique, gynecologists studied textbook plates, some in color, of drawings of different types of hymens classified by the shape of the openings in the membrane; there were many, and each had a different degree of "resistance," such as semilunar, crescentic, septate, sculptatus, cribriform, fimbrated, denticulate, annular, and imperforate.[16] (Only the latter type, a hymen without any opening, caused real medical problems, because it blocked the normal flow of menstrual blood from within the vagina.) Gynecologists had to familiarize themselves with all types, because they were sometimes asked by interested parties, other than the patient, to report the "true" condition of a hymen. As in Braille, a patient's hymen was supposed to be "read" by the doctor with his deft, skilled fingers.

In 1896, the first photograph of a "virginal vaginal outlet" was published in John Montgomery Baldy's *An American Textbook of Gynecology,* which was intended for clinicians in the field and students studying to enter the specialty. Baldy, a gynecologist at Pennsylvania Hospital in Philadelphia, was extremely sensitive to the issue of modesty involved in pelvic exams, so he warned his readers that many women would find the experience "distasteful and onerous." He also saved himself and other doctors from charges of indecency by using a black woman model for the clinical pictures in the text. African-American women were assumed to be hypersexual and without normal feminine modesty, so medicine's clinical appropriation of their bodies seemed only natural to late-nineteenth-century white Americans whose racism ran deep.[17]

Physicians wanted pictures and photographs because the hymen was something of a mystery. The membrane was not found very often in the cadavers they saw in medical school, and most of the married women they saw in clinical practice had already lost the membrane. In their professional journals, nineteenth-century physicians repeatedly pondered a number of questions: Did the hymen have nerve endings? If not, what accounted for the pain that accompanied defloration? Did all hymeneal membranes tear in exactly the same way? Did Negro and white women have the same kind? And most often: Did the absence of a hymen, or a hymen that admitted the doctor's finger or a speculum, always mean that the patient has experienced "sexual congress," as most laypeople thought?[18]

Among themselves, doctors readily agreed that the hymen was an unreliable indicator of whether or not a girl had ever had intercourse. "Its presence can never prove that she has not, nor its absence that she has," concluded a 1906 summary of medical opinion on the subject.[19] In the effort to blunt the idea that medicine could diagnose chastity, they told one another pointed stories about prostitutes whose hymens were intact, married women whose husbands had organs incapable of penetration, and girls born without the membrane who were considered "ruined" for life. Yet despite their limited knowledge and a lack of consensus on what constituted virginity, physicians got involved in policing the private parts of American girls. In an era when virginity was so highly revered, doctors were frequently called upon to provide scientific testimony about the condition of the membrane. Sometimes these expert readings occurred at the request of the courts. In 1904, Chicago physician James W. Walker was asked to testify for the defense about the "private parts" of twelve-year-old Irene Callahan, who had allegedly been raped by a forty-year-old bachelor teacher. Walker, however, definitively told the court that the girl was a virgin: "Her sexual organs, compared with those of a child of her age, were normal." In the detention centers established by the juvenile court system in California, female doctors also read the hymens of "morally suspect" working-class girls in order to determine who was chaste, and who was not. (It was easier for physicians to intervene in this manner when the case involved a poor immigrant girl rather than a girl who came from a polite middle-class home.)[20]

Although professional gynecologists understood the uncertainty in this kind of "reading," the American public continued to regard the hymen as a moral marker well into the twentieth century. For that very reason, American physicians took stringent precautions not to rupture or stretch the critical membrane when giving examinations. Because the pelvic exam was so repugnant, doctors constantly faced resistance, even in cases where virginity seemed irrelevant. In 1933, for example, the mother of a forty-year-old virgin still "would not permit any form of treatment which might injure her [daughter's] hymen."[21] As a result of this kind of anxiety, gynecologists in the late nineteenth and early twentieth centuries adapted their clinical technique to what *they thought* were the sensibilities of polite middle-class mothers and daughters.

Instead of vaginal exams, doctors promoted rectal exams, in the belief that they were better suited to the psychology and physiology of unmarried girls. For example: "In virgins, care should be taken not to tear the hymen and a rectal exam may have to suffice" or "Examine virgins by the rectum in order to avoid stretching the hymen."[22] Although patients probably found the rectal exam equally unpleasant, a predominantly male profession heralded it as the right thing to do, especially when the patient was a young, white, middle-class woman accompanied by her mother: "It is of special value in the examination of a virgin, as most pathological conditions of importance can thus be determined without causing the patient much pain or leaving the sense of having been examined."[23]

The rectal exam catered to the fears of traditionalists who worried not only about the integrity of the hymen but also about the vaginal exam's capacity to "shock" the modesty of the young. In the gynecologist's office, "the girl is subjected to a treatment of which she really should know nothing," said a midwestern doctor, "and her attention is called to organs of which she should not think at all."[24] (Calling attention to the rectum seemed to be more acceptable in a culture where vaginal intercourse was the accepted form of sexuality.) Many doctors and laypeople believed that a rectal exam was preferable to a vaginal exam because the latter stimulated sexual desire and directed "morbid attention" to the genitals.

As a result of these concerns, in the years after 1870, anesthesia became an important part of gynecological practice because it blotted out the experience of the pelvic exam, and it also allowed doctors to perform the diagnostic probe that was the defining characteristic of their specialty.[25] In the name of science, and with anesthesia as an aid, medicine enlarged its jurisdiction over female genitalia. But there was always some resistance and disquiet, even among doctors. In 1903, at the meeting of the American Medical Association, Dr. Florus F. Lawrence, a physician from Columbus, Ohio, felt the need to assure his colleagues that the science of gynecology was not incompatible with girlhood virginity. Instead, Lawrence suggested that gynecology was really a form of patriotism that yielded "fruitage" for the nation in the form of healthier women, happier wives, and more devoted mothers.[26]

Not everyone in the audience agreed with Lawrence's liberal views on vaginal exams. Dr. J. H. Carsten, a general practitioner from Detroit, was profoundly troubled by the idea of any "tinkering" with the reproductive organs of young women. Carsten told the same meeting: "If young girls are let alone and live a moral life, they will not require the gynecological finger."[27] Over the next few decades, many general practitioners came to understand the need for gynecologists and pelvic exams, but the reticence of middle-class patients and their families was always a factor whenever a referral was made. Some girls had to endure these difficult procedures, and the historical silence about them in the years before the 1920s suggests a deep level of embarrassment, as well as an inability to describe what was actually happening to their bodies.

Technically a Nice Girl

At the turn of the twentieth century, nice girls did not talk about sex or the body, but by the Roaring Twenties they did. For the first time, young women began to mention what had been unspeakable: their own sexuality. Although they did not speak or write with the frankness of today's teenagers, many described their own sexual awakening and recorded the details of intimate interactions with boys. This new language of sex and the self was generated by America's first great "sexual revolution" in the early decades of the twentieth century, a critical cultural event that signaled the decline of Victorian reserve.[28] Some of the behavioral change was artless and unself-conscious; some of it was not. But the fact that young women found the words to talk about sex suggests a profound transformation in their approach to their own bodies. That new perspective moved them into the arms—and stirrups—of professional gynecology.

Yvonne Blue, the same Chicago teenager whose diet I described in chapter 4, wrote a great deal about what it meant to come of age in the midst of the first American sexual revolution. As a student at the University of Chicago, Yvonne led a sheltered life. She lived at home with her parents in a new house in suburban Flossmoor, and she did not begin to date until the age of eighteen. Yet her diary conveys the physical pleasure she took from the relationship with her first boyfriend, Peter MacDonald, a handsome neighbor who was a year younger than she.[29]

Despite Prohibition and a watchful, middle-class mother, Yvonne's initial sexual interactions with Peter almost always involved the consumption of alcohol and the use of a car. In her case, as in countless others, the automobile was an important spur to premarital intimacy of all kinds. In the early 1950s, Alfred Kinsey's study of female sexual behavior revealed that 41 percent of women who had premarital intercourse did so in a car. But in the summer of 1930, nineteen-year-old Yvonne was not ready for intercourse, although she was primed for more restrained forms of sexual negotiation and interaction such as necking and petting. One evening, before a date with her boyfriend, Yvonne described herself as "awfully excited even before I went. Before I got dressed I lay down in the dark and listened to dance music on the radio and even then I felt that I wanted to be 'loved.' "

Yvonne's desire for Peter was given shape and meaning by the culture in which she lived. Lying undressed in the dark, she was moved by the romantic music that filled the airwaves, and she contemplated what she would look like that hot summer night in yet another new, form-fitting silk dress. That night, Yvonne downed a number of mixed drinks: "I was just tight enough to get awfully worked up. I was frightfully ashamed of myself the next morning for letting him go so far, but I enjoyed myself. I do like Peter in that way alot. I enjoy just being with him, but I would much rather be petting because the only way he really attracts me is physically." On that particular steamy August evening, Yvonne's new dress was "ruined." Another time, she lost a critical button in the backseat of Peter's car, something she found difficult to explain to her mother.

Despite her honesty with herself about the pleasures of petting, Yvonne was not totally at ease with her emerging sexuality. Although petting was commonplace among adolescents of her age and class, she still worried about her reputation, because she knew that she had a lower opinion of other girls whenever she found out about their sexual exploits. She also used euphemisms such as "worked up" and "go so far," in order to avoid more explicit descriptions of what took place. Because Victorian notions of propriety still had some resonance for her, Yvonne felt the need to clarify in her diary just how far she had gone. "I'm still technically a 'nice girl,' " she wrote, but she vacillated between feeling guilty and happy about the experiences she had. "Once in awhile I feel slightly ashamed of myself for indulging in the greatest American sport but something must be the matter with me because while I *think* it's wrong I really, really can't *feel* that it is [emphasis in original]."

At twenty, Yvonne came close to losing her virginity under the influence of bootleg gin and a wilder, older, and more sophisticated Chicago crowd. After staying out all night with a man she met at a downtown party, she confessed: "I didn't realize what was happening at first; as soon as I did I *made* him stop." Apparently, her companion "went almost as far as it is possible to go," which left Yvonne wondering how to think about herself, since there had been no real penetration, only the attempt at it. "I suppose that I am not a virgin any longer, but I don't count it to myself because I fought him and it didn't last long."

Petting, and the prospect of intercourse before marriage, meant that young women like Yvonne thought about virginity in ways that were dramatically different from the ideas of previous generations. Yvonne certainly understood that her encounter was dangerous, but in the sexually liberal world of the 1920s intelligensia, virginity had lost much of its power because it was a symbol of the older Victorian order. Despite her unnerving experience, Yvonne repeated a joke that made her feel worldly and in step with the times: "They were going to have a virginity parade in Hollywood but one girl got sick and the other wouldn't march alone." This kind of sophisticated repartee, and its suggestion that virginity was "old hat," added to an already powerful complex of forces, such as fashion, moving pictures, popular music, magazines, and automobiles, that all but disinhibited female sexuality in the 1920s and 1930s. On the basis of her own experience, Yvonne grew to understand that not much separated a good girl from a bad one. In this new world, virginity was simply a social category and not a moral state.

The experience of Yvonne Blue and thousands like her had a profound effect on the bodies of American girls, and also on the practice of gynecology. In the wake of World War I, petting became so commonplace that many girls were touched by boys on the breasts and genitals before they ever encountered a gynecologist.[30] Young women who were stroked and penetrated by male hands before marriage were not as frightened of pelvic exams as their mothers had been at the same age. These sexual encounters also meant that "nice" young women came to the doctor's office with a very different point of view about their bodies, as well as the ability to distinguish medical from sexual interactions.

Gynecologists perceived the change in their patients. Dr. Howard Kelly's authoritative and well-known gynecology text of

1928 reflected his sense that prior sexual experience was more common by the 1920s, and that it made the doctor's job somewhat easier. "As a rule, the readiness with which a young woman approaches a digital examination conveys a broad hint as to the status of the hymen," he wrote. Other physicians such as Robert Latou Dickinson, a prominent New York gynecologist who advocated birth control and sex education, attributed the greater tolerance for pelvic probes to a general waning of Victorian modesty, a development he applauded. "In 1885, no nice women [had] any anatomy between her neck and her ankles. She would rather die than be examined," he wrote. In the 1890s, patients reportedly covered themselves as fully as possible with a sheet. But by the 1920s, Dickinson said, "full exposure [was] taken for granted [especially] by the young." The Kinsey report upheld Dickinson's idea that there was a deep change in the American attitude toward nudity in the early twentieth century. Apparently, a third of women born before 1900 usually remained clothed during sex; but in the 1920s cohort, only 8 percent did.[31]

The revolution in sexuality meant that there were fewer virgins on the examining table, and that the hymen was less in evidence than it had been before. Petting made it technically difficult to distinguish those who had had sexual intercourse from those who had not, since it was hard to tell if a hymen had been ruptured and stretched by insistent hands or an erect penis. Dr. J. P. Greenhill, a gynecologist who understood the winds of change, explained the decline in virginity in these terms: "In most of these cases the hymen was ruptured by digital exploration and friction during petting."[32] Greenhill's blunt language said it all. Petting was a formidable assault on the traditional sanctity of the vagina, and it paved the way for American girls to challenge the long tradition of familial ownership of their bodies.

Hymenotomies

Deflowering was long considered the prerogative of a husband, but in the wake of the first American sexual revolution, some women in their late teens and early twenties turned to gynecologists to help them "adjust" their membrane, even before they were married. The motivation was clear. By the 1920s and 1930s, more and more women wanted sexual gratification in marriage, but a resistant hymen could make that goal difficult, particularly in the first days or weeks. In an influential book of 1925, *The Revolt of Modern Youth*, by Ben R. Lindsey and Wainwright Evans, readers were told that the best marriages were held together by equality, mutual affection, and sexual attraction rather than moral duty or social pressure. This ideal of "companionate marriage" promised interpersonal satisfaction on many levels, but it made successful coitus the centerpiece of the honeymoon and marital adjustment.[33]

The expectation of sexual compatibility generated business for gynecology, especially among educated middle-class young women in their early twenties who planned to marry. Premarital consultations became common in this group, and doctors soon discovered that future brides were willing to expose themselves to internal probes, or even to surgical procedures, in order to ensure that there was no physical barrier to successful intercourse. These modern women expected sexuality to be pleasurable, not painful. And they needed to be sexually successful in order to meet the new dictates of the modern female role.

In the interest of sexual satisfaction, professional gynecology began to offer a premarital hymenotomy, a surgical procedure that incised the hymen, or cut a septum between its openings, prior to first intercourse. This was a stunning departure from traditional practice. Until the 1930s and 1940s, gynecologists had used surgery to lacerate the hymen only in cases of menstrual blockage (caused by an imperforate hymen) or extremely painful intercourse (dyspareunia). Now they made a very different kind of recommendation: "Where the hymen is tough it may prove to be an insurmountable obstacle in the newly wedded. A crucial incision best made under gas anesthesia quickly relieves the situation."[34]

The hymenotomy was justified on the grounds that medical intervention improved the quality of the wedding night and, consequently, of the marriage itself. An incised hymen was considered a preventive measure and a boost to the modern bride because it prevented hemorrhage, pain, and "honeymoon cystitis," an irritation of the urinary tract caused by repeated attempts to force an opening in the vagina. The hymenotomy was also a way to protect against innocent or boorish husbands who attempted intercourse without knowing anything about female psychology or physiology. With a simple office intervention, done at least ten days to two weeks before the marriage, young women could assure themselves of less trauma and discomfort on the most important day of their lives. In essence, modern gynecologists offered to do in their offices what had been the peculiar right of husbands for centuries—that is, deflower virgins.

When future brides asked for this service, gynecologists performed it. But their willingness was not a recognition of the right of women or girls to sexual freedom. Although surgical incision of the hymen became an acceptable practice, the dialogue between physicians and their patients revealed a lingering adherence to older, patriarchal values. Because doctors in the interwar years did not want to make premarital sex too easy, young women who came asking for the special surgery were likely to be interrogated about their marriage plans and the identity of the future husband. And some physicians wanted assurance that the bridegroom had given his approval, since "an occasional man might want to convince himself that his bride is a virgin." As late as 1939, gynecologists were advised to obtain the permission of the groom, since it was still assumed that he had a custodial right to the membrane.[35] As a historian, I had hoped to find an authentic bridegroom's "permission note," but I suspect that most of these approvals were given orally.

Tampons for Teens

Reverence for the once venerable hymen dissipated further in the 1930s and 1940s as a result of the adoption of mass-produced tampons, a sanitary product that was used first by adult women and later by adolescents. Invented by Dr. Earle Cleveland Haas, a general practitioner who said he was tired of picking his way through "those damned old rags," the first commercial intravaginal tampons were marketed under the brand name Tampax beginning in 1936. Obviously, there had been earlier prototypes developed by women, but Haas had the right credentials—he was a physician and he was male—so he got credit for the invention and was able to raise the money to get mass production off the ground.[36] The adoption of tampons by American women ultimately affected how adolescent girls felt about medical examinations of their body, as well as their own sexuality.

Because the tampon was worn internally, it was considered a threat to virginity and reviled by many as nothing more than a dildo. Yet hundreds of thousands of women flocked to the Tampax display in the Hall of Pharmacy at the 1939 World's Fair in

New York, where a registered nurse answered personal questions about tampon use after a general presentation on personal hygiene.[37] Working women and athletic women liked the new product because of its convenience, its comfort, and the way it allowed complete freedom of movement. By World War II, tasteful and discreet ads for tampons appeared in respectable magazines such as the *American Weekly* and *Ladies' Home Journal.* In a time of national emergency, tampons were sold as a boost to the efficiency of America's women workers.

But internal protection for young girls was more problematic, and most people required medical assurance that it was neither dangerous nor immoral. In 1945 Dr. Robert Latou Dickinson gave his imprimatur to internal protection for teens in the *Journal of the American Medical Association,* stating: "The tampon has a caliber [width] that does not impede standard anatomic virginity." He made his point with a schematic drawing of the relative size of the distended hymen in virgins, married women, and those who had borne children. He showed that a tampon took up no more room than a standard nozzle for douching and it was smaller than the average penis. As for the old Victorian bugaboo that anything in the vagina had to be "stimulating," Dickinson said that if there was any erotic stimulus it was both "momentary" and "negligible" compared to the constant rubbing of sanitary pads.[38]

After World War II, many parents and doctors began to abandon their cautious approach to the female adolescent pelvis. In textbooks, but also in articles for mothers in the *Ladies' Home Journal,* doctors such as Goodrich C. Schauffler, a gynecologist at the University of Oregon Medical School, promoted the idea that prudish attitudes about female genitalia led to ignorance, untreated disease, and sexual problems later in life. Adolescent girls who had a "morbid" attitude toward their sexual organs, Schauffler said, would inevitably suffer frigidity, dyspareunia, sterility, and hostility toward their spouses. In order to avoid such difficulties, a sensitive gynecologist ought to help a teenager learn about her genitals, and thereby reduce her fear and anxiety. Many doctors suggested that if mothers would only put aside their old wives' tales, and develop instead a scientific attitude toward genitalia, then America's adolescent girls would be unlikely to engage in "aberrant" behaviors such as masturbation and premarital intercourse. Some even went so far as to suggest pelvic exams beginning in infancy, so that girls would accept them as routine, much like inspections of the ears or throat.[39] Clearly, modesty was no longer a reason *not* to examine. Yet there were still physicians like J. Roswell Gallagher, the Boston doctor who founded the field of adolescent medicine, who worried that a pelvic exam might result in psychosexual trauma, and stunt a girl's development into her mature feminine role. "A vaginal exam should only be done for good and sufficient special reasons and after due consideration of its possible unfavorable emotional effects," he advised.[40]

With tampons available in local drugstores, many absolutely normal, and relatively young, teenage girls began to try them. In that process, of course, they learned more about their own genitalia. Alone in the bathroom, or in venues such as school or camp, wherever "girl culture" flourished, postwar teenagers experimented with tampons in the hope that they could eliminate soggy napkins and uncomfortable sanitary belts. In 1959, when I was fifteen, I remember sitting on a toilet in a stall at a summer camp in the Adirondacks and receiving instructions on "how to put it in" from a female counselor whom I adored, a junior at Syracuse University. The door was shut, so I had enough privacy to really feel around inside my body; I also talked the entire time with two other girls, doing the same exact thing, in stalls to the left and right of me. Tampax instruction was more fun than swimming instruction, and I remember that someone shouted: "I don't think I have that hole." We squealed with delight, and, when we were all finished, we walked gingerly out of the cabin, down to the dining hall, anxious to see what it felt like to accommodate this new presence within our bodies.

This kind of experience was repugnant to many in the older generation, because it meant that girls touched their genitals as if they were masturbating. Mothers raised before World War II often backed off from this kind of instruction, either because they did not use tampons themselves or because they found it too awkward to discuss the different apertures in an "unclean" area of the body. Some women also opposed internal protection for their daughters because tampons stretched the hymen, thereby preparing girls, they thought, for intercourse and immorality.

Questions about the compatibility of virginity and internal protection lingered well into the 1960s and 1970s. A Catholic guide to sex education in that era stated authoritatively: "Tampons are completely unsuitable as a form of sanitary protection for young girls." Over and over the same questions were asked, suggesting the cultural power of the hymen even in the midst of the nation's second sexual revolution. In 1964, a teenager named Barbara wrote to *Seventeen* asking for advice because of disagreement at home: "What about internal protection? I mean my mother won't let me use it because she says it breaks the membrane or something." Barbara's comments revealed that she had no sense of the traditional sanctity of the hymen, although her mother surely did.[41] (As late as 1990, the tampon industry still felt the need to address traditional concerns. An advertisement in *Seventeen* showed a pensive teen asking bluntly, "Are you sure I will still be a virgin if I use Tampax?")

Yet by the 1960s and 1970s, both medicine and the sanitary products industry supported the idea of tampons for teens. Most gynecologists wanted to encourage better hygiene, and they also sensed that a younger and younger clientele was beginning to need their services. In their offices, doctors offered to instruct adolescents on how to insert vaginal tampons. When a concerned mother asked *Today's Health,* "Is there any harm in my twelve-year-old daughter using tampons?," the doctors who wrote for the magazine answered in terms that only hinted at the issue of virginity: "It is perfectly safe for a girl this age to use tampons, as long as she can place them in her vagina without discomfort. There are sizes made for young girls that will fit without difficulty."[42] In order to provide reassurance for younger girls, the sanitary products industry began to offer "small"- and "junior"-size products developed especially for the vaginas of the young.

American girls liked wearing tampons so much that by the 1970s and 1980s they were used by nearly 25 percent of girls in fifth and sixth grade, and by almost 75 percent of those in the last two years of high school.[43] This development in personal hygiene meant that more girls knew the difference between the vagina and the urethra and that some may even have discovered the clitoris in the process. "I had never touched my vagina until the day I tried to put in a Tampax at Aunt Nola's," a twenty-year-old recalled as she described how she came to learn about the "secret of masturbation." In a 1981 guide for physicians on how to do a patient's first pelvic exam, Dr. Karen Hein, director of the Division of Adolescent Medicine at New York's Columbia Presbyterian Hospital, recommended an early and forthright question about tampon use. "If she responds 'Yuck, I would never put my finger in there!' then you have both a good idea of her comfort in exploring her body and a guide in presenting your diagnostic findings," Hein advised. On the other hand, a girl who said something like " 'Oh yes, my mother and I thought tampons were a good idea' " was probably more relaxed and knowledgeable about her body.[44]

Tampons eventually became so familiar that they were used as a common reference point for helping young patients deal with the introduction of the speculum in the modern gynecological exam. By the 1960s, progressive practitioners were using a diminutive speculum based on the vaginal measurements of adolescent girls rather than those of adult women.[45] This age-specific instrument was a symbol of postwar gynecology's profound interest in adolescent girls, a group that formed a growing segment of its clinical practice because of their experience with internal sanitary protection and increased sexual activity.

Tampons, like petting, widened the twentieth-century adolescent girl's experience of the body and, ultimately, made it easier to have both internal exams and intercourse. Repeated monthly use of tampons meant that young women became familiar with the idea of penetration, even if they had never had intercourse. In fact, each time a girl inserted a tampon she defied traditional notions about the vagina and the sanctity of the hymen. In the late twentieth century, this intimate and highly individual act is so routine that its historic connotation is nearly obscured. Whether the hymen is ruptured or merely stretched is of little significance today. We wear internal protection, often at an early age, without concern for the status of a body part that used to mean so much to girls and their families. Just like menstrual rags and corsets, this once hallowed membrane has been consigned to the junk heap of women's history.

The Sexually Active Girl

In the late 1960s, as the Vietnam War escalated, so did the level of sexual activity on the home front. On a Saturday in December

1969, an adolescent in Florida named Laura Ramirez wrote in her diary: "This morning I went to play tennis with Mike. We stayed an hour and a half in the woods. I let him do more than I ever have." Compared with Yvonne Blue forty years earlier, Laura was sexually precocious. When she was only fifteen, and still in high school, she felt little reserve about detailing the nature of her sexual intimacies with her boyfriend. "I let Mike feel me off everywhere inside. I even removed my shorts and let him undo my bra. It was a tremendous experience."[46]

Laura lived with her mother, her stepfather, and her college-bound older sister in a middle-class neighborhood in Melbourne, Florida. Her stepfather was a white-collar employee of a local corporation; her mother was a business teacher at the Catholic high school in town. Laura was a good student at the local public high school, and also a voracious reader who tended to cast her life in terms of the books she read. After the tryst with Mike near the tennis courts, she explained that she agreed to meet him "because last night I read [Kahlil Gibran's] *The Prophet* and it convinced me that there's nothing wrong with pleasure." Yet Laura was not a hippie, a rebel, or an antiwar activist. "I hate hippies," she wrote while listening to the group Chicago on her earphones, "but I love their bag. You know—acid-rock, incense, psyched-out clothes, etc. Everything but pot and mind-benders." Laura rooted for her school basketball team, attended Sunday services at the local Baptist church, and adored Richard Nixon. "I love him deeply. He is great and I am speechless," she wrote after hearing the president's explanation of his veto of a 1970 spending bill.

Despite her mainstream conservative orientation, Laura did not revere virginity, and she was sexually adventurous. In her diary, she graphically described the course of her sexual experiments with Mike: "He did what I guess you could call finger coitus for about twenty-five minutes and neither of us said anything during the whole time. It was fantastic and I enjoyed it immensely." (She was surprisingly uneasy, however, about certain kinds of kissing: "Mike frenched me to show me what it was like and its horrible, Yech!") Sometimes she took the lead and told her boyfriend what to do: "I have candidly taught Mike how I want him to make love to me: (1) Kiss alot (2) Kiss on the neck frequently (3) Press hard." After school one afternoon, in January 1970, the couple pledged to "commit coition" on a particular day in the summer of 1975. Both parties clearly had intercourse in mind for the future; but it was not meant to be, because they "broke up," as teenagers do.

A year later, Laura began to date Bob Hughes, a seventeen-year-old senior who was editor of the school yearbook, an active Boy Scout, and a leader in student government. Bob took her to homecoming and football games, and he gave her corsages, pictures, and other small gifts, which she liked a great deal. Bob was more romantic than any other boy she had known, and he told her explicitly that he "liked her body." Laura welcomed that kind of admiration, and it prompted her to take further risks in their sexual relationship. After a romantic picnic in a shady and secluded spot, she wrote: "We fixed the blanket just so and I ate a sandwich and we drank some orange juice and then we lay down and kissed. I took off my clothes and he took off his pants and we had sex. Everything went along smoothly and normal like we always do it. First he turned me on and when I was feeling pretty good then I sat up and turned him on." Whether Laura and Bob had intercourse, oral sex, or simply mutual masturbation is not entirely clear, but her tone indicates that the intimacies were familiar and very pleasurable. For a few months, passion and hormones reigned: "We have sex everytime we see each other now, if we have five minutes or five hours."

I use this diary account not to shock or titillate but to make a point about what was happening in the 1960s and 1970s even in "middle America." Physicians in this era saw thousands of girls like Laura Ramirez. As the rate of premarital coitus soared, gynecologists had to face a new reality in which premarital chastity was becoming the exception rather than the rule. This revolution in social values meant that doctors had to change both their language and their attitudes. Traditional moral pronouncements against sexuality in the young were not only ineffective but off-putting, and they drove young women away from medical services. Conservation of the hymen became a concern of the past, as doctors looked for ways to help girls make sensible, safe sexual choices in a style that was neutral and nonthreatening.

In the interest of establishing rapport with a new breed of patient, physicians cultivated a clinical style that put special emphasis on appearing nonjudgmental, no matter how young the patient or how flamboyant the sexual behavior.[47] The first step in creating an atmosphere that would neither intimidate nor condemn involved creation of a neutral language to describe the patient. To that end, doctors began to use the term *sexually active,* borrowed from the older family-planning movement, to designate adolescent females who were no longer virgins. *Sexually active* was an important semantic innovation because it described a social state without reference to morality. Older terms such as *ruined, wayward,* and *promiscuous* disappeared from the clinical case reports of medical and mental health professionals. The concept of a "sexually active girl" represented a sea change in American attitudes. It not only implied that sexual activity among female adolescents could be voluntary, autonomous, and guilt-free, but it also cast the hymen as irrelevant.[48]

Physicians, however, were in a tough spot. If they appeared to encourage recreational sex—by casually prescribing contraceptives, for example—they risked offending many parents, the clergy, and conservatives who accused them of fostering immorality and illegitimacy. But if they were too cautious or punitive, they lost opportunities to serve a clientele that needed contraception, treatment for venereal disease, and prenatal care. Because so many physicians felt uncomfortable handling the psychosocial side of adolescent sexuality, there were all kinds of clinical advisories about how to interact with teenage girls like Laura Ramirez. Dr. Ralph Lopez, director of the Division of Adolescent Medicine at Cornell Medical College, advocated direct questions: "Are you having sexual intercourse? If so, what form of birth control do you use?" But others thought it best to be indirect, and some still shied away from asking the question that eventually became the gynecological mantra of the 1970s and 1980s: "Are you sexually active?"[49]

Doctors no longer assumed virginity in the young. To the amazement of older, more conservative clinicians, most adolescent patients seemed more than willing to talk about their sexual experiences. "In this enlightened age, teenage girls not unusually offer this information spontaneously," explained a New York practitioner. In a well-known textbook on clinical practice, Dr. John Huffman confirmed that contemporary teenagers were "quite frank and matter-of-fact about their sexual activities."[50] Many physicians admitted that it was difficult to appear nonjudgmental about the sexuality of young girls, particularly when the spectrum of reported behaviors widened to include multiple partners, oral sex, and homosexuality. (By 1979, a California study revealed that a third of fifteen- and sixteen-year-olds, and almost half of seventeen- and eighteen-year-olds, had either given or received oral-genital stimulation.)[51] Some doctors were awkward and brusque with young female patients whose experience seemed to them "immoral, unaesthetic, or undisciplined."[52] The fact that so many young sexual adventurers came from "good," as opposed to "bad," homes only made doctors more uneasy, because it stimulated concern about what their own daughters, nieces, or babysitters might be doing.

Given these difficulties, some physicians hid behind the law. In the 1960s, most states still had laws that made it illegal to administer medical treatment to minors without parental consent.[53] These "parental consent" barriers made most doctors extremely cautious about treating sexually active patients under the age of eighteen. In a 1970 article in *Redbook* entitled "Why I'll Give My Daughter the Pill," a young mother from Decatur, Georgia, told the unhappy story of how she found herself pregnant before marriage, and she pleaded for greater availability of contraceptives. But only a few progressive clinics, such as the one associated with the Division of Adolescent Medicine at Boston's Children's Hospital, were publicly willing to touch this sensitive issue before 1972.[54] Although it was hard for some people to accept, the behavior of teenagers was forcing medicine to rethink its traditional allegiance to parents, and their right to control the bodies of unmarried adolescent daughters.

Parents everywhere were losing authority as adolescents in this era pushed for greater sexual autonomy. In the summer of 1971, after reading an article in *Seventeen* about Boston's Adolescent Clinic, a sexually active seventeen-year-old from Connecticut wrote to Dr. Robert P. Masland at Children's Hospital asking him for help. Like most girls her age, she wrote about her boyfriend and the nature of their romance: "We have been dating for quite a few months. I really love him and as of late, we have spent a few nights and weekends together. We thought of getting married some time in the future, but neither of us is really sure we can hack it. He's taken care of any birth control means before (condom) but now I feel that we need something that will offer us more security." The girl then stated her predicament: "I am a minor, but in need of help for securing some form of contraception. I don't want to become pregnant [because] that would probably ruin my chances for a good education (I am still attending high school) and generally make things bad for John [her boyfriend], my friends and family. Will you help me obtain some means of birth control? What I had specifically in mind was the Pill."[55]

The following year, in *Eisenstadt* v. *Baird*, the Supreme Court put aside the model of "joint ownership" of girls' bodies that had prevailed since the nineteenth century. In this historic case, the court upheld the rights of minors to seek and obtain contraceptives without parental approval. In its assertion that minors had the right to control their own reproductive processes, the Court symbolically denied parents their traditional interest in the virginity of their teenage daughters. After 1972, gynecologists—who had once refused to give oral contraceptives to underage girls, or had given them grudgingly on the grounds that they were good for acne or reduced menstrual cramps—could openly write prescriptions without fear of prosecution. This decision was a landmark in the "contraceptive revolution," and it had important consequences for the autonomy, as well as the anatomy, of America's female adolescents.

The End of Parental Rights

Within the next decade, middle-class mothers were eased out of their traditional supervisory and counseling roles in the pelvic examination. Despite the new openness about sexuality, concerned doctors realized that many girls were still silent and secretive in the presence of a parent. As a consequence, they developed a new clinical protocol in which they took a patient's history and did the internal, both without the mother present. A supportive, but neutral, nurse or female assistant remained instead. In cases where a mother stayed in the examining room because of a daughter's preference, physicians were advised to "push the mother into the background by asking her only such questions as the girl herself cannot answer."[56]

In sharp contrast to Victorian doctors, who advised using the mother as an aide to the clinical examination, gynecologists at the end of the twentieth century treated the adolescent female as if she were independent of her parents. Even the very youngest girls no longer had to wear the historic mantle of maternal supervision. "Questions concerning sexual behavior should not be asked of a thirteen-year-old girl in the presence of her mother," one doctor advised. Reports from gynecologists claimed that their adolescent patients preferred the new protocol and "rarely" wanted their mothers to remain.[57] At the end of an independent examination, the responsible doctor tipped his hat to the traditional family context by asking simply, "What would you like me to share with your parents concerning your visit?"

Once vilified, feared, and monitored by mothers, the pelvic exam of an adolescent was now a confidential interaction between the girl and her doctor. By the 1970s and 1980s, breaches of confidentiality were justified only in a life-threatening emergency. Loss of virginity was not a justification. Forsaking their longstanding respect for parental rights in a daughter's body, gynecologists in the late twentieth century allied themselves with girls, even girls whose sexual behavior they might not condone. In

1988, the American College of Obstetricians and Gynecologists issued an important statement, "Confidentiality in Adolescent Health Care," that urged its professional membership to honor the adolescent's need for privacy and pay no special deference to mothers or fathers. Although parents continued to give directives, such as "See if my daughter is a virgin," the enlightened gynecologist now resisted that request because it was considered "inappropriate."[58] The state of a girl's hymen was nobody's business but her own and her doctor's.

In a world where the hymen was "disempowered," the typical pelvic exam for an adolescent became an educational experience rather than a test of virginity. In doctors' offices and in Planned Parenthood clinics, young women were taught about their internal reproductive organs and the physiology of heterosexual intercourse. Doctors and nurses developed visual aids appropriate to the cognitive abilities of modern teenagers; instead of line drawings and sketches, they relied on three-dimensional models of body parts, and they eliminated medical illustrations of female pathologies in frightening or exaggerated colors. Many girls also learned for the first time that masturbation was a legitimate form of sexual pleasure, and that it was not something they had to fear or feel guilty about. (Judy Blume first broached the topic in her widely read story *Deenie,* published in 1973.)[59] In some offices, patients were encouraged to spread their own genitalia, insert the speculum, and "get to know" their cervix by using mirrors. This strategy reflected the feminist push for self-determination in medical care, made popular by *Our Bodies, Ourselves,* published in 1973, and adopted by many women's self-help groups. This "hands-on" pedagogy was important because it demystified girls' bodies and helped to remove the taboos upon which veneration of the hymen and virginity depended.[60]

Coming Out in College: Ellen Anderson's Struggle

In a climate where sexual expression in girls was valued rather than denied, more girls than ever before began to consider lesbianism a viable option. In the 1970s and 1980s, American girls began to write openly in diaries about their struggles with sexual identity. Although lesbian women characteristically define themselves as such in their early twenties, in the 1970s some girls who were still teenagers began to express discomfort with heterosexual norms and acknowledge their emotional and erotic preference for their own sex. Within the past twenty years, sexual orientation—just like most sexual experiences—has become an issue, and a choice, earlier in life.

From both a historical and a psychological perspective, an emotional attachment to other women and girls is not unusual in adolescence. In the Victorian era, many girls, such as Lou Henry (Hoover), had brief crushes on their female teachers in the years before they married; others—such as M. Carey Thomas, later president of Bryn Mawr College—showed a determined preference for their own sex, rejected marriage, and established intimate relationships with other women throughout their lives.[61] What was new in the 1970s was the ability of adolescent women to express erotic as well as emotional interest in other women. Instead of remaining celibate, entering convents, making unhappy marriages, or leading furtive lives, by the 1970s a sizable number of young women became self-identified, sexually active lesbians. Their ability to accept and express their own sexual desire was facilitated by the women's movement and by the emergence of an openly gay culture, both of which provided young lesbians with role models and a vocabulary for understanding themselves.[62]

The diary of Ellen Anderson reveals a great deal about the "coming out" struggle and the ways in which lesbian sexuality was expressed and learned in the United States by the late 1970s. As a girl growing up in Greensburgh, Pennsylvania, Ellen led a life that was characteristic of many small-town, middle-class Protestant girls. Her father was an administrator and fund-raiser for the Young Men's Christian Association; her mother was a homemaker who sometimes did substitute teaching. Although both parents were liberal Presbyterians, Ellen became involved in Young Life, an evangelical youth outreach program that was based on social values far more conservative than those of her own parents. At fourteen, Ellen spent long hours writing in her diary about her hopes for a good Christian life, which, at that point, included marriage and a family.[63]

But Ellen's friends, especially her girlfriends, were always a major preoccupation in her life. In eighth grade, while she was playing tuba in the school band, she met Michelle, a French horn player, whom she described as "the smartest and most popular girl in [her] class." Ellen's diary reveals that she idolized Michelle but that her affection and loyalty were never repaid. At the age of fifteen, in 1970, Ellen and her family moved to Elmhurst, Illinois, where she was thrown into a high school environment that left her feeling lonely and very much like an outcast. Although she had acquaintances at school, received good grades, and was active in the town's Christian youth fellowship, she had difficulty finding a social group because she was not as interested in boys as were the other girls. When Ellen told her minister that she was unhappy because she was not popular, he responded by saying that she was "too mature mentally for most high school boys." Ellen and her family attributed some of her difficulty to the fact that although she was pretty, she was tall—almost five feet nine—and athletic, rather than traditionally feminine.

In moments of depression, when her sense of difference was overpowering, Ellen turned to her religious faith, hoping for an answer. But her spirituality always led her to the issue of her relationships with other girls. "If you like someone, how do you tell her so?" she wrote wistfully. "If you admire her, how can she know? If you want to talk to her, how can you, if you're afraid she'll laugh?" By the time she was a senior, Ellen had a special friendship with Susan, a girl from her church, but the relationship ended bitterly. In the aftermath of that friendship, before she graduated from high school and embarked for Japan as a foreign exchange student, Ellen was comforted by two other girls from her high school, Judi and Joanne, who also felt "different." In fact, Judi and Joanne were together so much that the adviser to the cheerleading squad asked Judi, who was a cheerleader, to give up her friend because they were becoming "too close," a familiar euphemism for fears about lesbianism.

In 1974, after she returned from Japan, Ellen entered the University of Illinois at Champaign-Urbana, and she chose to live in Allen Hall, a dormitory associated with liberal social causes. Although she began to date a few young men, she was never really comfortable with conventional undergraduate life and its heterosexual emphasis. Ellen admitted in her diary that she occasionally developed an interest in a particular boy, but she also described herself as "contemptuous of girls who let themselves get wrapped up in a guy." Typically, her dating relationships and her friendships with males ebbed whenever they took a romantic turn: "Yesterday Ken and I talked for awhile. Then he started getting physical. I like him and all but I guess I warm up slowly. I don't even feel like that about him." Ellen's distaste for sexual overtures, and her lack of response to them, made her wonder where she fit in a world in which most people her age were enthusiastically pairing off as heterosexual couples.

As time passed, Ellen became aware of a pattern in her life—that she wanted exclusivity in relationships with girls rather than boys. Her dissatisfaction with traditional dating, combined with her sense that she was "neither very feminine or poised," also stimulated her interest in events in the local women's community. Once a week she went to Treno's, a local bar, to hear Kristin Lems, founder of the National Women's Music Festival, an event that Ellen attended in its early years; she joined a group devoted to female spirituality where she read a feminist version of the Bible under the direction of a female minister; and she also accompanied her high school friend Judi, now "out" as a lesbian, to Augie's, an all-women's bar in Chicago. "I'm glad I went with [Judi]," Ellen wrote, "because I've rarely felt the completely unthreatening security of acceptance and anonymity as there. Women were talking, dancing, being—warmly, as friends, as lovers. Everything seemed very natural. Maybe I was deluded but feelings seemed very sincere there. More so than in coed bars where the men and women are really out to make impressions."

By the spring of 1976, when Ellen was twenty years old, she began to write openly about the issue of her own sexual orientation. At first, she was ambivalent about sexual relationships with women, although the possibility was clearly in her mind. In May, after she had a dream in which a woman made a sexual pass at her, she responded with both curiosity and denial. "I've never been propositioned," she wrote after mentioning the dream, "although I am sure there are women I know who would sleep with me if I suggested it. I won't. Somehow female-female affection (which is healthy and valid) becomes sickening as it becomes sexual. Maybe I'm just brainwashed by a heterosexual society." As she thought about the issue of sex with women, she used the *L* word for the first time in her diary: "Lesbians are usually not monogamous," she explained, "and that takes part of the validity out of the relationship, I think. [But] I really shouldn't talk. What do I know?"

By midsummer, Ellen's struggle was focused on the question of which sex best fulfilled her needs. "Physically a man can do anything for me that a woman could, and more," Ellen wrote, revealing that she was wondering about what it meant to make love to a woman as compared with a man. In terms of emotional sustenance, Ellen clearly ranked men below women: "The question is whether a man's emotional makeup is such that it would be fulfilling for me." As the summer progressed, Ellen zeroed in on what she wanted and the issues that were involved: "I'd rather like having an intense one-to-one 'love affair' type relationship with someone. I'm not sure if I care if that person is male or female."

Despite this admission, Ellen was not certain how to think about women as sexual partners. In her diary she wrote that she was still "sexually attracted to men" but "rarely loved them like she did women." Women seemed to her "more worthy" of her love but problematic in terms of what she knew about making love. (Ellen was a virgin.) But instead of denying her interest in this question, Ellen began to spend less time with her straight roommates, Kathy and Jane, and more time with friends who were openly gay. By early August, she was feeling some confidence about the path that was emerging: "I'm learning more about my own sexuality and about my feelings about interpersonal relationships and I'm convinced now of the validity of falling in love with someone of your own sex."

For her twenty-first birthday, in August 1976, Ellen went to New York City to visit her old friend Judi, who was renting a room in an apartment with a group of gay women. With Judi, she attended a women's self-defense class in Greenwich Village and then a lively potluck supper with "real lesbians" who sang special gay music by the rising star Chris Williamson. This visit helped to confirm Ellen's emerging sense of herself. "In New York," she wrote, "I was surrounded by women the whole time, most of them were Radical Lesbian Feminists. It was a real growing experience for me. They see lesbianism as being the result of more than sexual preference, but also as a political statement. They don't need men." At the potluck, Ellen experienced her first sexual overture from a woman who was older and more experienced. "They call her the bulldozer," Ellen reported. "She really moved in fast. She wanted me to go home with her." Although Ellen was attracted to this woman, she felt she was "not ready" for "that kind of relationship," so nothing happened. Instead, she returned to the Midwest with a T-shirt that said A WOMAN WITHOUT A MAN IS LIKE A FISH WITHOUT A BICYCLE and planned to "come out" to others, now that she had "come out" to herself.

Strengthened by what she saw in gay women's culture, Ellen decided to attend a lesbian dance that she read about in the university newspaper, *The Daily Illini.* "I went by myself. Scared shitless," she wrote afterward. For Ellen, the event was an enormous success because she felt comfortable and had a wonderful time: "Dancing with women I just loosen up and move. Especially slow dancing. You can just feel your two bodies flow together." Although the dance was a joyous declaration of her sexuality, Ellen understood that there were problems ahead: "Going there was the first time I actually admitted that I love women. I can't say I can't love or won't love men, but first I love women. The problem with this setup is, of course, that it's socially unacceptable. Women who love women are weird—no, 'queer'—outcasts. You can lose a job for that crime. It's sickening." The implications of Ellen's choice seemed clear: "This is the beginning of a new hidden lifestyle. It will take guts, but I am sure it's worth it, being true to my feeling and my own understanding of who I am."

Ellen's new "lifestyle" did not remain hidden for very long. Within a month of her return from New York City, she was involved in a physical and emotional relationship with Rachel, a rugby player whom she met at the dance. Rachel was more experienced than Ellen, at least in terms of lesbian sexuality. "At first she was hesitant about extending a relationship with me—such a rookie," Ellen wrote. "She was concerned that all I wanted from her was to learn how to make love with a woman." When they finally did make love, Ellen described her reaction to their physical intimacy: "It was all so natural and easy and innocent in the sense that it was clean and not 'premeditated' like I felt with Ken. Sometimes I would just hold her and she would hold me back, or stroke me gently in just the right places—my neck, back, face. It was incredible how she responded to me just as I would have responded to her had she done the same things to me."

In a rush of happiness about the relationship with Rachel, Ellen began to "come out" to heterosexual friends at the university, such as her roommate, Kathy, who showed no disapproval, although she was "surprised" and "worried about the implications." Ellen also told a few old friends by phone, but she could not find the courage to tell her acquaintances at the faculty center where she worked as a waitress, because she feared she would lose her job if they knew the truth. As happy as she was about her relationship with Rachel, Ellen's elation was always tempered by the reality that lesbian love was neither familiar nor acceptable to many people, particularly her own family. "I'm really paranoid about people finding out that I love Rachel," Ellen explained, "yet the more people that know the happier I am." The semester after she came out, Ellen took her first women's studies course and began to frequent the Balloon Saloon, a local gay bar, where she and Rachel found a supportive community. In her senior year, Ellen and Rachel lived as a couple in a household that included gay men.

Ellen graduated from the university in 1978 with a degree in linguistics. Soon after that, she left with Rachel, who was Jewish, for a two-year adventure living and working in Israel. At this point, Ellen had told her siblings that she was lesbian, but she had not told her parents. However, while she was away in Israel, Mrs. Anderson read a letter Ellen had written to her minister in Elmhurst suggesting that the church was bigoted in its treatment of homosexuals and disclosing her own sexuality. This news was so unsettling to Ellen's mother that she stopped writing her usual weekly letters and was silent for over two months. When Ellen heard from her mother again, she learned that her mother had not yet told her father because she feared his reaction to the news about her sexuality. Mr. Anderson was eventually told the truth, but his reaction was a familiar mix of contradictions: while he did not approve of "gay bashing," he hoped that Ellen's lesbianism was only a stage and that she would eventually "grow out" of it. (She did not. Today, at forty, she lives in a settled, loving relationship with a woman who has been her partner for almost fifteen years.)

Like many middle-class adults who came of age before the social revolution of the 1960s and 1970s, Ellen Anderson's mother and father were adrift in a world with an expanded sexual repertoire that left them confused, unhappy, and sometimes very angry. Although they loved their thoughtful, sensitive daughter, they had to think about her in a profoundly new way—as a sexual being whose sexual choices ran "against the grain." "Coming out" was hard for adolescents like Ellen Anderson, and also for their families, but it was not uncommon in the 1970s and 1980s, when

American society had to face the full flowering of the second American sexual revolution born of the 1960s. Gay girls were a logical but unanticipated consequence of our commitment to the normality and the value of sexual expression in adolescence.

The Era of Sexual Liberalism: Deborah Perry's Diaphragm

For a brief moment, in the time between *Eisenstadt* v. *Baird* and the emergence of the HIV virus in the 1980s, there were few constraints on sexually active girls so long as they used contraceptives reliably and avoided pregnancy. In this new world, sexual expression was seen as a critical personal right to which even adolescents were entitled. According to observant doctors, the second American sexual revolution generated adolescent girls who were explicit about their interest in intercourse and more confident about their own sexuality. In urban centers, particularly in medical practices that drew from a middle-class clientele, doctors encountered a new kind of American girl. "The increasing number of young adolescent girls who are taking birth control pills has resulted in a new situation," wrote Dr. Masland of Boston in the early 1980s. What impressed Masland was not just the frequency of premarital intercourse but the attitude of his teenage patients: "Heretofore, the young boy had always been thought of as the aggressive one, but now we find adolescent girls on the pill may be equally aggressive in their desire for sexual activity."[64] In Philadelphia, Dr. Albert Bongiovanni noted a related change: "Many more young women are less concerned about whether to participate in coitus than was the case a generation ago. [Now] they are more concerned about the nature of their relationships. Decisions often involve not whether the young woman should have sex, but with whom."[65]

The diary of Deborah Perry provides vivid testimony to the freewheeling spirit of sexually active girls in the early 1980s. Deborah was only fourteen years old in 1982 when she, and many of her friends at Stuyvesant High School in New York City, began to talk about losing their virginity.[66] Even before she had her first date, she considered the possibility of intercourse: "It's pretty strange to think that my first date ever is going to be with Brad Muller, a superstar [at our school]. I'm pretty nervous but I know I don't have to be because he's the kind of person you could say 'Let's wait' to." Deborah did not have sex with Brad on their first date, but her diary reflects the extent to which intercourse was a subject of concern among her thirteen- and fourteen-year-old friends. A boy, who was a classmate, told her on the phone that "if he didn't lose it [his virginity] by June," he would "fuck anybody." Deborah wrote repeatedly in her diary about her crush on a boy named Josh, but she dreamed of more than sweet kisses: "I really want to lose my virginity with him, that's for sure." Talk about boys and sex percolated constantly throughout her diary. By the time she was fourteen, she had already decided to use a barrier method of birth control, rather than the Pill, because she feared the weight gain associated with oral contraceptives.

When Deborah first began to write about intimate adventures with boys, she was two years younger than Laura Ramirez in the 1960s, and five years younger than Yvonne Blue in the 1920s. "Tuesday Pete and I were alone for about six hours, three of which we were making love," she reported in early September before she returned to school for her sophomore year. "I'm still a virgin but we tried," she wrote. Apparently, penetration was awkward, so Deborah became concerned about the size of her body; she never mentioned her hymen, though, and she was more expectant than afraid. "I have to go to the gynecologist to get a diagrahm [sic] and see how small my vagina is. I love Pete sooo much! He's the best kisser in the world. I love the way he tastes."

Within the month, Deborah made a visit to her mother's gynecologist, a woman who was "really nice," who assured her that her vagina was of normal size. "She gave me a prescription for a size 70 diagrahm [sic]," Deborah wrote excitedly, misspelling the word again. When she finally got the diaphragm, she said that it looked like a "Frisbee," and she waited expectantly for a reunion with Pete so she could try it out: "I can't wait! Gonna get some mileage on my diagrahm." Although Deborah was ripe and ready, the relationship was not consummated because the couple could not get enough time alone together. Six months later, when she met another boy whom she liked a great deal, Deborah began to wear the diaphragm almost continuously, in order to be prepared for sex whenever it might occur. By the time she was sixteen, Deborah had had experience with a number of different sexual partners, and she continued to protect herself from pregnancy, the major worry of adolescents, in a world where the HIV virus was lurking but generally unknown.

Deborah's sexual autonomy was rooted in her peer group, in a sexually stimulating popular culture, and in the general decline of protective supervision and nurturance of girls that had been going on since the late nineteenth century. In the 1980s, even the advice columns in such teenage magazines as *Seventeen* began to allow that protected sex—that is, intercourse with contraceptives—might be an appropriate personal decision in adolescence, so long as a young woman felt safe and comfortable sharing her body in this intimate way. This new sexual freedom was aided and abetted by parental and medical neutrality. Parents like the Perrys did not prohibit sexuality in their young daughter's life, perhaps because their own upbringing had been repressive and they wanted something different for her. As they listened to Deborah's stories about her romantic travails and sexual exploits with boys, they made no moral pronouncements and insisted only on consistent use of birth control. At the gynecologist's office, Deborah was also treated as an adult, even though she regarded her "diagrahm" as if it were a new bike or a piece of camping gear. She went to the gynecologist on her own, and when she was alone with her doctor she discussed the mechanics of heterosexual penetration in a matter-of-fact, clinical way. Had she wanted a hymenotomy, she probably could have had one, even at her tender age. A clinical textbook in the 1980s advised that doctors "should not arbitrarily tell the adolescent to wait until marriage" if she is interested in a hymenotomy.[67]

Sexual Pressure at School: The Ordeal of Sarah Compton

The "hands off" attitude of parents and doctors may have been an improvement over the censorious overprotection of earlier times, but it has a negative side in a world where girls' bodies are, literally, more accessible and also more vulnerable. In a culture like ours, where girlhood virginity is now an archaic ideal, adolescent girls are subject to more sexual pressure than ever before; they are more likely to become sexually active before they are sixteen; and all of this activity makes them more vulnerable to multiple medical risks. In addition to the possibility of AIDS, they are exposed to a wide range of venereal diseases that their mothers generally did not face. There is the old standby, gonorrhea, but also an increase in chlamydia, herpes, perineal warts, and human papillomavirus, all of which are linked to increased sexual activity. And the earlier a girl begins to have intercourse, and the more sexual partners she has, the greater her risk for cervical cancer.[68]

Unfortunately, in this new disease environment, girls must also handle an increase in sexual pressure, often at a very early age. National data reveal that fourteen and fifteen are two of the peak ages for becoming a victim of sexual assault; approximately 50 percent of rape victims are between ten and nineteen, and half of this group are under sixteen.[69] A national study in 1995 by the Alan Guttmacher Institute, a research and public policy group that studies fertility and population issues, suggests that heightened adult male interest in the bodies of young girls is not a figment of the feminist imagination. In fact, a startling number of teenage girls are having sex with adult men, instead of with boys their own age. In California, among teenage mothers eleven to fifteen, only 9 percent of the partners were junior high school boys; 40 percent were in high school, and 51 percent were adults.[70] But sexual pressure comes in many different forms, from schoolboys as well as experienced men. During the summers of 1994 and 1995, the police in New York City had to deal with a new "game," called whirlpooling, in which a group of teenage boys surround a girl in a swimming pool and try to remove her bathing suit in order to "grope" her or have sex.[71] Less violent, but equally unsettling, verbal violations happen every day, even to middle-class girls in supposedly safe environments.

Consider the case of Sarah Compton, who, in chapter 1, called up her friends to tell them that she had *finally* gotten her period, at the advanced age of thirteen. Although Sarah wrote with enormous pleasure about getting her period and developing breasts, her diary reveals that there was a cloud over the experience of biological maturation, and it had to do with the adolescent culture at her middle school in Ithaca, New York.[72] In seventh grade, the boys began to use a ranking system (associated with the popular 1979 Bo Derek film, *10*) to describe the bodies of their female classmates. Although the girls facilitated this kind of talk by passing it around—for example, Sarah told her friend Julie that "Scott said Lisa was an '8' "—the rankings made them uneasy because it gave boys the power to establish their value on the basis of their bodies. Whether they were thin or fat, had breasts, or seemed "sexy" was becoming as important as how they rode a bike or performed in school. Sarah was disheartened by the fact that a classmate at school considered her only a "3" while a boy she met during the summer in Georgia thought she was a "10." It did not matter to her that the boys who did the rankings were as young, inexperienced, and gawky as the girls. The boys took their authority from popular culture, which made male perspectives on female bodies all-important.

On the bus and in school, Sarah had some provocative and upsetting interactions with boys. In English class, a boy named Mike sent her a note with an imaginary contract saying he wanted "total control of her body" for a movie called "Foreplay in the Corner." This pseudo-sophisticated joke made Sarah realize that she didn't like Mike very much, so she tried to drop out of a joint class project. But Mike was not deterred; in front of other kids, he told her that she would have to become either his "personal pleasure servant" or a "prostitute" in order to get out of the project. When Sarah heard this, she replied, "Go to hell," but the boys who were listening laughed uproariously and told her she could make a great deal of money that way.

Sarah's developing body provoked suggestive talk despite the fact that she dressed in loose, comfortable clothing, and wore only blush and a touch of lipstick. When she was at the mall one day with a group of girls and boys, she called her mother from a pay phone to arrange a ride home. To her amazement, a boy whom she had always considered nice and a good friend opened the phone booth door and yelled: "Tell her we're molesting you and she'll come right away!" Sarah joked in her diary about boys who were "sex maniacs," but the joke soured when she had to deal with one who called her slut, whore, and bitch. "As I left the bus, he [Eric] said again, 'Bye Bitch.' I should have slapped him hard," Sarah wrote, "so hard that it would make him feel the way I did, hurt, angry and about to cry. I should have slapped him so hard that his face would swell up till it looked like he had one-sided mumps." The same boy plagued her in the halls: "Do you want to make love, or just fool around?" he sneered one morning. That comment prompted her to write: "Eric talks like he is going to rape me, and that's really scary." Sexual innuendo and harassment made school difficult for Sarah, but with her mother's help, she began to develop some perspective on the reactions her new body provoked. "He [Eric] is reducing me to a sex object and that is an awful feeling," she wrote at the end of eighth grade, when she was only fourteen. The reluctance of many school officials to take seriously the problem of verbal harassment in early adolescence sets the stage for more serious difficulties—such as acquaintance rape—in high school and college.

It is no wonder that teenage magazines today are filled with stories of sexual violation, as well as inquiries about how to fend off unwelcome comments, touching, and outright physical intimidation. A girl who was grabbed and then French-kissed by a boy she barely knew wrote with annoyance to *Seventeen:* "I felt almost like my mouth was raped," but she followed her admission of disgust with the question: "Am I just being a prude?" And another, whose boyfriend pushed her into oral sex, was unsure if she should express her displeasure: "Two weeks ago when we were making out, he unzipped his pants and sort of guided my head down there. I'd never done that before and didn't want to, so I sort of held back, but I was too embarrassed to say no. Afterward he was so sweet and thankful, but I hated it. I feel really stupid because all my friends say they do it with their boyfriends and I'm going to lose him if I don't."[73] Teenage magazines try to assure girls that pressure from boyfriends and peers should never make them do anything they do not feel comfortable doing, but many girls sound as if they are swimming upstream against a powerful current.

Coercion, Not Consent

As always, the bodies of girls are a symbol of new sexual attitudes and behaviors. Adolescent experience with oral sex is a case in point. These days, many adolescent girls experience fellatio and cunnilingus, behaviors their mothers saved for the intimacy and trust of long-standing marital relationships.[74] But recent developments in popular culture, ranging from increased knowledge about homosexuality to a musical genre known as "sex rock" or "cock rock," has reduced the taboo on oral sex. Songs with suggestive titles, such as "I Want'a Do Something Freaky to You" or "Do It Any Way You Wanna," are common fare on MTV, along with explicit lyrics, such as Lou Reed's, about a lover who "never lost her head while giving head."[75] Whether one approves or not, young women growing up at the end of the twentieth century face an expanded repertoire of erotic possibilities. This means that some look for new and different pleasures to enhance or supplement "traditional" intercourse. In the world of the 1990s, both fellatio and cunnilingus can be natural and enjoyable, although they were once considered perverted, unnatural, and immoral. In practice, however, a girl's sexual pleasure is usually not the motivating factor. The few studies that exist on oral sex among teenagers indicate that although teenage girls perform fellatio more often than in the past, they do so *without* pleasure, usually to please their boyfriend or to avoid the possibility of impregnation. (Some also believe, mistakenly, that oral sex is "safe sex.")

Coercion, not consent, is often a reality in the lives of today's sexually active girls. As girls mature and begin to date, the psychological pressures often increase and become more complicated, in an emotional sense, because a partner's demands are often tied up with the issue of love. Recent studies of violence in adolescent dating, conducted at high schools and colleges throughout the country, indicate that a substantial number of adolescent girls have experienced some form of sexual violence in their dating relationships. Yet when they are asked about their attitudes toward these behaviors, girls, as well as boys, revealed a surprising level of tolerance for sexual coercion. Thirty-two percent of the girls believed that forced sex was actually acceptable if a couple had dated for a long time. And 40 percent of the boys believed that forced sex was acceptable if the "guy" spent a lot of money on the date. Given this kind of thinking, it is no wonder that the American College of Obstetricians and Gynecologists feels the need to tell its membership that they should ask another question of the current adolescent generation: "Has anyone tried to make you have sex?"[76] This is as realistic a query as "Are you sexually active?" was twenty years ago.

In the past century, we have undergone enormous changes in our thinking about a piece of elusive anatomy that once symbolized the ultimate female ideal, virginity in youth. According to the June 1994 *Seventeen*, "most girls have little or no hymen left by the time they start menstruating."[77] The reason for this historic change in girls' bodies is complex, as this chapter has suggested. Because contemporary girls are more active physically, they are apt to use tampons instead of napkins; many also pet and masturbate without fear of punishment; and over 50 percent have intercourse, voluntarily or under pressure, before they are even out of high school. In effect, twentieth-century social and cultural changes have altered the female body, so much so that a membrane that was once a primary concern is not only culturally extraneous, it has all but "disappeared."

And yet there is one notable exception. The hymen is still discussed by those who work in the difficult and often frightening world of child protective services. The hymen still has some importance for pediatricians, nurse practitioners, and social workers—that is, professionals who deal with the signs of sexual abuse in little children, not adolescents.[78] Ugly pictures of ripped hymens and brutalized perineums, along with glossaries of medical terms and descriptions of prepubertal genitals, are all a necessary part of this unhappy world because they provide physical evidence for criminal prosecution. This shift in the discussion of the hymen from gynecology to pediatrics is a disturbing red flag that signals how girls' bodies are eroticized in our culture at an increasingly early age. (Along with fourteen- and fifteen-year-olds, the other main victims of sexual abuse are girls of only five and six—that is, little girls, like JonBenet Ramsey, who was found murdered and possibly sexually abused in her Colorado home the morning after Christmas 1996.)

The social history of the hymen helps us to see one of the tragic ironies of late-twentieth-century life: that girlhood is now something of an endangered status, threatened by all kinds of biological as well as social forces. Although American girls have generally profited from the historic exchange between the disappearance of the ideal of virginity and the right to sexual expression, their early-maturing bodies now face greater risks than they did back in 1900. In practice, this means that progress is fraught with ambiguities, particularly in the case of sexually maturing girls.

In the 1990s, the rule book on sexual behavior is slim, and it is summarized quite easily: all sex, no matter what it is, should be mutual, consensual, and protected. This is a fine ideal, worthy of constant repetition, but it is not what has happened. In a world where men and women still have unequal power and resources, it is hard for many to overcome the gender imbalance, or even to assert themselves, in the domain of intimate relations with men. As we approach the millennium, we need to acknowledge that American girls are both the beneficiaries and the victims of a century of change in sexual mores and behaviors.

CHAPTER SIX

Girl Advocacy Again

Photos on p. 193: *(left)* Permission of Duke University, Special Collections, Cowherd Collection; *(right)* permission of Lois Lamphere Brown and Anna Brown.

At the end of the twentieth century, living in a girl's body is more complicated than it was a century ago. When the students in my seminar described how they managed the "bikini-line area," they were admitting, in a backhanded way, that their generation had taken on the burden of perfecting yet another body part. Their informed commentary on diet and exercise strategies, body sculpturing, liposuction, and mammoplasty all revealed that they had internalized the contemporary imperative for a perfect body, even as they stood apart from it and tried to understand it as a social and cultural phenomenon.

I was struck by the confusion they felt. On the one hand, their parents and teachers told them that being female was no bar to accomplishment. Yet girls of their generation learned from a very early age that the power of their gender was tied to what they looked like—and how "sexy" they were—rather than to character or achievement. Because of the visual images they had absorbed since they were toddlers, they invariably wanted to be thinner, a desire that motivated them to expend an enormous amount of time and energy controlling the appetite and working on their bodies, all the while thinking about food. Although they were aware that diet and exercise regimens could become obsessive and lead to eating disorders, in their own lives they walked a narrow line between the normal and the pathological. Almost all of them admitted that they did battle, on a daily basis, with what therapists in the eating disorders world call "bad body fever," a continuous internal commentary that constitutes a powerful form of self-punishment. "I'm gross," "My thighs are disgusting," "My stomach hangs out" are all typical refrains among the current generation, regardless of whether they are fat or thin.[1] Marketers recognize these anxieties and play them to the hilt. For example, a 1990 advertisement for the popular hair product Dep simply assumed that girls did not like their bodies and that they worried about cellulite and saddlebag thighs.

My students were exquisitely sensitive to the cultural pressures surrounding them. They understood that their relationship to food and the body had been shaped by what they saw as little girls on television, at the movies, and in advertising. They were especially savvy in their analysis of marketing strategies, and adept in their ability to "deconstruct" messages about women in any ad, ranging from Oil of Olay to Calvin Klein to Jeep Cherokees. I really had little to teach them about what it means to live in a culture of unrelenting objectification where women's bodies are used to sell everything. Because of their age, and the nature of the developmental process, they already felt the pressure emanating from American popular culture, sometimes more acutely than I did.

But when it came to a historical understanding of their situation, they had little to say, except for a few naive claims about how much better things became for American women as a result of the demise of the corset and the emergence of more sexual freedom. Neither my students nor the many adult audiences to whom I have spoken since the publication in 1988 of my book on the history of anorexia nervosa really understood the historical process by which women exchanged external controls of the body for internal controls—or the ways in which the body became a central paradigm for the self in the twentieth century, thereby altering the experience of coming of age in some fundamental ways. This lack of attention to the historical roots of the "body problem" is what inspired me to write this book, and to articulate at its conclusion what is unique and dangerous about our present predicament.

Contemporary girls are in trouble because we are experiencing a mismatch between biology and culture. At this moment in our history, young women develop physically earlier than ever before, but they do so within a society that does not protect or nurture them in ways that were once a hallmark of American life. Instead of supporting our early-maturing girls, or offering them some special relief or protection from the unrelenting self-scrutiny that the marketplace and modern media both thrive on, contemporary culture exacerbates normal adolescent self-consciousness and encourages precocious sexuality. Too often popular culture and peer groups, rather than parents or other responsible adults, call the cadence in contemporary teenage life. Contemporary girls *seem* to have more autonomy, but their freedom is laced with peril. Despite sophisticated packaging, many remain emotionally immature, and that makes it all the more difficult to withstand the sexually brutal and commercially rapacious society in which they grow up.

The current vulnerability of American girls is linked to the decline of the Victorian "protective umbrella" that sheltered and nurtured them well into the twentieth century. Victorian society could be repressive and unkind, and many mothers failed their daughters by not talking about normal physiological functions, but girls today are failed in a different way. On the basis of what we know from their diaries, there has been a curious decline in maternal involvement and supervision of girls over the past century. Although middle-class parents are invested more than ever before in the health and education of their adolescent girls, one of the most intimate aspects of the mother-daughter relationship—menarche and menstruation—had been relegated to medicine and to the marketplace by the time of World War II. After the war, there were also important economic changes that led to a broad retreat from girls and their social needs: more mothers had to work outside the home, so they had fewer hours to volunteer in community and church groups for young women. At the same time, nuclear family life also became more private and more isolated. By the 1950s, a married woman's primary allegiance was to her own children, not to those of others. Today, sustained involvement with girls other than one's own daughters is unusual in the world of middle-class women, unless these relationships are structured by their professional responsibilities as teachers and professors, nurses and doctors, nutritionists, psychologists, and social workers.

We also think about equality differently, and that has had an impact on how we handle adolescent girls and issues of sexuality. Beginning in the late 1960s and 1970s, the traditional notion that women need special protections because of their biology was discredited. In 1972, Congress passed the influential Title IX legislation, which made it illegal to discriminate on the basis of sex in most aspects of American life. This long-awaited gain, which opened up new areas of education, employment, and sports, meant that efforts to protect and nurture girls in special ways now seemed old-fashioned, if not reactionary. In the interest of fairness, feminists like myself wanted no part of any educational program or organization that treated adolescent girls differently from boys. This was an understandable reaction to the "ovarian determinism" that used biology to rationalize female inequality. We agitated for the abolition of discriminatory, old-fashioned rules that required curfews for girls but not boys because we wanted our daughters to have the same social and sexual equality that we demanded for ourselves. We also were willing to relent on statutory rape laws, a favorite cause of Progressive reformers who struggled to protect the innate "virtue" of girls from the well-known "vices" of men by raising the age of consent from ten and twelve to eighteen or twenty. As columnist Ellen Goodman rightly points out, our desire to overturn the "double standard" of sexuality allowed us to put these laws into "mothballs" and transformed adolescent girls from "jailbait" into "fair game."[2]

In the effort to be different from our staid and sometimes repressive mothers and fathers, many of us also changed the ways in which we parent. According to Tufts University psychologist David Elkind, our current postmodern style of family nurturance pays little deference to the old ideal of protecting children from life's vicissitudes or adult knowledge. Today's "harried parents" expect their "hurried children" to be autonomous, competent, and sophisticated by the time they are adolescents. This pseudosophistication leads adults to abandon the traditional position of setting limits and forming values, particularly in matters of sex, that characterized previous generations of parents, teachers, and female mentors. Adolescents raised in this permissive environment become extremely stressed precisely because they have been denied a comfortable envelope of adult values that allows them time to adjust emotionally to their developing bodies and new social roles.[3] This situation is made even more troublesome by the fact that we do not prepare girls adequately for the range of sexual choices existing in the United States in the 1990s. Instead, they absorb a great deal of erroneous information from popular culture (the "entertainment" model of sex education) or they are lectured about the virtues of abstinence (the "just say no" model).

As a society, we edged down the road of sexual liberalism without giving much thought to the situation of girls or to changing historical circumstances. What no one could foresee in the 1970s was the way in which early sexual maturation, our commitment to adolescent sexual expression, and the HIV virus would all coincide within the next two decades. In the 1990s, adolescent sexuality is more dangerous than ever before because the players are so young and the disease environment is so deadly. And the peril in this biological state of affairs is heightened by our social arrangements and our televisual environment. We have backed off from traditional supervision or guidance of adolescent girls; yet we sustain a popular culture that is permeated by sexual imagery, so much so that many young women regard their bodies and sexual allure as the primary currency of the realm.

Many different kinds of social critics now agree that American girls make the trip from menarche into adulthood without either knowledgeable guides or appropriate protective gear. For that reason, we may want to borrow at least one operating principle from our Victorian ancestors and consider the idea that young women deserve to be eased into womanhood more slowly than is the case today. In the 1990s, though, we cannot buy time with silence, the way Victorian mothers did. Contemporary girls need to be educated about the worst excesses of a society saturated with sex, such as the popular notion that violence is "sexy," or that the capacity for instant "intimacy" is a desirable personal characteristic. While contemporary girls enjoy many expressive freedoms that older women were denied when they were young, there is growing evidence that sexuality can be extremely dangerous when there is no system of responsible adult nurturance or guidance. From a historian's perspective, our timing has been off: as a society, we discarded the Victorian moral umbrella over girls before we agreed upon useful strategies and programs—a kind of "social Gore-Tex"—to help them stay dry. We live now with the consequences.

Although this book is primarily about middle-class girls and their bodies, the mismatch between biology and culture plays itself out among the poor as well as the privileged. In our public discussions of the one million teenage girls who get pregnant in America every year, attention is rarely paid to the ways in which our "epidemic" of teenage pregnancy is related to the confluence of early sexual maturation with a particular kind of social and economic environment associated with urban poverty.

In the case of "girl mothers," there is a general misunderstanding of the data. Contrary to stereotype, there is no epidemic, most pregnant teens are not African-American, and adolescent childbearing is actually less prevalent today than it was in the 1950s. How can this be? Not all of the one million pregnancies come to term; in fact, only 45 percent result in the birth of an infant that has to be cared for by the mother or her family. Abortion, miscarriage, and adoption account for the difference. What is new and different about contemporary teenage mothers is that they are more likely to remain unmarried than in the 1950s, especially if they are African-American. And they are also more likely to become mothers earlier in life. In the United States, *girls under fifteen* are at least five times more likely to give birth than girls of the same age in other industrialized countries.[4]

The ways in which a society regards and manages its adolescent girls is always an indication of its fundamental values and priorities.

But the way in which a society handles young girls in trouble is even more revealing. Although most Americans agree that teenage pregnancy is regrettable, we have enormous differences over why it occurs and what to do about it. The explanations vary, but they are almost always loaded with political meaning. Some people cast the unmarried teenage mother as an unwitting "breeder," while others portray her as quite deliberate. In the eyes of conservative critics of the welfare system, the unmarried adolescent mother is nothing more than a "welfare queen," giving birth to more and more children because the system allows her to claim support for herself and her children rather than work for a living. In this scenario, social programs to support poor young mothers are unnecessary and unwise. Less cynical approaches are based on the belief that teenage pregnancy is a complex social issue that has to do with the reactions of peers and family to the girl's developing body, the age at which dating begins, a girl's level of social and intellectual functioning at school, the availability of birth control, and how girls think about what it means to be an adult woman when their bodies become fertile. Since all of these factors operate whether or not welfare checks are available, cutting off government monies will probably result in more suffering children, not in fewer out-of-wedlock pregnancies.[5]

In the contentious and sometimes nasty public debate over how we should (or should not) help unmarried mothers, the relevance of age, combined with race and social class, is too often overlooked. Motherhood at eighteen or nineteen is different from motherhood at thirteen or fourteen, and if the teenager is poor and black, that experience is qualitatively different from that of a middle-class, white unmarried mother of the same age. In the 1950s, a sizable number of American women had children in their late teens; but few people objected then, because so many were white, and they generally got married to men who supported them and kept them off the welfare rolls.[6] But today's girl mothers are considered especially problematic when they are black and Hispanic, unmarried, and with a tenuous economic relationship to the fathers of their children. Because of poverty and discrimination, a powerful double whammy, most of the fathers have little reliable income to contribute. Without work, or much hope of employment, young African-American males cannot marry or assume normal adult roles, and as a result, they turn to crime and to temporary liaisons—both of which have profound implications for the young women they choose as their sexual partners.[7]

What do we really know about the lives of these girl mothers whom politicians glibly chastise for their immoral and irresponsible use of their bodies? For reasons that are not yet clear, African-American and Hispanic girls typically reach puberty a few months earlier than girls of Caucasian descent. Although many of these early-maturing girls have high aspirations, they have little opportunity in adolescence to experiment with forms of self-expression other than sexuality and maternity. In a world of poverty, inadequate schools, and pervasive crime, teenage motherhood becomes emotionally attractive. Being a mother and taking care of a child is understandably more interesting and rewarding than the dead-end, debilitating jobs to which poor women, and especially minority women, are most often consigned. A baby can mean status and love to a teenage girl, and it can provide an important connection to a young man—even though he is unable to marry and is likely to end up in prison. (In 1994, one third of African-American males between eighteen and thirty were behind bars.)[8]

We also know that many of our girl mothers—black and white—did not experience reliable, responsible parenting. Sexual victimization is often part of their early life experience, and they usually are impregnated by men who are at least five years older.

Half of the babies born to mothers between the ages of fifteen and seventeen had fathers who were over twenty. In a particularly horrific type of situation, impregnation by a "boyfriend" provides a way out of abuse at the hands of a predatory stepfather or older relative. Both of these scenarios raise questions about whether coitus is coercive or freely chosen, or whether adolescent girls can find the strength to resist the wishes of others, particularly in a world where it is accepted that being "grown up" means having sex.[9]

Not surprisingly, age matters in shaping the outcome of sexual activity. The younger a girl is when she begins to have intercourse, the less likely she is to use contraception. Even when sexual intercourse is not coercive, in early adolescence it is usually not experienced as a self-conscious decision. "It just happened," most girls say, reflecting their infatuation with the power of romance, and the fact that it is hard for them to admit intentionality in this domain. These are the young women who use Coke as a postcoital douche, or who think that conception is impossible the first time you "do it," or if you are standing up. Barely out of childhood, looking for love, and certain that they are immune to diseases that affect others, young girls cannot always comprehend the negative outcomes of a single sexual act.[10]

Studies of risky behavior in adolescence reveal that boys and girls from all social classes experience a lag between the body's capability and the mind's capacity to comprehend the consequences of sex.[11] In other words: adolescents are capable of reproduction, and they display sexual interest, *before* their minds are able to do the kind of reasoning necessary for the long-term, hypothetical planning that responsible sexuality requires. (How would I care for a baby? What would we do if I became pregnant?) But the lag has its most profound implications among poor minority girls of twelve, thirteen, and fourteen who live often without responsible adult supervision and guidance, in a world where family and community life have been eroded by unprecedented joblessness and violent crime. In ghetto environments, such as the South Bronx in New York or Chicago's West Side, the normal gap between biological and cognitive development becomes even more dangerous than it is in suburbs such as Scarsdale or Winnetka.

Regardless of what some politicians think, reproduction at an early age is not an opportunistic move, and girl mothers do not profit from having babies. In our society, childbirth in adolescence has serious costs to both mother and child, especially where there are limited family and community resources to buffer the economic and social consequences. Some studies show that children born to teenage mothers are more likely to be of low birth weight, at risk for serious medical and learning problems, and prone to poverty-associated traumas such as crime and drug abuse. Others argue that it is not age alone but *poverty combined with age* that makes early motherhood a formidable educational and economic handicap in life.[12]

Whether girls begin to have sex in their early teens ultimately depends upon the social and cultural environment in which they develop. But the younger they are when they begin to menstruate, the greater the risk. And the younger they are when they bear their first child, the more likely it is that both mother and child will experience negative outcomes. In peer groups where heterosexual intercourse is regarded as a critical sign of maturity and status, the pressure is on for girls as young as eleven and twelve to try out their powerful new equipment, particularly if they think they are in love, as they often do. These are the girls who most need nurturance and protection, but when they have limited resources and family life is under stress, they are unlikely to get it. In this environment, the body is often the only capital a girl will ever have.

Our current problem with girl mothers is neither natural nor inevitable. Although out-of-wedlock births are also on the rise in Western European countries, only the United States has so many very young teenage mothers. Our girl mothers are a telling indication of how we have failed as a society to protect the most vulnerable segment of our population: young women from historically disadvantaged groups who live in a social environment where families, churches, and neighborhoods have lost their efficacy. In our public discussions of teenage mothers, we need to acknowledge that early biological maturation has profound social consequences in a society like ours, where sex is used so extensively to sell, entertain, and exert power. The risks are real for all girls, but they are clearly greater and more devastating for girls who are already economically marginalized. At the end of the twentieth century, girl mothers are a telling symbol of the mismatch between early maturation and the exigencies of life in a hard-core culture of poverty that persists, to our shame, within a society of unparalleled plenty. Our Victorian ancestors would be shocked by this situation, and by our lack of commitment as a nation to keeping girls free from the responsibilities of adult female sexuality.

Many people think that the answer to our problems with girls is simply to turn the clock back. Some folks plainly liked it better when the hymen was the Maginot Line of virginity, and young women were punished for even minor breaches of feminine decorum. Admittedly, there are enormous risks for adolescent girls in the contemporary world, but this is not sufficient cause to turn the clock back to an era when it was acceptable to treat women as though they were asexual objects living in divinely inspired subordination to men. Besides, it's impossible. There have been too many deep changes in our economic and social life, changes that are irrevocable now that they are embedded in our daily lives as well as our minds. Although we can learn from the past, at the end of the twentieth century we need to fashion a new strategy of girl advocacy that acknowledges the convergence of earlier sexual maturation with our current cultural imperatives.

One of the first things we need to clarify is what it means to be an adolescent girl in a sexually permissive society. If you are not convinced that our culture has been sexualized, spend a morning at home watching the most popular talk shows and see how often sexual behavior, and explicit talk about sexual acts and sexual orientation, is the focus of discussion. Then watch some prime-time television at night, and count the number of times sexual innuendo, sex acts, and sexual violence are central to both comedy and drama. Growing up in this kind of environment is vastly different from what it was like to grow up a century ago, when middle-class girls like Lou Henry lived securely in a culture of modesty, the product of a high level of sexual repression. But it is also distinctly different from what many of us experienced even as late as the 1960s, when things really began to "loosen up." Today, the standard of modesty and decorum is extremely low, at least on television, and that fact has profound implications for how adolescents handle their bodies, regardless of gender. Our contemporary immodesty, however, is more problematic for girls, because it is their bodies, not the bodies of boys, that are consistently evaluated, displayed, and brutalized. Because we no longer maintain any special structural or ideological protections for them, many adolescent girls are alone and unattended in this environment as they struggle to make sense of their own sexuality and what it means to be an adult woman.

As long as there is no special support system for girls, life in a sexually permissive society is both confusing and dangerous for adolescents. This is a hard fact for many of us to admit, given our commitment to sexual expression. But facing the hard reality of HIV, we probably need, at least, to refine our idea that sexual activity in adolescence is inevitable and intrinsically worthwhile. In fact, right now, a totally permissive attitude may be as unthinking as the reactionary approach that preaches a rigid return to Victorian standards of virginity. In the university town where I live, I often hear the "pro sex" argument, usually from feminists like myself. Many of my friends maintain that sexual expression is as important an American right as those guaranteed in the Bill of Rights and the Constitution. In this view, adolescent girls should be totally autonomous in their sexual decision making; by contrast, among conservatives, adolescent sexuality is a matter for firm parental control.

As a historian with a long-standing interest in developmental psychology, I question both approaches because they ignore the relevance of age, and the ways in which popular culture has evolved in the past thirty years. Although I applaud the social freedom and economic opportunities enjoyed by the current cohort of high school and college girls, their "autonomy" seems to me to be oversold, if not illusory. Many young women, particularly those under twenty, do not have the emotional resources to be truly autonomous or to withstand outside pressures from peers and boyfriends, whom they desperately want to please. They are also locked into a commercially driven television culture that exploits female bodies in unprecedented and, increasingly, violent ways. By their own admission, this environment of slick images and quick seductions shapes their desires, and their sense of self, even if they try to resist. As we consider ways to respond to the predicament of our girls, we need to acknowledge these facts: teenagers do not always understand their own self-interest. And real autonomy may be impossible in a society where adolescents' expectations and desires are determined so consistently by media and advertising. How can we expect adolescent girls to be in charge of their sexuality when adult women are still struggling for equality in this domain?

Given what we know about the deep commercial investment in girls' bodies, and also the tenor of our contemporary culture, it seems unrealistic to think that young girls can operate independently, without parental or adult assistance, or that they should be expected to. Like Carol Gilligan, I think that most girls desire and profit from connection with their mothers, their aunts, their women teachers, and even their friends, and that individual autonomy has been oversold as a model for female development and for social life in general. Because of what we know about girls, and the ways in which the failure to set limits leaves them dangerously afloat, I am no longer quiet around ideologues who make sexual freedom and autonomy the ultimate value for adolescent girls. While they are still in their teens, there are other freedoms from which girls would profit even more, such as the freedom to be heard at school in an equal way with boys, or the freedom to develop their bodies without constantly measuring themselves against some artificial, airbrushed ideal. These would help girls overcome the well-known "confidence gap" that not only stymies their performance in life but also leads them into sexual liaisons where there is little equality or pleasure.[13]

As we prepare girls for life in the twenty-first century, we need to initiate a larger multigenerational dialogue that speaks to the reality of earlier maturation, the need for sexual expression, and the nature of contemporary culture. These discussions must offer more than such simplistic axioms as "Just say no," and more than logistical instruction about how to hold off male advances or practice safe sex. Whether at home or at school, our discussions need to be responsive to the developmental needs of girls, needs generated by their biological and emotional growth as well as the popular culture in which they live. This is the terrain on which liberals and feminists should do battle with the forces of reaction. Although many people will not like it, American girls should be presented, as they mature, with the full range of sexual options that young women now experience, including lesbianism as well as heterosexuality, and also thoughtful discussions of female pleasure as well as danger. In the teen years, the focus should not be on finalizing a clear-cut sexual identity—Are you straight or are you gay?—but on helping young women evolve a standard of sexual ethics that has integrity, regardless of the gender of their partners.

Sexual ethics—that is, a coherent philosophy about what is fair and equitable in the realm of the intimate—is what girls need in a society that treats women's bodies in a sexually brutal and commercially rapacious way. Instead of "shock talk" television, the vehicle Americans now use to explore the most lurid, flamboyant side of the sexual revolution, female professionals—particularly social workers, psychologists, nurses, doctors, and teachers like myself—need to create a national forum for developing a code of sexual ethics for adolescent girls in a postvirginal age. This discussion will not be easy, but I think most Americans can agree on at least two things: the discussion must include girls themselves, and the goals should be safety, reciprocity, and responsibility in all forms of human intimacy.

Sexual intercourse during the high school years is dangerous—most Americans would agree on that—but we will never be able to restrict it legally, by age, the way we restrict other adult privileges such as driving and drinking. One way to curb sexual activity is to make it harder for young people to be alone in seductive situations—by imposing rules and curfews, for example—but even this kind of control can backfire, since some teenagers make "breaking rules" an end in and of itself. In a society like ours, where teenagers of both sexes have an unprecedented amount of social freedom, traditional mechanisms of social control are hard to reinstitute and also inadequate to the job. While they are still in their early and middle teens, adolescent girls may find comfort in sensible parental constraints, such as curfews, but they will ultimately need something more than rules to help them navigate a successful passage into adulthood. What they need is a code of personal ethics that helps them make sense of their own emotions, as well as the social pressures that are part of the postvirginal world.

For parents, sexual ethics means facing up to our responsibilities to nurture and protect our young, even if it means that we must take an unfashionable stand against the vulgarity of popular culture and the power of adolescent peer groups. Although knowledge is always preferable to misinformation, we need to recognize that simply providing clear-cut, visually interesting materials about contraception or "safe sex" is not the same as helping young women develop a sense of what is a fair, pleasurable, and responsible use of their bodies. Freedom of information helps, but it does not always lead to healthy decision making, especially in the realm of youthful female sexuality. Adolescent girls simply are not mature enough, or sufficiently in control of their lives, to resist all the social and commercial pressures they face in our hypersexual, televisual environment. For that reason, I think there are plenty of "values" that sensible liberal people can agree upon without allowing conservative ideologues to act as if they have a monopoly in the "moral values" business. For example, responsibility means not having kids unless you are prepared to support them emotionally and economically.

But before we try to initiate this critical discussion about sexual ethics for girls, we need to acknowledge something critical about their experience. As long as they feel so unhappy with their bodies, it is unlikely that they can achieve the sexual agency that they need for complete and successful lives in the contemporary world. Girls who do not feel good about themselves need the affirmation of others, and that need, unfortunately, almost always empowers male desire. In other words, girls who hate their bodies do not make good decisions about partners, or about the kind of sexual activity that is in their best interest. Because they want to be wanted so much, they are susceptible to manipulation, to flattery, even to abuse. Body angst is not only a boost to commerce, as this book has shown; it makes the worst forms of sexual flattery acceptable, which explains why some girls feel ambivalent about sexual harassment and do not know how to respond.

I am not the first person to make a link between girls' bodies and cultural values. Even before Elizabeth Cady Stanton broached the subject in her famous lecture "Our Girls," there were other Americans who understood this critical connection. In 1871, in a book that was called *Our Girls,* a Boston physician and health reformer named Dioclesian Lewis argued that America's adolescent girls needed to develop greater confidence in their bodies in order to become effective students, teachers, and mothers. In this popular book, and also on the lecture circuit, Dr. Lewis tried to redirect young girls away from idle pursuits (such as piano playing and French lessons) and fashions (such as tight lacing and narrow shoes), because he believed that these interests encouraged indolence and fragility. Lewis, like Stanton, was more than just an opponent of the corset; he was an advocate for girls, and his enthusiasm for their potential was boundless. "My hopes of the future rest upon the girls," Lewis wrote optimistically. "My patriotism clings to the girls. I believe America's future pivots on this great woman revolution."[14]

Although the forms of girl advocacy change over time—in the 1990s we uphold rights to personal freedom and expression that were unthinkable in the 1870s—we need to consider being "girl advocates" again. For this reason, I admire the style of both Stanton and Lewis, and I also support the traditional idea of collective responsibility implied by the words "our girls." In the 1990s, we need to make an investment in *all* American girls, not just our own middle-class daughters.

The hope of Stanton and Lewis that America's adolescent girls would put aside trivial body projects for more creative and meaningful pursuits has not, unfortunately, been realized. Neither the outspoken feminist nor the eccentric doctor could foresee that as American women shed their corsets, they would adjust their waistlines to a different set of expectations and constraints that would be even harder and tougher than cotton laces and whalebone stays. Over the course of the twentieth century, girls' bodies have been a critical index of our social and economic life, in ways that we are just beginning to understand. The rise of scientific medicine, the decline of parental and community supervision, the triumph of a visual consumer culture, and the changing nature of intimacy in our society are all encoded in their youthful flesh, and in the social problems they now face. Although evolution in fashion is part of this story, there is more at stake here than simply changing hemlines or bustlines.

In reality, there is an interaction between biology and culture that is shaping the experience of contemporary girls in some critical and troublesome ways. More than any other group in the population, girls and their bodies have borne the brunt of twentieth-century social change, and we ignore that fact at our peril. It is time for us to talk—squarely and fairly—about the ways in which American girlhood has changed and what girls must have to ensure a safe and creative future.

NOTES

Introduction: The Body as Evidence

1. Joan Jacobs Brumberg, "Coming of Age at Kensington: Victoria as an Adolescent Girl," Keynote Address, New York State Association of European Historians, University of Rochester, October 1, 1993. See Viscount Esher, *The Girlhood of Queen Victoria,* 2 vols. (London, 1912), which is an edited version of Victoria's adolescent diaries, and Elizabeth Longford, *Victoria R.I.* (London, 1964); Lucy Larcom, *A New England Girlhood, Outlined from Memory* (Boston, 1889), p. 166.
2. Simone de Beauvior, *Memoirs of a Dutiful Daughter* (New York, 1959), p. 101.
3. Margaret Mead, *Coming of Age in Samoa* (New York, 1928).
4. On the relationship between body size and social class, see Joan Jacobs Brumberg, *Fasting Girls: The Emergence of Anorexia Nervosa as a Modern Disease* (Cambridge, Mass., 1988). My reading of the body styles of the nineteenth century is based on Thorstein Veblen, *The Theory of the Leisure Class* (New York, 1899); Sanford Dornbusch et al., "Sexual Maturation, Social Class, and the Desire to Be Thin Among Adolescent Females," *Journal of Developmental and Behavioral Pediatrics* 5 (December 1984): 308–14; Albert J. Stunkard, "Social Factors in Obesity," *Journal of the American Medical Association* 192 (1965): 97–102.
5. Of course, denial and repression led to anxiety that fueled a number of psychiatric disorders, such as hysteria and conversion disorder, characteristic of nineteenth-century women. On the history of these nineteenth-century psychopathologies, see Ann Douglas, "The Fashionable Diseases: Women's Complaints and Their Treatment in Nineteenth-Century America," in *Clio's Consciousness Raised,* Mary S. Hartman and Lois Banner, eds. (New York, 1974), pp. 1–22; Carroll Smith-Rosenberg, "The Hysterical Woman," *Social Research* 39 (1972): 652–78; Elaine Showalter, *The Female Malady: Women, Madness and English Culture, 1830–1880* (New York, 1985); Ellen Bassuk, "The Rest Cure: Repetition or Resolution of Victorian Women's Conflicts," in *The Female Body in Western Culture,* ed. Susan Sulieman (Cambridge, Mass., 1985), pp. 139–51;

Nancy J. Tomes, "Historical Perspectives on Women and Mental Health," in *Women, Health and Medicine in America: A Historical Handbook,* ed. Rima Apple (New York, 1990), pp. 143–71; Nancy J. Tomes, "Devils in the Heart: Historical Perspectives on Women and Depression in Nineteenth-Century America," *Transactions and Studies of the College of Physicians of Philadelphia* 5 (1991): 363–86.

6. Quoted in Jane Hunter, "Inscribing the Self in the Heart of the Family: Diaries and Girlhood in Late Victorian America," *American Quarterly* 44, no. 1 (March 1992): 63.
7. Because so many of the diaries I used have no consistent dating or page numbers, I give the best approximation I can of when the entry appears. Diaries that are in historical archives are so noted with standard manuscript and collection numbers; others are indicated as "poa," in possession of their author. Many diarists chose to develop a pseudonym (pseud.) rather than use their real name; pseudonyms were developed with an eye to preserving the ethnic heritage of the author. Diary of Deborah Perry (pseud./poa), January 1982.
8. Teenagers in the United States spent $63 billion in 1994; next to fashions, girls spend most of their money on personal-grooming items. For the best analysis of teenage consumer habits see Peter Zollo, *Wise Up to Teens: Insights into Marketing and Advertising to Teenagers* (Ithaca, N.Y., 1995); see also Robin Pogrebin, "Magazines Learning to Take Not-So-Clueless (and Monied) Teenagers More Seriously," *The New York Times,* November 4, 1996: D8.
9. Susan Nolen-Hoeksema, *Sex Differences in Depression* (Stanford, Calif., 1990), pp. 179–81; Ann C. Petersen et al., "Adolescent Depression: Why More Girls?," *Journal of Youth and Adolescence* 20 (April 1991): 247–71; Bonnie Leadbetter, "Gender-Linked Vulnerabilities to Depressive Symptoms, Distress, and Problem Behavior in Adolescents," *Journal of Research on Adolescence* 5 (1995): 1–29. The fact that early-maturing girls are more prone to depression is discussed in Jill Rierdan and Elissa Koff, "Depressive Symptomatology Among Very Early Maturing Girls," *Journal of Youth and Adolescence* 20 (August 1991): 415–25.
10. Carol Gilligan, Nona Lyons, and Trudy J. Hanmer, eds. *Making Connections: The Relational Worlds of Adolescent Girls at Emma Willard School* (Cambridge, Mass., 1990); Carol Gilligan and Lyn Mikel Brown, *Meeting at the Crossroads: Women's Psychology and Girls' Development* (Cambridge, Mass., 1992); Mary Pipher, *Reviving Ophelia: Saving the Selves of Adolescent Girls* (New York, 1994). Some other analyses that confirm the contemporary crisis in female adolescence are: Emily Hancock, *The Girl Within* (New York, 1989); Ruth Sidel, *On Her Own: Growing Up in the Shadow of the American Dream* (New York, 1990); Peggy Orenstein, *School Girls: Young Women, Self-Esteem and the Confidence Gap* (New York, 1994).
11. Data are from Hillary Carlip, *Girl Power: Young Women Speak Out* (New York, 1995), p. 53; Naomi Wolf, *The Beauty Myth* (New York, 1991); Rebecca Barry, "Body Obsessed," *Seventeen,* May 1995, pp. 112–15. On race differences in "body image," see Shelia Parker, Mimi Nichter, et al., "Body Image and Weight Concerns Among African American and White Adolescent Females:

Differences That Make a Difference," *Human Organization* 54 (Summer 1995): 103–14.

12. For my analysis of why there is so much more anorexia nervosa today, see Brumberg, *Fasting Girls,* and "From Psychiatric Syndrome to 'Communicable Disease': The Case of Anorexia Nervosa," in *Framing Disease: Studies in Cultural History,* Charles E. Rosenberg and Janet Golden, eds. (New Brunswick, N.J., 1992). On evaluating body image in adolescent girls, see Stephen L. Franzoi and Stephanie Shields, "The Body Esteem Scale: Multidimensional Structure and Sex Differences in a College Population," *Journal of Personality Assessment* 48 (1984): 173–78; Susan J. Paxton et al., "Body Image Satisfaction, Dieting Beliefs and Weight Loss Behaviors in Adolescent Boys and Girls," *Journal of Youth and Adolescence* 20 (June 1991): 361–79; David I. Ben-Tovim and M. Kay Walker, "Women's Body Attitudes: A Review of Measurement Techniques," *International Journal of Eating Disorders* 10 (1991): 155–67. The best review of the psychological literature on the importance of beauty to adolescent female mental health is Rita Jackway Freedman, "Reflection on Beauty as It Relates to Health in Adolescent Females," in *Health Care of the Female Adolescent,* ed. Sharon Golub (New York, 1984), pp. 29–45.
13. The diary of Ruth Teischman (pseud.) is now in the collection of the Schlesinger Library at Radcliffe College, AT265.
14. For discussion of girlhood diaries in the late nineteenth century, see Hunter, "Inscribing the Self in the Heart of the Family"; for analysis of girls' diaries in the 1920s, see Joan Jacobs Brumberg, "Coming of Age in the 1920s: The Diaries of Yvonne Blue and Helen Laprovitz," in *New Viewpoints in Women's History: Papers from the 50th Anniversary Conference of the Schlesinger Library,* ed. Susan Ware (Cambridge, Mass., 1994), and for a comparison between the 1920s and the 1950s, see Joan Jacobs Brumberg, "The 'Me of Me': The Voices of Jewish Girls in Adolescent Diaries in the 1920s and 1950s," in *Developing Images: Representations of Jewish Women in American Culture,* ed. Joyce Antler (forthcoming). On diaries as a female genre, see Margo Culley, *A Day at a Time: The Diary Literature of American Women from 1764 to the Present* (New York, 1985), and *The Norton Book of Women's Lives,* ed. Phyllis Rose (New York, 1993).
15. Diary of Lou Henry (Hoover), Box 65, January 1 and November 4, 1891; June 14, 1892, Hoover Presidential Library, West Branch, Iowa.
16. Diary of Antha Warren, Autumn of 1868. Cornell University Archives, #4815.
17. Anne Frank, *The Diary of a Young Girl* (New York, 1952), p. 143. On the publishing history of the diary, see *The Diary of Anne Frank: The Critical Edition,* prepared by the Netherlands State Institute for War Documentation (New York, 1989). The material on menstruation and sexuality was reintroduced in the latest 1994/95 edition: *The Diary of a Young Girl: The Definitive Edition,* Otto H. Frank and Miriam Pressler, eds., trans. Susan Massotty (New York, 1995).
18. Diary of Ruth Teischman, November 26, 1959; Diary of Eve Sullivan (pseud./poa), January 6, 1954.

19. Diary of Gabby Brown (pseud./poa), March 26, 1982; *Seventeen*, May 1995, p. 68. There is almost no scholarly work on the changing language of adolescent sexuality. Two important works on the general history of adult sexuality are John D'Emilio and Estelle Freedman, *Intimate Matters: A History of Sexuality in the United States* (New York, 1988), and Thomas Laqueur, *Making Sex: Body and Gender from the Greeks to Freud* (Cambridge, Mass., 1990).
20. For a handwritten version of this speech, see Reel 45, frames 1–74, in the microfilm collection *The Papers of Elizabeth Cady Stanton and Susan B. Anthony* (Wilmington, Del., 1991).

CHAPTER ONE

The Body's New Timetable

1. Abigail Adams to Sarah Smith Adams, January 20, 1808, Johnson Family Papers, Cornell University Archives, #4928, Box 1, Folder 1.
2. Diary of Sarah Compton (pseud./poa), September 1982. Regardless of how much a girl wishes for her periods to start, she cannot control the tempo of development. The sequence of events, however, is fixed and predictable: breast buds and pubic hair are the earliest signs of puberty; menstruation, typically, begins about two and a half years later. J. M. Tanner, "Sequence, Tempo, and Individual Variation in Growth and Development," in *Adolescent Behavior and Society*, 4th ed., ed. Rolf E. Muuss (New York, 1950), pp. 39–51; R. V. Short, "The Evolution of Human Reproduction," *Proceedings of the Royal Society of London*, Series B, 195 (1976–77): 3–24.
3. Although girls tend to follow their mothers in age at menarche, as well as in size, living conditions seem to supersede genetics over the course of a number of generations. P. E. Brown, "The Age at Menarche," *British Journal of Preventive and Social Medicine* 20 (1966): 9–14; Leona Zacharias, William Rand, and Richard Wurtman, "A Prospective Study of Sexual Development and Growth in American Girls: The Statistics of Menarche," *Obstetrical and Gynecological Survey* 31 (1976): 325–37. P. Eveleth and J. Tanner, *Worldwide Variation in Human Growth* (New York, 1976); R. E. Frisch and R. Revelle, "Height and Weight at Menarche: A Hypothesis of Critical Body Weights and Adolescent Events," *Science* 169 (1970): 397–99; R. E. Frisch, "A Method of Prediction of Age at Menarche from Height and Weight at Ages 9 Through 13 Years," *Pediatrics* 53 (1974): 384–90.
4. My general thinking about menarche has been influenced by Jeanne Brooks-Gunn and Diane Ruble, "Menarche: The Interaction of Physiological, Cultural and Social Factors," in *The Menstrual Cycle: A Synthesis of Interdisciplinary Research*, ed. Alice Dan (Urbana, Ill., 1980). On the declining age at menarche, known as the "secular trend," see James M. Tanner, *Growth at Adolescence* (Springfield, Ill.,

1962); John Money and A. E. Ehrhardt, *Man and Woman, Boy and Girl: The Differentiation and Dimorphism of Gender Identity from Conception to Maturity* (Baltimore, 1972); Grace Wyshak and Rose E. Frisch, "Evidence for a Secular Trend in Age at Menarche," *New England Journal of Medicine* 36 (April 29, 1982): 1033–35; P. E. Brown, "The Age at Menarche," *British Journal of Preventive and Social Medicine* 29 (1966): 9–14; Short, "The Evolution of Human Reproduction"; Leona Zacharias, Richard Wurtman, and Martin Schatzoff, "Sexual Maturation in Contemporary Girls," *American Journal of Obstetrics and Gynecology* 108 (1970): 833–46; Zacharias, Rand, and Wurtman, "A Prospective Study of Sexual Development and Growth." For a criticism of the idea of the declining age at menarche by a historian, see Vern Bullough, "Age at Menarche: A Misunderstanding," *Science* 213 (July 1981): 365–66. Despite Bullough's objections, there seems to be general agreement that improved nutrition in infancy and childhood and the decline of infectious diseases has produced larger, healthier young women who menstruate earlier. On age at first intercourse today, see C. Hayes, ed., *Risking the Future: Adolescent Sexuality, Pregnancy and Childbearing,* vol. I (Washington, D.C., 1987); Herant Katchadourian, "Sexuality," in *At the Threshold: The Developing Adolescent,* S. Shirley Feldman and Glen R. Elliot, eds. (Cambridge, Mass., 1990), pp. 330–51. On changes in adolescent sexuality see chapter 5 of this volume.

5. On the developmental work of adolescence, see Eric Erikson, "Identity and the Life Cycle," *Psychological Issues* (1959): 1–171; John Hill and W. Palmquist, "Social Cognition and Social Relations in Early Adolescence," *International Journal of Behavioral Development* (1978): 1–36; Barbel Inhelder and Jean Piaget, *The Growth of Logical Thinking from Childhood to Adolescence* (New York, 1958). On the relationship between earlier sexual maturation and depression, substance abuse, crime, and early parenting, see Michael Rutter and David Smith, eds., *Seriously Out of Order: Psychosocial Disorders in Young People* (London, 1995); Kimberly Christie Burke, Jack Burke, Donald Rae, and Darrel Regier, "Comparing Age at Onset of Major Depression and Other Psychiatric Disorders by Birth Cohorts in Five U.S. Community Populations," *Archives of General Psychiatry* 48 (September 1991): 789–94.
6. On the decline in fertility in the nineteenth century, see Robert Wells, *Revolutions in Americans' Lives: A Demographic Perspective on the History of Americans, Their Families and Their Society* (Westport, Conn., 1982); Carl Degler, *At Odds: Women and Family in America from the Revolution to the Present* (New York, 1980).
7. This summary of what was happening to adolescent girls in the nineteenth century is based on work by Joseph Kett, *Rites of Passage: Adolescence in America, 1790 to the Present* (New York, 1977); Nancy Cott, "Young Women in the Second Great Awakening in New England," *Feminist Studies* 3 (Fall 1975): 15–29; Michael B. Katz, *The People of Hamilton, Canada West: Family and Class in a Mid-Nineteenth-Century City* (Cambridge, Mass., 1975); Mary Ryan, *Cradle of the Middle Class: The Family in Oneida County, New York, 1790–1855* (New York, 1981); Laurence Glasco, "The Life Cycles and Household Structure of American Ethnic Groups: Irish, Ger-

man and Native-Born Whites in Buffalo, New York, 1855," in *A Heritage of Her Own: Toward a New Social History of American Women*, Nancy F. Cott and Elizabeth Pleck, eds. (New York, 1979), pp. 268–89. I am indebted to Constance Nathanson, *Dangerous Passage: The Social Control of Sexuality in Women's Adolescence* (Philadelphia, 1991), for the demographic insight. See also Irene B. Taeuber and Conrad Taeuber, *People of the United States in the 20th Century. Census Monograph* (Washington, D.C., 1971).

8. A.F.A. King, "A New Basis for Uterine Pathology," *American Journal of Obstetrics and Diseases of Women* 8 (August 1875): 237–56; W. H. Studley, "Is Menstruation a Disease? A Review of Dr. King's Article," *American Journal of Obstetrics and Diseases of Women* 7 (November 1875): 487. On the history of ideas about menstruation, see Patricia Crawford, "Attitudes to Menstruation in Seventeenth-Century England," *Past and Present* 91 (May 1981): 47–73; Vern Bullough and Martha Voght, "Women, Menstruation and Nineteenth-Century Medicine," *Bulletin of the History of Medicine* 47 (January–February 1973): 66–82; Elaine Showalter and English Showalter, "Victorian Women and Menstruation," *Victorian Studies* 14 (1970): 83–91; R. O. Valdiserri, "Menstruation and Medical Theory: An Historical Overview," *Journal of the American Medical Women's Association* 38 (1983): 66–70.

9. Granville Stanley Hall, *Adolescence; Its Psychology and Its Relations to Physiology, Anthropology, Sociology, Sex, Crime, Religion, and Education*, vol. I (New York, 1904), p. 480. For an early discussion of the relationship between hormones and the onset of menstruation, see Robert T. Frank et al., "The Female Sex Hormone: An Analysis of Factors Producing Puberty," *Journal of the American Medical Association* 85 (November 14, 1925). On Allen, see his biography in *Dictionary of Scientific Biography*, vol. I, ed. Charles C. Gillispie (New York, 1970), p. 123. In 1905, Ernest Starling, Jodrell Professor of Physiology at University College, London, introduced the term *hormones* to designate the chemical messengers carried in the blood. The best synthesis of the early history of research on hormones and its relationship to the understanding of menstruation is in Margaret Marsh and Wanda Ronner, *The Empty Cradle: Infertility in America from Colonial Times to the Present* (Baltimore, 1996), pp. 134–48.

10. Victorian medicine's ideas about the female body are described in Carroll Smith-Rosenberg and Charles Rosenberg, "The Female Animal: Medical and Biological Views of Woman and Her Role in Nineteenth-Century America," *Journal of American History* 60 (September 1973): 332–56; John S. Haller and Robin Haller, *The Physician and Sexuality in Victorian America* (Urbana, Ill., 1974).

11. Edward Clarke, *Sex in Education; Or, A Fair Chance for the Girls* (New York, 1873).

12. Marion Harland (pseud.), *Eve's Daughters; or Common Sense for Maid, Wife and Mother*, reprint of 1882 edition, with an Introduction by Shelia Rothman (Farmingdale, N.Y., 1978), pp. 86–87.

13. Most of these reports were done by British physicians although they were clearly read by Americans. Between 1832 and 1850, John Robertson, a surgeon in Man-

chester, England, wrote a series of articles for the *Edinburgh Medical and Surgical Journal* that laid out the inquiry. See, for example, his "An Inquiry into the Natural History of the Menstrual Function" (October 1832); "On the Period of Puberty in Negro Women" (July 1842); "On the Alleged Influence of Climate on Female Puberty in Greece" (July 1844), and "On the Period of Puberty in Hindu Women" (July 1846). Some other British reports are: Edward John Tilt, "Reflections on the Causes which Advance or Retard the Appearance of First Menstruation in Woman," *Monthly Journal of Medical Science* 11 (October 1850); J. Fayere, "European Child-Life in Bengal," *Medical Times and Gazette,* May 24, 1873; Charles Roberts, "The Physical Maturity of Women," *The Lancet,* July 25, 1885; Mrs. B. Sheldon Elgood, "The Age of Onset of Menstruation in Egyptian Girls," *Journal of Obstetrics and Gynecology* 16 (October 1909); J. C. Holdrich Leicester, "Menstruation in Europeans, Eurasians and East Indians in India," *Journal of Obstetrics and Gynecology* 17 (May 1910).

14. Joan Jacobs Brumberg, "Chlorotic Girls, 1870–1920: A Historical Perspective on Female Adolescence," *Child Development* 53 (1982): 1468–77.
15. Joan Jacobs Brumberg, "Zenanas and Girlless Villages: The Ethnology of American Evangelical Women," *Journal of American History* 69 (September 1982): 347–71; George H. Napheys, *The Physical Life of Women* (Philadelphia, 1876), pp. 46–48, 67; *Ladies' Home Journal,* April 1910, p. 5.
16. Emma Goldman, *Living My Life* (New York, 1931); Simone de Beauvoir, *Memoirs of a Dutiful Daughter* (New York, 1959); Audre Lorde, *Zami: A New Spelling of My Name* (Freedom, Calif., 1982).
17. My interpretation of the Colonial period is based on Judith Walzer Leavitt, *Brought to Bed: Childbearing in America, 1750 to 1950* (New York, 1986); Cornelia Dayton, "Taking the Trade: Abortion and Gender Relations in an Eighteenth-Century New England Village," *William and Mary Quarterly,* 3rd series, 68 (January 1991): 19–49; Laurel Thatcher Ulrich, *A Midwife's Tale: The Life of Martha Ballard* (New York, 1990).
18. Norbert Elias, *The Civilizing Process,* trans. Edmund Jephcott (Oxford, 1994).
19. Edward Tilt, *On the Preservation of the Health of Women at Critical Periods of Life* (London, 1851), quoted in Hall, *Adolescence,* p. 481.
20. My analysis of menstrual preparedness is based on all of the following: Helen P. Kennedy, "Effects of High School Work Upon Girls During Adolescence," *Pedagogical Seminary* 3 (June 1896): 469–82; Clelia Duel Mosher, *The Mosher Survey: Sexual Attitudes of Forty-five Victorian Women,* James Mahood and Christian Wenburg, eds. (New York, 1980); A. Louise Brush, "Attitudes, Emotional and Physical Symptoms Commonly Associated with Menstruation in One Hundred Women," *American Journal of Orthopsychiatry* 8 (1938): 286–301; Carney Landis, *Sex in Development* (New York, 1940); Natalie Shainess, "A Re-evaluation of Some Aspects of Femininity Through a Study of Menstruation: A Preliminary Report," *Comprehensive Psychiatry* 2 (1961): 20–26; W. G. Shipman, "Age at Menarche and Adult Personality," *Archives of General Psychiatry* 10 (1964): 155–59; and Frances Y. Dun-

ham, "Timing and Source of Information About, and Attitudes Toward, Menstruation Among College Females," *Journal of Genetic Psychology* 117 (1970): 205–17.

21. Burt Wilder, *What Young People Should Know: The Reproductive Function in Man and Lower Animals* (Boston, 1875), p. 168. On the history of women's higher education, see Thomas Woody, *A History of Women's Education in the United States* (New York, 1929); Barbara Miller Solomon, *In the Company of Educated Women: A History of Women and Higher Education in America* (New Haven, Conn., 1985); Charlotte Conable, *Women at Cornell, the Myth of Coeducation* (Ithaca, N.Y., 1977); Patricia Palmieri, *In Adamless Eden: The Community of Women Faculty at Wellesley* (New Haven, Conn., 1995).
22. Harland (pseud.), *Eve's Daughters*, pp. 83–84.
23. Mrs. E. R. Shepherd, *For Girls: A Special Physiology* (New York, 1884), pp. 9–10; Kennedy, "Effects of High School Work," pp. 472–73; Mosher Survey, nos. 41 and 35.
24. Karen Lystra, *Searching the Heart: Women, Men and Romantic Love in Nineteenth-Century America* (New York, 1989); Ellen Rothman, "Sex and Self-control: Middle-Class Courtship in America, 1770–1870," *Journal of Social History* 15 (1982); William Goode, "The Theoretical Importance of Love," *American Sociological Review* 24 (1959): 38–47.
25. On this point, see Joan Jacobs Brumberg, " 'Ruined' Girls: Changing Community Responses to Illegitimacy in Upstate New York, 1890–1920," *Journal of Social History* 18 (Winter 1984): 247–72; Nathanson, *Dangerous Passage*, p. 82.
26. There is no history of the large complex of religious and secular girls' groups that characterized American society from the late nineteenth century to the end of World War II. On the Girl Scouts, the best recent studies are Wendy Sterne, "The Formation of the Scouting Movement and the Gendering of Citizenship," unpublished Ph.D. dissertation, University of Wisconsin, Madison, 1993; Margaret Jennings Rogers, "From True to New Womanhood: The Rise of the Girl Scouts, 1912–1930," unpublished Ph.D. dissertation, Stanford University, 1992; Mary Rothschild, "To Scout or to Guide? The Girl Scout–Boy Scout Controversy, 1912–1941," *Frontiers* 6 (1981): 115–21. For a history of adult women's voluntary organizations, see Anne Firor Scott, *Natural Allies: Women's Associations in American History* (Urbana, Ill., 1991), and Karen J. Blair, *The Clubwoman as Feminist: True Womanhood Redefined, 1868–1914* (New York, 1980). Neither Scott nor Blair deals explicitly with the "junior" groups that were often attached to adult women's organizations.
27. From the Friendly Society Constitution in the 1890s. Quoted in Linda Larach, "Organizing American Girls: 1870–1950," seminar paper, Cornell University, 1992.
28. On the early effort to raise age of consent, see David J. Pivar, *Purity Crusade, Sexual Morality, and Social Control* (Westport, Conn., 1973); Ruth Bordin, *Woman and Temperance—The Quest for Power and Liberty, 1873–1900* (Philadelphia, 1981);

Mary Odem, *Delinquent Daughters: Protecting and Policing Adolescent Female Sexuality in the United States, 1885–1920* (Chapel Hill, N.C., 1995).

29. Diary of Lou Henry (Hoover), November 23, 1891; March 25, 1891.
30. For the literature on "bad" girls, see Brumberg, " 'Ruined' Girls," and Barbara Brenzel, *Daughters of the State: A Social Portrait of the First Reform School for Girls in North America, 1856–1905* (Cambridge, Mass., 1983); Steven Schlossman and Stephanie Wallach, "The Crime of Precocious Sexuality: Female Juvenile Delinquency in the Progressive Era," *Harvard Educational Review* 48 (February 1978): 65–93; Rickie Solinger, *Wake Up Little Susie: Single Pregnancy and Race Before Roe v. Wade* (New York, 1992); Odem, *Delinquent Daughters;* Nicole Han Rafter, "Chastising the Unchaste: Social Control Functions of a Woman's Reformatory, 1894–1931," in *Social Control and the State,* Stanley Cohen and Andrew Scull, eds. (New York, 1983), pp. 288–311; Ruth Alexander, *The Girl Problem: Female Delinquency in New York, 1900–1930* (Ithaca, N.Y., 1995).
31. For a critical approach to the iconography of American girls, see Martha Banta, *Imaging American Women: Ideas and Ideals in American Cultural History* (New York, 1987); Caroline Moseley, "The Maids of Dear Columbia: Images of Young Women in Victorian American Parlor Song," *Journal of American Culture* 6 (Spring 1983): 18–32. For visual examples of this trend, see Charles Dana Gibson, *The Gibson Girl and Her America* (New York, 1969); Howard Chandler Christy, *Artist and Illustrator of Style* (Allentown, Pa., 1977); Fairfax Davis Downey, *Portrait of an Era as Drawn by Charles Dana Gibson* (New York, 1936). In *Dimity Convictions: The American Woman in the Nineteenth Century* (Athens, Ohio, 1976), Barbara Welter notes the "girl fetish" of late-nineteenth-century America (p. 3). An earlier, but equally notable, archetype of the American girl was Daisy Miller, the title character in Henry James's 1878 story first published in *The Cornhill Magazine;* for a more sentimental point of view, at the end of the century, see James Whitcomb Riley's poetry about girls and romance.
32. George Whythe Cook, "Puberty in the Girl," *American Journal of Obstetrics and Diseases of Women and Children* 46 (December 1902): 805; George Julius Engelmann, "The American Girl of Today. The Influence of Modern Education on Functional Development," *Transactions of the American Gynecological Society* 25 (1900): 33.
33. George Julius Engelmann, "Age of First Menstruation on the North American Continent," *Transactions of the American Gynecological Society* 26 (1901).
34. Dr. Tilt made this point back in 1850; see Edward John Tilt, "Original Communications," *Monthly Journal of Medical Science* 2 (October 1850): 290. On childlessness, see Marsh and Ronner, *Empty Cradle,* pp. 92–93, 143.
35. These data are from Henry P. Bowditch, "The Growth of Children," Massachusetts State Board of Health, Eighth Annual Report (January 1877), p. 284; Engelmann, "Age of First Menstruation," pp. 8–44; Robert Latou Dickinson, *A Thousand Marriages: A Medical Study of Sexual Adjustment* (Baltimore, Md., 1931), p. 43; Laurence Steinberg, *Adolescence,* 3rd ed. (New York, 1993), p. 37. In statis-

tical terms, the "secular trend" resulted from a change in the *range* of ages at which first menstruation occurred.

36. Marion M. Maresh, "A Forty-Five-Year Investigation for Secular Changes in Physical Maturation," *American Journal of Physical Anthropology* 26 (1972): 103–109; P. K. Poppleton and P. E. Brown, "The Secular Trend in Puberty: Has Stability Been Achieved," *British Journal of Educational Psychology* 36 (1966): 95–100.
37. John W. Huffman, *The Gynecology of Childhood and Adolescence,* 2nd ed. (Philadelphia, 1981), p. 60.
38. See Ellen Goodman's excellent analysis, "Adult Men Must Not Be Left Out of the Teen Pregnancy Equation," *Ithaca Journal,* February 9, 1996.
39. At a conference that I attended on "Girls and Girlhood" in Amsterdam in June 1993, this was a persistent theme: adolescent girls in these particular Western European democracies are able to combine sexual activity without the problems we see here in the United States.

CHAPTER TWO

Sanitizing Puberty

1. See "Private-Label Gains Scare Feminine Hygiene Leaders," *Advertising Age* (September 28, 1994): 42.
2. Alice Stone Blackwell, *Growing Up in Boston's Gilded Age: The Journal of Alice Stone Blackwell, 1872–74* (New Haven, Conn., 1994), entries for May 21, June 27, and July 23 and 26, 1872.
3. Diary of Ruth Teischman (pseud.), September 1959; Schlesinger Library, Radcliffe College, AT265.
4. See Lynn Whisant and Leonard S. Zegans, "A Study of Attitudes Toward Menarche in White Middle-Class American Adolescent Girls," *American Journal of Psychiatry* 132 (August 1975): 809–14; and Lynn Whisant, Leonard S. Zegan, and Elizabeth Brett, "Implicit Messages Concerning Menstruation in Commercial Educational Materials Prepared for Young Adolescent Girls," *American Journal of Psychiatry* 132 (August 1975): 815–20; Jeanne Brooks-Gunn and Diane Ruble, "Menarche: The Interaction of Physiological, Cultural and Social Factors," in *The Menstrual Cycle: A Synthesis of Interdisciplinary Research,* ed. Alice Dan (Urbana, Ill., 1980). Much of the basic information in this chapter appeared in Joan Jacobs Brumberg, " 'Something Happens to Girls': Menstruation and the Emergence of the Modern Hygienic Imperative," *Journal of History of Sexuality* 4 (July 1992): 99–127.
5. Peter Zollo, *Wise Up to Teens* (Ithaca, N.Y., 1995), p. 33. In Margaret Mead, "Adolescence in Primitive and Modern Society," in *The New Generation,* Victor

Francis Calverton and Samuel Schmalhausen, eds. (New York, 1930), pp. 169–88, Mead claimed that Americans had no menstruation rituals. By "rituals," Mead obviously meant something formal, explicit, and derived from religion, not the broad, secular usage common today. For an anthropological reading of menarche and menstruation in other cultures, see Thomas Buckley and Alma Gottlieb, eds., *Blood Magic: The Anthropology of Menstruation* (Berkeley, Calif., 1988), and Chris Knight, *Blood Relations: Menstruation and the Origins of Culture* (New Haven, Conn., 1991).

6. For the classic statement on medicalization, see Irving K. Zola, "Medicine as an Institution of Social Control," *Sociological Review* 20 (1972): 487–504. The nineteenth-century case follows the model of medicalization provided by C. K. Reisman, "Women and Medicalization: A New Perspective," *Social Policy* 14 (1983): 3–18. The expansion of medical control over menarche and menstruation is similar to medicine's expansion elsewhere and should be seen as part of the push for cultural authority described in Paul Starr, *The Transformation of American Medicine* (New York, 1982).
7. Clelia Duel Mosher, *The Mosher Survey: Sexual Attitudes of Forty-five Victorian Women*, James Mahood and Christian Wenburg, eds. (New York, 1980), survey, no. 24. "Tokology" was used as a generic term for a book about the body and sex, even by physicians. See George H. Napheys, *The Physical Life of Women* (Philadelphia, 1876), p. 57.
8. Mrs. E. R. Shepherd, *For Girls: A Special Physiology* (New York, 1884), p. 8.
9. In this respect, menarche follows the classification model described by Michel Foucault in *The History of Sexuality*, trans. Robert Hurley (New York, 1978). For an important overview of nineteenth-century medicine's view of the female life course, see Carroll Smith-Rosenberg, "From Puberty to Menopause: The Cycle of Femininity in Nineteenth-Century America," *Feminist Studies* I (1973): 58–72.
10. Shepherd, *For Girls*, pp. 129–30. Other rare descriptions are in Mary Wood-Allen, *What a Young Woman Ought to Know* (Philadelphia, 1905), p. 149, and Emma Frances Angell Drake, *What a Young Wife Ought to Know* (Philadelphia, 1908), pp. 194–95. Male writers did not speak of such things.
11. The idea of "invisible cleanliness" and the notion that washing obliterated microbes usually is associated with Louis Pasteur and Joseph Lister; on Pasteur, see Gerald Geison, *The Private Life of Louis Pasteur* (Princeton, N.J., 1995). See also George Vigarello, *Concepts of Cleanliness: Changing Attitudes in France Since the Middle Ages* (Cambridge, 1983), and also Richard L. Bushman and Claudia Bushman, "The Early History of Cleanliness in America," *Journal of American History* 74 (1988): 1213–38. The term *hygiene* was not used in the eighteenth century; it is a nineteenth-century innovation. On the subject of domestic hygiene, see Nancy J. Tomes, "The Private Side of Public Health: Sanitary Science, Domestic Hygiene and the Germ Theory, 1870–1900," *Bulletin of the History of Medicine* 64 (Winter 1990): 509–39, and "The Wages of Dirt Were Death: Women and Domestic Hygiene, 1870–1930," unpublished OAH paper, April 1991. According to Vi-

garello, pp. 107–11, the insistence on feminine cleanliness became explicit for the first time in the 1770s as part of a larger turn to intimate washing of body parts. The story of the elaboration of menstrual hygiene practices fits the general model suggested by Norbert Elias in *The Civilizing Process: The History of Manners,* trans. of 1939 German edition (Oxford, 1978). Joseph H. Greer, *The Wholesome Woman* (Chicago, 1902), p. 172.

12. On technological innovation in this area, see Laura Kidd Klosterman, "Menstrual Technology in the United States, 1854 to 1921," unpublished Ph.D. dissertation, Iowa State University, 1994; Vern L. Bullough, "Technology and Female Sexuality and Physiology: Some Implications," *Journal of Sex Research* 16 (February 1980): 59–71; Fred E. H. Schroeder, "Feminine Hygiene, Fashion, and the Emancipation of American Women," *American Studies* 17 (Fall 1976). Menstrual pads may have been one of the first disposable products in our "throwaway" culture. The 1895 catalog from Montgomery Ward advertised the "Faultless Serviette or Absorbent Health Napkin," which was "antiseptic . . . required no washing . . . [and was] burned after using." The 1897 Sears, Roebuck catalog featured two different menstrual aids: a "Ladies Elastic Doily Belt" (made of silk trimmings and elastic) and "Antiseptic and absorbent pads" (made from cotton, gauze, and bandage).
13. Winfield Scott Hall, "Daughter, Mother, and Father: A Story for Girls" (Chicago, 1913), pp. 4–14. The author was a professor of physiology at the Northwestern University Medical School; the publication was the fourth in the Sex Education series issued by the Council on Health and Public Instruction of the American Medical Association.
14. Krause Collection, Historical Society of Western Pennsylvania (hereafter cited as HSWP), #I9A. See Corrine Azen Krause, *Grandmothers, Mothers and Daughters: An Oral History of Ethnicity, Mental Health and Continuity of Three Generations of Jewish, Italian and Slavic American Women* (New York, 1978). Krause reported that 40 percent of her sample did not know about menstruation before it occurred.
15. HSWP, #I1B. The same scenario appears in S11B and S2B, but the mother provides some explanation after finding the telltale blood.
16. Kate Simon, *Bronx Primitive* (New York, 1982); Helmi Hiltunen Biesanz, *Malvis Helmi: A Finnish American Girlhood* (St. Cloud, Minn., 1989).
17. HSWP, #J3A; Biesanz, *Malvis Helmi,* p. 179; HSWP #S10A.
18. HSWP, #S2A.
19. The biblical heroine Queen Esther said: "Thou knowest that I abhor the sign of my high estate [her crown] . . . as a menstrous rag." On niddah, "the state of uncleanness," see "Niddah," *The Jewish Encyclopedia,* vol. 16, ed. Isidore Singer (New York, 1901), p. 301.
20. Onnie Lee Logan, *Motherwit: An Alabama Midwife's Story* (New York, 1980), p. 51.
21. HSWP, #I1A.
22. Theodora M. Abel and Natalie F. Joffe, "Cultural Backgrounds of Female Puberty," *American Journal of Psychotherapy* 4 (1950): 91–92.

23. Cellucotton was the invention of Ernest Mahler, a chemist at Kimberly-Clark; it was derived from wood pulp and it was twice as absorbent as surgical cotton. As a result it was shipped to the allied troops in World War I, where it was "discovered" by Red Cross nurses as an effective form of sanitary protection. Kimberly-Clark actually set up the International Cellucotton Production Company to market Kotex because they did not want to be publicly associated with their product. The Kimberly-Clark name was not in Kotex advertisements and/or promotions until the 1950s. See Margot Kennard, "The Corporation in the Classroom: The Struggles Over Meanings of Menstrual Education in Sponsored Films, 1947–1983," unpublished Ph.D. dissertation, University of Wisconsin, 1989.
24. HSWP, #18B and #11A. See also #11B and #16B for cases where Italian-American girls were using rags well into the 1930s. This was the pattern, not the exception.
25. Anna C. Arbuthnot, "Physiology and Sex Hygiene for Girls in the Technical School, Cleveland, Ohio," *School Science and Mathematics* 11 (1911): 106.
26. A German proverb quoted in C. F. Hodge, "Instruction in Social Hygiene in the Public Schools," *School Science and Mathematics* 11 (1911): 304. The discussion about where menstruation and sex should be taught can be found in Lo Ree Cave, "Domestic Science as an Opportunity for Sex Education," *Bulletin of the Kansas State Board of Health* (April 1920): 67–72; Benjamin Gruenberg, *High Schools and Sex Education: A Manual of Suggestions on Education Related to Sex* (Washington, D.C., 1922). Emil Novak, *Menstruation and Its Disorders* (New York, 1921), p. 108. On the history of sex education, see Bryan Strong, "Ideas of the Early Sex Education Movement in America, 1890–1920," *History of Education Quarterly* 12 (1972): 129–61; Wallace H. Maw, "Fifty Years of Sex Education in the Public Schools of the United States, 1900–1950," unpublished Ph.D. dissertation, University of Cincinnati, 1953; Jeffrey P. Moran, "Modernism Gone Mad: Sex Education Comes to Chicago, 1913," *Journal of American History* 83 (September 1996): 481–513.
27. Fannie Moulton McLane, *A Home Study Course in Scouting for Girl Scout Leaders* (New York, 1921); see also "Health Winner Badge," *Girl Scout Handbook* (1934).
28. Kotex advertisement, *Good Housekeeping* 80 (1925), p. 190. See also the popular ad for "Marjorie May's Twelfth Birthday," *Parents' Magazine*, February 1939, p. 49. These ads follow what Roland Marchand calls the "vacuum of advice" argument. See Roland Marchand, *Advertising the American Dream: Making Way for Modernity, 1920–1940* (Berkeley, Calif., 1985). Another stage in the industry's advertising strategy, the transformation from shame to liberation, is described in Ann Treneman, "Cashing In on the Curse: Advertising and the Menstrual Taboo," in *The Female Gaze: Women as Viewers of Popular Culture*, Lorraine Gamman and Margaret Marshment, eds. (Seattle, 1989), pp. 153–65.
29. Kennard, "Corporation in the Classroom." Throughout the 1950s, the Disney film was advertised regularly in *The Leader*, the magazine for Girl Scout leaders.

30. *Seventeen,* March 1952, p. 38. Menarcheal competition among bourgeois girls was described in *A Young Girl's Diary: With a Letter by Sigmund Freud,* trans. Eden Paul and Cedar Paulk, with an introduction by Sigmund Freud (New York, 1921).
31. Diary of Sandra Rubin (pseud./poa), April 21, 1950.
32. Joseph D. Waddersug, "A Doctor Fills You In on Facts," *Seventeen,* March 1955, p. 116.
33. "The objective was to make each girl a confirmed Kotex user, which would provide more business in the long run than convincing a thirty-five-year-old woman to switch to Kotex." Quoted in Kennard, "Corporation in the Classroom," p. 77.
34. Houston L. Mapes, "Growing Pains," in "Book Week," *The Washington Post,* October 31, 1965, p. 41; Mary Gaver, "Realism and Children's Books," *Teachers College Record* 68 (February 1967): 451.
35. On Judy Blume, see Maryann Weidt, *Presenting Judy Blume* (Boston, 1989); Hilary Wilce, "Dear Judy, You're Brilliant," (London) *Times Educational Supplement,* February 4, 1994, pp. SS 1–2. Sales figures were provided by Harold Ober Associates, Blume's agent.
36. "We Shamelessly Talk About Our Periods," *Sassy,* October 1989, pp. 56–57. After this column appeared, Playtex ran a special promotion in *Sassy* in 1990–91 called "The Most Embarrassing Moment in Your Menstrual History Contest."
37. Diary of Deborah Perry (pseud./poa), June 1982; diary of Heather Ellis (poa), Spring 1989.
38. HSWP, #JI5B.

CHAPTER THREE

Perfect Skin

1. Edwin Rosenthal, "The Medical Treatment During the Adolescent Period of Girls," *American Journal of Surgery and Gynecology* 14 (1900–1901): 180–81.
2. Granville Stanley Hall, *Adolescence; Its Psychology and Its Relations to Physiology, Anthropology, Sociology, Sex, Crime, Religion, and Education,* vol. II (New York, 1904), p. 5.
3. All of the material that follows is from L. Duncan Bulkley, *Acne. Its Etiology, Pathology and Treatment* (New York, 1885), pp. 41–42 and Chapter 6. See also George Thomas Jackson, *The Ready Reference Handbook of Diseases of the Skin* (New York, 1896).
4. Girls get pimples earlier than boys do because they mature sexually at a younger age. But acne is actually more severe in boys at all ages. By seventeen or eighteen, when the worst acne years are over for girls, boys are just beginning their most difficult period. On the epidemiology of acne, see Josephine Hinrichsen and A. C. Ivy, "Incidence in the Chicago Region of Acne Vulgaris," *Archives of Dermatology and Syphilology* 37 (June 1938): 976.

5. My argument about parental investment in American girls follows themes laid out in Viviana A. Zelizer's *Pricing the Priceless Child* (New York, 1985).
6. Charles Capper, *Margaret Fuller: An American Romantic* (New York, 1992), p. 65.
7. Simon-André Tissot wrote the first book on masturbation in the eighteenth century; an anonymous American translation appeared in the early nineteenth century: *Onanism* (New York, 1832). On the history of medical ideas about masturbation, see E. Hare, "Masturbatory Insanity: The History of an Idea," *Journal of Mental Science* 108 (January 1962): 2–25; H. Tristam Engelhardt, "The Disease of Masturbation: Values and the Concept of Disease," *Bulletin of the History of Medicine* 48 (1974): 234–48.
8. John Thomas Crissey and Lawrence Charles Parish, *The Dermatology and Syphilology of the Nineteenth Century* (New York, 1981).
9. Bulkley, *Acne,* p. 69.
10. W. A. Haraway, *Manual of Skin Diseases* (Philadelphia, 1892), p. 24.
11. Wallace Marchall, "The Psychology of the General Public With Regard to Acne Vulgaris," *Canadian Medical Association Journal* 44 (June 1941): 600; conversation with Dr. Lawrence Parish, February 1996. There is a similar theme in Sigmund Greenbaum, "That Troublesome Acne," *Hygeia* 7, no. 2 (February 1929): 133.
12. Ferdinand Ritter von Hebra, *On Diseases of the Skin* (London, 1874), p. 294.
13. Sears, Roebuck & Company Catalog (1908) #117, 797.
14. Lucy Larcom, *A New England Girlhood, Outlined from Memory* (Boston, 1889), p. 106.
15. On the history of bathing and personal cleanliness, see Richard Bushman and Claudia Bushman, "The Early History of Cleanliness in America," *Journal of American History* 74 (1988): 1213–38; and Jacqueline Wilkie, "Submerged Sensuality: Technology and the Perception of Bathing," *Journal of Social History* 19 (1986): 649–64. On the impact of department stores on women and girls, see Elaine Abelson, *When Ladies Go A-Thieving: Middle-Class Shoplifters in the Victorian Department Store* (New York, 1989); and Susan Porter Benson, *Counter Cultures: Saleswomen, Managers and Customers in American Department Stores, 1890–1940* (Urbana, Ill., 1986). Dermatologists have long understood that it was hard to be obsessive about something one could not easily see. In the 1940s, a Pittsburgh specialist advised that in treating adolescent girls with acne, "it was a good plan to strictly forbid the use of a looking glass." Lester Hollander, "Dermatologic Problems of the Adolescent," *American Pracitioner* 3 (January 1949): 296.
16. Diary of Lou Henry (Hoover), 1890 and 1891, Hoover Presidential Library, West Branch, Iowa; on the history of girls and American high schools, see David Tyack and Elizabeth Hansot, *Learning Together: A History of Coeducation* (New Haven, 1990); Susan B. Carter and Mark Prus, "The Labor Market and the American High School Girl, 1890–1928," *Journal of Economic History* 42 (March 1982): 163–71. Court plaster was named for its use by ladies at court to cover patches or discoloration on the face. See Marion Harland (pseud.), *Eve's Daughters; Or, Common Sense for Maid, Wife, and Mother* (New York, 1882), p. 110.

17. N. H. Shehadeh and A. M. Kligman, "The Bacteriology of Acne," *Archives of Dermatology* 88 (December 1963): 829–31.
18. Emma Walker, "Pretty Girl Questions," *The Ladies' Home Journal,* May 1909, p. 48.
19. Joseph Grindon, "The Cutaneous Accidents of Puberty," *St. Louis Medical Review* 60 (January 1911): 6–8.
20. In *The Fashioned Self* (Philadelphia, 1991), Joanne Finkelstein demonstrates that the notion that character is revealed by an individual's physical appearance is deeply embedded in Western culture. On the change from Victorian to modern concepts of beauty, see Lois Banner, *American Beauty* (Chicago, 1983), and Beth Haiken, "Plastic Surgery and American Beauty in 1921," *Bulletin of the History of Medicine* 68 (1994): 429–53. On the transformations from "character" to "personality" in American culture, see Warren Susman, *Culture as History: The Transformation of American Society in the Twentieth Century* (New York, 1973). Also relevant are Richard Wrightman Fox and T. Jackson Lears, eds., *The Culture of Consumption: Critical Essays in American History, 1880–1980* (New York, 1983), and Joan Shelly Rubin, "Salvation as Self-Realization," *Reviews in American History* 20 (1992): 505–21.
21. Kathy Peiss, "Making Faces: The Cosmetics Industry and the Cultural Construction of Gender, 1890–1930," *Genders* 7 (Spring 1990): 143–69; Laura M. Mueller, *Collector's Encyclopedia of Compacts* (Padukah, Ky., 1994).
22. On yeast and acne, see Rachel Palmer and Sarah Greenberg, *Facts and Frauds in Women's Hygiene* (Garden City, N.Y., 1936), p. 94; Howard Fox, "Dermatologic Quackery," *Archives of Dermatology and Syphilology* 13 (January 1926): 8; Sigmund Greenbaum, "That Troublesome Acne," *Hygeia* 7 (February 1929): 134; H. H. Hazen, "Acne Vulgaris Following the Taking of Yeast," *Journal of the American Medical Association* 100 (March 18, 1933): 837.
23. Fox, "Dermatologic Quackery," p. 10. After 1938 there were critical licensing laws that severely limited the practice of cosmetology. See Herman Goodman, *Principles of Professional Beauty Culture* (New York, 1938); for an attack on the cosmetic industry, see M. C. Phillips, *Skin Deep: The Truth About Beauty Aids—Safe and Harmful* (New York, 1934).
24. Board certification in dermatology did not occur until 1932, according to Dr. Lawrence Charles Parish, editor in chief of the *American Journal of Dermatology.*
25. Eleanor Crehore Bedell, Smith College Archives, Box 1806, February 1919. This information was pointed out to me by Kathy Peiss.
26. Jeffrey C. Michael, "Roentgen-Ray Treatment of Acne Vulgaris," *Archive of Dermatology and Syphilology* 17 (May 1928). "The majority of dermatologists of this country follow the plan outlined by McKee," said Michaels, a physician from Texas, who proclaimed the Roentgen ray "the most effective remedy for acne" available in 1928. Everyone in the medical world seemed to know that "glandular therapy" was not as well developed, but estrogen was given to many blemished young women nevertheless. On estrogen treatments, see Jeffrey C. Michael,

"Observations on the Treatment of Acne Vulgaris," *Journal of the American Medical Association* (August 3, 1935): 327–33; M. T. Van Studdiford, "Effects of Hormones of the Sex Glands on Acne," *Archives of Dermatology and Syphilology* 31 (1935): 333–42; Theodore Rosenthal, "Acne and Its Relations to the Endocrines," *Lancet* 56 (September 1936): 496–99; Lee McCarthy and Oscar Hunter, "Failure of Therapy with Glandular Preparations in Acne Vulgaris," *Archives of Dermatology and Syphilology* 37 (February 1937): 211–25; Udo J. Wylie et al., "Studies of Sex Hormones in Acne," *Archives of Dermatology and Syphilology* 39 (February 1939): 195–210; Charles H. Lawrence and Nicholas T. Wethessen, "Treatment of Acne with Orally Administered Estrogens," *Journal of Clinical Endocrinology* 2 (November 1942); Harry O. Nyvall, "Treatment of Adolescent Acne with Endocrines," *Urologic and Cutaneous Review* 47 (December 1943): 685–89. Hormones also got mentioned in popular advice literature such as Edwin F. Patton, "Complexion Ills of the Teens," *Parents' Magazine,* January 1936, pp. 25, 76.

27. "What Was Your Father's Name?" *The Nation* 115 (October 4, 1922): 332. Of course, this quotation refers to Jewish boys; on anti-Semitism directed against young Jewish women, particularly their looks and voices, see Ruth Markowitz, *My Daughter the Teacher: Jewish Teachers in the New York City Schools* (New Brunswick, N.J., 1993). For a general history of anti-Semitism, see David Gerber, *Anti-Semitism in American History* (Urbana, Ill., 1986), and Leonard Dinnerstein, *Antisemitism in America* (New York, 1994).
28. Diary of Helen Laprovitz (poa), September–October 1922.
29. Dr. Frank Combes graduated from University and Bellevue Hospital Medical College in 1918. He was director of dermatology and syphilology at Bellevue and a consultant to a number of Westchester County hospitals; see Marquis–Who's Who, *Directory of Medical Specialists,* vol. 7 (Chicago, 1955), p. 118.
30. Diary of Helen Mitrano (pseud./poa), 1932.
31. Gwendolyn Brooks, *Report from Part One* (Detroit, Mich., 1972), pp. 37–38. In *Balm in Gilead: Journey of a Healer* (Boston, 1988), pp. 20–21, Sarah Lawrence Lightfoot describes the ways in which her grandmother, at the turn of the century, recognized her good fortune in having light-skinned daughters who could pass for white.
32. Jessie Redmon Fauset, *Plum Bun: A Novel Without a Moral,* with an introduction by Deborah MacDowell (Boston, 1990), p. 53.
33. I am indebted to Rebat M. Halder, professor and chair, Department of Dermatology, Howard University, for my understanding of the special skin problems of young black women, particularly a letter of October 31, 1995.
34. See, for example, *Ebony* for 1945–47. Color is still an issue; see Karen Grisby Bates, "The Color Thing," *Essence,* September 1994, and the letters that appeared in the "Letters" column in the months that followed. On the difference between *Ebony* and *Jet,* see Jacqueline Goldsby, "The High and Low Tech of It: The Meaning of Lynching and the Death of Emmett Till," *Yale Journal of Criticism* (forthcoming).

35. For a current analysis of the color issue, including the recent privileging of "blue-black" skin, see Lisa Jones's essay "Faded Attraction" in Lisa Jones, *Bulletproof Diva* (New York, 1994), pp. 153–56.
36. Theodore Cohen and Richard O. Pfaff, "Penicillin in Dermatological Therapy," *Archives of Dermatology and Syphilology* 51 (March 1945): 172–77. Both were lieutentants in the United States Navy and their research was based on 100 cases in the Pacific theater during World War II.
37. Alfred Adler (1870–1930), *The Neurotic Constitution* (New York, 1917) and *The Practice and Theory of Individual Psychology* (London, 1929); on the new language of psychology in the 1920s, see John Burnham, "The New Psychology: From Narcissism to Social Control," in *Change and Continuity in Twentieth-Century America: The 1920s,* John Braeman, Robert H. Bremner, and David Brody, eds. (Columbus, Ohio, 1968), pp. 351–98.
38. Patton, "Complexion Ills of the Teens," pp. 25, 76; Inis Weed Jones, "The Plague of Youth," *Hygeia* 16 (October 1938): 881–83, 956–57; Norman Goldsmith, "Acne: The Tragedy of Youth," *Hygeia* 23 (April 1945): 266–67, 318.
39. Hazel Rawson Coates, "Manual of Good Looks," *Woman's Home Companion,* October 1936, p. 101.
40. Jeanette Eaton, "Good Looks for Daughters," *Parents' Magazine,* September 1934. For an example of the appeal to mothers, see Herman Bundesen, president of the Chicago Board of Health, "What to Do About Acne," *Ladies' Home Journal,* November 1950, pp. 133–34.
41. J. Mace Andrews, "School and Health," *Hygeia* 14 (December 1936): 1131.
42. Diary of Jane DeWalt (poa), May 1946. See Rima Apple, *Vitamania: Vitamins in American Culture* (New Brunswick, N.J., 1996).
43. Lester Hollander, "Dermatologic Problems of the Adolescent," *American Practitioner* 3 (January 1949): 290.
44. Diary of Ruth Teischman (pseud.), Schlesinger Library, Radcliffe College, AT265; John Stokes and Thomas Sternberg, "A Factor Analysis of the Acne Complex with Therapeutic Comment," *Archives of Dermatology and Syphilology* 40 (September 1939): 363; Hollander, "Dermatologic Problems of the Adolescent," 290.
45. Diary of Ruth Teischman (pseud.), November 1959.
46. David A. Tartaglio, "Your Job: Does It Really Pay Off?," *Seventeen,* November 1980, pp. 148–49.
47. *Seventeen,* October 1951. The manufacturer was Eastco, Inc., in White Plains, New York.
48. Clearasil was a "white" product in more than just a symbolic way, however. African-American teenage girls used their own "race products" because this popular over-the-counter medication contained resorcinol, a chemical alleged to cause skin discoloration in people of color. In the 1950s, Clearasil was firmly rooted in a world where skin care was highly segregated and there was little "crossover" market. Moreover, by keeping all the "personalities" wholesome and

white, the advertisements symbolically reinforced the purity of their product and those who used it. In the 1950s, no one expected the "Clearasil Personality of the Month" to be sexually active. By the 1960s, however, her wholesome demeanor was clearly outdated, and the once-popular contest disappeared quietly from the pages of *Seventeen.*

49. Joe Graedon, *The People's Pharmacy* (New York, 1978), p. 336. "Those Precious 13-Year-Old Girls," *Brandweek,* January 25, 1993; *Oxford Dictionary of Modern Slang* dates the term *zit* to 1966; see also *The New Dictionary of American Slang,* ed. Robert I. Chapman (New York, 1986), p. 484.
50. David G. Welton and Bernard G. Greenberg, "Acne: Additional Data from a National Survey," *Archives of Dermatology* 87 (February 1963); Dr. Rebat Halder of Howard University confirms that girls make up 85 percent of the acne patient population.
51. On dermabrasion, see Mary Ellen Flynn, "Acne: Hope for Tomorrow," *Seventeen,* February 1957, pp. 83–113; "Aid for Acne," *Newsweek,* April 3, 1950, p. 46; "Rough Stuff," *Time,* March 13, 1950, p. 51; Herman N. Bundesen, "What to Do About Acne," *Ladies' Home Journal,* November 1950, pp. 133–34; Veronica Lucey Conley, "Beauty Hints for Teenagers," *Today's Health,* February 1957, p. 38; "A Clear Skin," *Seventeen,* May 1953, pp. 127–29. Another popular, but controversial, remedy in the early 1960s was a product called Acnotabs. See Rima Apple, "Science in the Marketplace: Acnotabs and the Food and Drug Administration," *Public Understanding of Science* 2 (1993): 59–70, for an analysis of marketing to teens in the 1960s, and the way in which the claims of the Pannett Company, the producer of Acnotabs, were evaluated by the U.S. Food and Drug Administration.
52. "Letters to the Editor," *Archives of Dermatology* 89 (June 1964): 898, and 90 (September 1964): 375; Donald M. Pillsbury, "How Teenage-Skin Problems Should Be Treated—and How They Shouldn't," *Ladies' Home Journal,* January 1967, p. 42; Jean Liebman Block, "Some Helpful Answers to Worrisome Questions You Ask about Acne," *Seventeen,* October 1974, pp. 116, 190.
53. Diary of Heather Ellis (pseud./poa), April 1989; oral history interview with Susan Segal, MacDowell Colony, January 1995.
54. Richard Restak, "Pseudotumor Cerebri, Psychosis and Hypervitaminosis A," *Journal of Nervous and Mental Disease* 155 (1972): 72–75.
55. "Danger from Acne Medication," *USA Today,* October 1984, p. 13; "An Acne Drug That's Not for Everybody," *U.S. News & World Report,* May 2, 1988, p. 11; Stuart Nightingale, "From the Food and Drug Administration: Isotretinoin Restrictions," *Journal of the American Medical Association* 260 (July 15, 1988): 315; Charles Marwick, "FDA Ponders Approaches to Curbing Adverse Effects of Drug Used Against Cystic Acne," *Journal of the American Medical Association* 259 (June 10, 1988): 3225.
56. "Those Precious 13-Year-Old Girls," p. 13; Laura Zinn, "Teens: Here Comes the Biggest Wave Yet," *Business Week,* April 11, 1994, pp. 76–86.

57. Donald A. Davis, "Skin Care Roundup," *Drug & Cosmetic Industry* 152 (January 1993): 22–26.
58. Diary of Sarah Compton (pseud./poa), March 1982; diary of Heather Ellis (pseud./poa), 1989.

CHAPTER FOUR

Body Projects

1. Thorstein Veblen made this point about women in *The Theory of the Leisure Class* (New York, 1899). Rita Freedman discusses the clinical implications of objectification in *Beauty Bound* (Lexington, Mass., 1986).
2. The best summary of recent scholarship on the body is available in Chris Shilling, *The Body and Social Theory* (London, 1993). See also Michael Featherstone, "The Body in Consumer Culture," *Theory, Culture and Society*, vol. 1 (1982): 18–33; Bryan Turner, *The Body and Society* (London, 1984); Norbert Elias, *The Civilizing Process*, vols. 1 and 2 (Oxford, 1939).
3. Quoted in Margaret A. Lowe, "From Robust Appetites to Calorie Counting: The Emergence of Dieting Among Smith College Students in the 1920s," *Journal of Women's History* 7 (Winter 1995): 37.
4. On this point I am indebted to Betsy Lynam, "From Grace Harlow to Sweet Valley High: Body Image and Romance in Serial Fiction for Girls, 1910–1989," undergraduate paper, Cornell University, 1989.
5. Joan Jacobs Brumberg, "Modern Dieting" in *Fasting Girls: The Emergence of Anorexia Nervosa as a Modern Disease* (Cambridge, Mass., 1988); Roberta Pollack Seid, *Never Too Thin: Why Women Are at War with Their Bodies* (New York, 1989); William Bennett and Joel Gurin, *The Dieter's Dilemma* (New York, 1982); Hillel Schwartz, *Never Satisfied: A Cultural History of Diet, Fantasies and Fat* (New York, 1986). Each of these sources discusses other reasons, besides fashion, for the emphasis on slimness in the twentieth century.
6. For example, "Holding the Interest of Our Girl Scouts," *The Leader*, March 1927, p. 8.
7. All of the quotes that follow are from the diary of Yvonne Blue, 1923–28, Schlesinger Library, Radcliffe College.
8. On calories, see Brumberg, *Fasting Girls*, pp. 236–37, 340; on scales, see Schwartz, *Never Satisfied*, pp. 168–75. Although bathroom scales were introduced at the turn of the century, sales did not take off until the 1920s. In 1925, Detecto, one of a number of companies, claimed to have sold one million.
9. In *Black Ice* (New York, 1991), Laurene Cary describes how she also changed her handwriting in adolescence as a way of experimenting with her identity.
10. Doris Langley Moore, *Techniques of the Love Affair* (New York, 1928).

11. Kate Simon, *Bronx Primitive* (New York, 1982); Jamaica Kincaid, *Annie John* (New York, 1983).
12. It has been suggested that breasts occupy a greater importance in female adolescent consciousness because of the relative lack of visibility of female genitals. See M. Rosenbaum, "The Changing Body Image of the Adolescent Girl," in *Female Adolescent Development*, ed. M. Sugar (Lexington, Mass., 1979); Jane M. Ussher, *The Psychology of the Female Body* (London, 1989). For works that describe the changing cultural emphasis on breasts, see Lois Banner, *American Beauty* (New York, 1983); Valerie Steele, *Fashion and Eroticism: Ideals of Feminine Beauty from the Victorian Era to the Jazz Age* (New York, 1985); Ann Hollander, *Seeing Through Clothes* (New York, 1978); Donna R. Danielson, "The Changing Figure Ideal in Fashion Illustration," *Clothing and Textiles Research Journal* 8 (Fall 1989): 35–48.
13. Elizabeth Ewing, *Dress and Undress: A History of Women's Underwear* (London, 1978); Alison Carter, *Underwear: The Fashion History* (London, 1992).
14. Helmi Hiltunen Biesanz, *Mavis Helmi, a Finnish American Girlhood* (St. Cloud, Minn., 1989); Jenny Oppenheimer, "Popularized Images and the Ready-to-Wear Industry: Adolescent Girls and Control Over Personal Dress Selection, 1900–1930," unpublished paper, Cornell University, 1990.
15. On the history of the ready-to-wear industry and its leveling effects, see Claudia Kidwell and Margaret C. Christman, *Suiting Everyone: The Democratization of Clothing in America* (Washington, D.C., 1974); Margaret Walsh, "The Democratization of Fashion: The Emergence of the Women's Dress Pattern Industry," *Journal of American History* 66 (September 1979); Stuart Ewen and Elizabeth Ewen, *Channels of Desire: Mass Images and the Shaping of American Consciousness* (New York, 1982).
16. "Dear Beauty Editor," *Seventeen*, October 1952, p. 42.
17. *Today's Health* 29 (February 1951); *Seventeen*, September 1951, p. 58.
18. Frank H. Crowell, "When Your Daughter Matures," *Parents' Magazine*, August 1952. Medical emphasis in the 1950s on the capacity to breast-feed is peculiar given that so many postwar mothers chose not to do so; in fact, adult women in this era worried that nursing the young would ruin the line or uplift of their breasts. See Rima Apple, *Mothers and Medicine: A Social History of Infant Feeding, 1890–1950* (Madison, Wis., 1987).
19. This line is from a popular ad in the 1950s. See also "Bras and Girdles for Teenagers," *Good Housekeeping*, November 1956, p. 289.
20. "For Juniors, It's Away All Hips," *Women's Wear Daily*, May 31, 1957, p. 26; *Compact*, November 1953, n.p.
21. "Strong Promotion Urged to Build Junior Sales," *Women's Wear Daily*, January 13, 1955, p. 29; "Plan for a Prettier Bosom," *Seventeen*, May 1959, p. 108.
22. A copy of "Figure Forum" (1955) is in the Warner Company Archives, Burroughs Library, Bridgeport, Connecticut.
23. Sarah Dunbar, "Teenage Operation Needs Maker-Aids, Buyer Says," *Women's Wear Daily*, May 31, 1957, p. 60. Diary of Gloria James (pseudo./poa), February 28, 1957.

24. Dunbar, "Teenage Operation," p. 60; Evelyn Friedman, "Texas Shop Finds Teens Demand Foundation Wear," *Women's Wear Daily*, May 31, 1957, p. 30.
25. See *Compact*, February, May, and December 1955.
26. Diary of Sandra Rubin (pseud./poa), 1950–51, 1954–55.
27. Diary of Ruth Teischman (pseud.), Schlesinger Library, Radcliffe College, AT265.
28. See, for example, *Seventeen*, February 1953, p. 146.
29. On the history of the distinction between clothing for children and for adults, see Karen Calvert, *Children in the House: The Material Culture of Childhood, 1600–1900* (Boston, 1992).
30. Shelia Parker, Mimi Nichter et al., "Body Image and Weight Concerns Among African American and White Adolescent Females: Differences That Make a Difference," *Human Organization* 54 (1995): 103–14; Linda Villarosa, "Body and Soul," *Essence*, December 1994, pp. 66–71.
31. Diary of Heather Ellis (pseud./poa), April 1989. Heather was not alone. Many young women fear going away to college because they expect to gain the "freshman 15." According to a recent study, this is more myth than fact: most female students do not gain weight in their first year of college and, if they do, the average gain is about seven pounds. Carole Nhu'y Hodde, Linda A. Jackson, and Linda A. Sullivan, "The 'Freshman 15': Facts and Fantasies About Weight Gain in College Women," *Psychology of Women Quarterly* 17 (1993): 119–26.
32. All of the quotations that follow are from the diary of Carol Merano (pseud.), 1967–68, Schlesinger Library, Radcliffe College.
33. Although Christina Hoff Sommers maintains that feminists have inflated statistics and thereby created an eating disorders epidemic, epidemiologists and mental health professionals generally agree that eating disorders have actually accelerated in the past thirty years. See Christina Hoff Sommers, *Who Stole Feminism? How Women Have Betrayed Women* (New York, 1994), and critical reviews, such as Nina Auerbach in *The New York Times Book Review*, June 12, 1994, and Barbara Ehrenreich in *Time*, August 1, 1994; Judith Rodin, Lisa Silberstein, and Ruth Streigel-Moore, "Women and Weight: A Normative Discontent," in *1984 Nebraska Symposium on Motivation*, ed. Theodore Sonderegger (Lincoln, Neb., 1985); Judith Rodin, *Body Traps: Breaking the Binds That Keep You from Feeling Good About Your Body* (New York, 1992).
34. "All the Things You Wouldn't Tell Your Friends," *Sassy*, August 1989, pp. 78–79.
35. On mammoplasty, see Patricia Braus, "Boomers Against Gravity," *American Demographics*, February 1995, pp. 50–57; Carole A. Potter and Ilene Springer, "Breast Downsizing: A Growing Trend," *Good Housekeeping*, April 1995; Marjorie Rosen, "Now I Can Be Free," *People*, April 26, 1993. Eighty percent of the breast implants done in the United States over the past thirty years have been for cosmetic reasons. Reduction mammoplasty used to be done only on young women of nineteen or twenty; but today the operation is sometimes performed on girls

of fourteen or fifteen who have what medicine describes as "gross" breasts (i.e., the surgeon can extract a pound of flesh from each). In general, reputable plastic surgeons hold the line, preferring not to do either reduction or augmentation mammoplasty on anyone under sixteen. Patricia McCormack, "Too Much Too Soon?," United Press International, September 16, 1992.

36. On Rockettes, see Vernon Scott, "One, Two, Three Kick," United Press International, October 13, 1982.
37. Stephanie Mansfield, "A Great Body Is Fine, but a Business Mind Is a Joy Forever," *The Washington Post,* May 1, 1983.
38. United Press International, September 12, 1982; *People,* September 19, 1983; United Press International, June 15, 1985; United Press International, August 29, 1984.
39. Mark Stultz, "Majorette, 1 Pound Too Heavy, Marches," United Press International, October 1, 1982; *The New York Times,* October 10, 1982; *People,* August 2, 1982.
40. "Now Faster... Thinner Thighs," *Young Miss,* March 1995, p. 24. On cellulite and thigh creams, see John Schieszer, "The Quest for the Magic Cream," *St. Louis Dispatch Sunday Magazine,* June 11, 1995; Mary Tannen, "The Way of All Flesh," *The New York Times,* May 14, 1995, Sec. 6, p. 44; "Can a Cream from 'Down Under' Work on Your Down Under?," *Business Wire,* March 9, 1995; Pete Born, "The Beauty Report," *Women's Wear Daily,* January 13, 1995, p. 9; Laura Castenada, "Beauticontrol Does Leg Work on Body Cream," *Dallas Morning News,* December 3, 1994, p. 1F.
41. Seymour Fisher, *Body Consciousness* (Englewood Cliffs, N.J., 1973); Karen L. LaBat and Marilyn De Long, "Body Cathexis and Satisfaction with Fit of Apparel," *Clothing and Textiles Research Journal* 8 (Winter 1990): 43–48; David I. Ben-Tovim and Mary Walker, "Women's Body Attitudes: A Review of Measurement Techniques," *International Journal of Eating Disorders* 10 (1991): 155–67; Paul F. Secord and Sidney Jourard, "The Appraisal of Body-Cathexis: Body Cathexis and the Self," *Journal of Consulting Psychology* 17 (1953): 343–47. Secord and Jourard's findings demonstrated for the first time that a woman's self-concept, more than a man's, depended upon her own evaluation of certain body parts. There is also psychological literature about the perceptual prominence of different body parts and how people distribute their attention to body terrain. See Seymour Fisher, *Development and Structure of Body Image* (Hillsdale, N.J., 1986). This literature does not, however, take the changing cultural milieu into account.
42. There is very little social or cultural analysis of adolescent female behavior in the dressing room. Market research companies probably study this aspect of teenage behavior, but they do not make that information available without cost. For my understanding of what goes on in the dressing room, I found all of the following useful: John Fiske, *Understanding Popular Culture* (Boston, 1989), especially Chapter 1; Marc Frons, "The Jeaning of America," *Newsweek,* October 6, 1980, p. 83; P. Gibian, "The Art of Being Off Center: Shopping Center Spaces and

Spectacles," *Tabloid* 5 (1981): 44–64; Elaine Underwood, "Jean-etics," *Brandweek*, August 19, 1992, p. 14–15; Alice Welsh, "Teenagers' Wants," *Women's Wear Daily*, May 25, 1995, p. 8.; Catherine M. Daters, "Importance of Clothing and Self-esteem Among Adolescents," *Clothing and Textiles Research Journal* 8 (Spring 1990): 45–50; A. W. Koester and J. K. May, "Profiles of Adolescents' Clothing Practices: Purchase, Daily Selection and Care," *Adolescence* 20 (1985): 97–113; B. Smucker and A. M. Creekmore, "Adolescents' Clothing Conformity, Awareness and Peer Acceptance," *Home Economics Research Journal* 1 (1972): 92–97; George P. Moschis, *Acquisition of the Consumer Role by Adolescents*, Research Monograph #82 (Atlanta, Ga., 1978). At Cornell, my colleagues Susan Ashdown and Susan Watkins taught me about the history and vagaries of sizing in the American garment industry. For the original so-called voluntary standards, see Ruth O'Brien and William Shelton, *Women's Measurements for Garment and Pattern Construction*, Bureau of Home Economics (Washington, D.C., 1942). There was some revision of the anthropometric data in a 1970 update, but it was minimal and based only on a small sample of military women. See Jane E. Workman, "Body Measurement Specifications for Fit Models as a Factor in Clothing Size Variation," *Clothing and Textiles Research Journal* 10 (Fall 1991): 31–36; M. Gaetan, "Bringing Anthropometric Data into the Twentieth Century," *Apparel Manufacturer*, November 1989, pp. 24–31; Glenn Rifkin, "Digital Blue Jeans: Our Data and Legs into Customized Fit," *The New York Times*, December 8, 1994, pp. 1ff.

43. On race differences in trying on clothes, see Parker, Nichter et al., "Body Image and Weight Concerns," p. 108. There are sex differences in consumer behavior very early; by age seven, girls recognize the importance of clothing in group norms and personal identity. We also know that class matters: upper- and middle-class families are more likely to supervise buying clothes in an effort to socialize their children into class norms. Data on contemporary teenage buying patterns, particularly the fact that most twelve- to eighteen-year-olds still shop for jeans with their mothers, was supplied to me through Teenage Research Unlimited in Northbrook, Illinois.

44. Diary of Heather Ellis (pseud./poa), April 1989; Grace Kyung Won Hung, "Why We Don't Like Our Bodies," *Sassy*, December 1990.

45. Until very recently, those who pierced their bodies in Western societies were considered to be involved in "self-mutilation," and this was attributed to either homosexuality, sadomasochism, or psychosis. My understanding of body piercing has been enriched by Erika Sussman, "Body Piercing in the 1990s: The Hole Story," unpublished paper, Cornell University, 1995. Interviews were conducted by Ms. Sussman under my direction. See also Michael Kimmelman, "Tattoo Moves from Fringes to Fashion: But Is It Art?," *The New York Times*, September 15, 1995, sec. C, pp. 1, 27. For some relevant scholarly analysis, see O. P. Joshi, ed., *Marks and Meaning: The Anthropology of Symbols* (Jaipur, India, 1992); F. Mascia-Lees and P. Sharpe, *Tattoo, Torture, Mutilation and Adornment: The Denaturalization of the Body in Culture and Text* (Albany, 1992); James Meyers, "Nonmainstream Body

Modification: Genital Piercing, Branding, Burning and Cutting," *Journal of Contemporary Ethnography* 21 (1992): 267–306. In *Fetish: Fashion, Sex and Power* (New York, 1996), Valerie Steele argues that the line between the "normal" and the "perverse" is blurring.

46. C. Vale and Andrea Juno, eds., *Modern Primitives: An Investigation of Contemporary Adornment and Ritual* (San Francisco, 1989); "Jewelry for Exotic Piercing," Gauntlet catalog.
47. Dennis Altman, *The Homosexualization of America/The Americanization of the Homosexual* (New York, 1978).
48. "Our Gender Specific Poll," *Sassy,* August, 1994, pp. 52–58.

CHAPTER FIVE

The Disappearance of Virginity

1. "Lynn Minton Reports," *Parade,* November 7, 1993, p. 10; the same theme is echoed in "Virgins Are Cool," *Sassy,* November 1988, pp. 34–35, 92; Debra Kent, "Sex & Your Body," *Seventeen,* January 1991, pp. 34–35; Ann Patchett, "Virginity," *Seventeen,* June 1994, pp. 117–19.
2. See, for example, Peter Mayle, *What's Happening to Me* (New York, 1989), and Mavis Jukes, *It's a Girl Thing* (New York, 1996).
3. Paolo Mantegazza, *The Physiology of Love* (New York, 1917), p. 85.
4. Robley Dunglison, *Dictionary of Medical Science* (Philadelphia, 1874), pp. 519–20; Harold Richard and Patrick Dickson, *The Arab of the Desert* (London, 1951), p. 204.
5. E. S. McKee, "The Hymen Anatomically, Medico-Legally and Historically Considered," *Lancet-Clinic* 99 (February 29, 1908): 240–41.
6. For some recent work on the hymen in literary studies, see Leslie Wahl Rabine, "The Unhappy Hymen Between Feminism and Deconstruction," in *The Other Perspective in Gender and Culture: Rewriting Women and the Symbolic,* ed. Juliet Flower MacCannell (New York, 1990), pp. 20–38; Linda K. Hughes, "Fair *Hymen* Holdeth Hid a World of Woes: Myth and Marriage in Poems by 'Graham R. Tomson,' " *Victorian Poetry* 32 (Summer 1994): 97–120.
7. McKee, "The Hymen Anatomically," p. 246. According to anthropological theory, the value attached to chastity is directly related to the degree of property ownership and social hierarchy in a society. See Lawrence Stone, *The Family, Sex, and Marriage in England, 1500–1800* (New York, 1977), p. 401.
8. On nineteenth-century medical views of the female adolescent, see Joan Jacobs Brumberg, "Chlorotic Girls, 1870–1920: A Historical Perspective on Female Adolescence," *Child Development* 53 (1982): 1469–77, and *Fasting Girls: The Emergence of Anorexia Nervosa as a Modern Disease* (Cambridge, Mass., 1988). On the

emergence of scientific imperatives in nineteenth-century society and medicine, see Charles E. Rosenberg, *No Other Gods: On Science and American Social Thought* (Baltimore, 1976); Bruce Haley, *The Healthy Body and Victorian Culture* (Cambridge, Mass., 1978); John Harley Warner, *The Therapeutic Perspective: Medical Practice, Knowledge and Identity in America, 1820–1885* (Cambridge, Mass., 1986).

9. The best survey history of gynecology is Judith M. Roy, "Surgical Gynecology," in *Women, Health, and Medicine in America,* ed. Rima D. Apple (New Brunswick, N.J., 1990), pp. 173–95. An older history, James V. Ricci's *One Hundred Years of Gynecology, 1800–1900* (Philadelphia, 1945), is also useful although it is primarily a list of medical advances in the field. See also Richard Leonardo, *History of Gynecology* (New York, 1944), and Harvey Graham, *Eternal Eve* (London, 1950). In the 1970s, as part of the Second Wave of feminism, gynecology came under attack for its insensitive and paternalistic treatment of women. The best-known exponents of this "victimization" history are Barbara Ehrenreich and Deirdre English, *Complaints and Disorders: The Sexual Politics of Sickness* (Old Westbury, N.Y., 1973), and G. J. Ben Barker-Benfield, *The Horror of the Half-Known Life* (New York, 1976), both of which portrayed gynecologists as villains intent on excluding and subordinating women. Edward Shorter's *A History of Women's Bodies* (New York, 1982) also emphasizes the ways in which women were controlled by their body and sexuality until the twentieth century. Regina Morantz Sanchez offered an insightful early corrective to the victim approach in "The Perils of Feminist History," *Journal of Interdisciplinary History* 4 (1973): 649–60. Gynecology and obstetrics were separate fields well into the twentieth century. See Pamela S. Summey and Marcia Hurst, "Ob/Gyn on the Rise: The Evolution of Professional Ideology in the Twentieth Century—Part II," *Women and Health* 11 (1986): 103–22. For a symbolic analysis of the characteristic contemporary internal examination, see James M. Henslin and Mae A. Biggs, "Dramaturgical Desexualization: The Sociology of the Vaginal Examination," in *The Sociology of Sex,* James M. Henslin and Edward Sagarin, eds. (New York, 1978), pp. 141–70.
10. Catharine Beecher, quoted in *The Roots of Bitterness,* ed. Nancy Cott (New York, 1972), p. 268.
11. R. W. Shufeldt, "Popular and Medical Opinions in Regard to the Hymen," *Pacific Medical Journal* 49 (January 1906): 1–9. This chapter is based on research done while I was a fellow at the American College of Obstetricians and Gynecologists, Washington, D.C., in April 1991. My original research covered the period 1880 to 1950. For the period after 1950, I learned a great deal from my collaboration with my former graduate student Heather Munro Prescott, who was an ACOG fellow in 1994.
12. Working-class girls accused of sexual improprieties were an exception. For a description of the use of pelvic exams in juvenile detention centers in the early twentieth century, see Mary Odem, *Delinquent Daughters: Protecting and Policing Adolescent Female Sexuality in the United States, 1885–1920* (Chapel Hill, N.C., 1995). J. M. Baldy, *An American Textbook of Gynecology: Medical and Surgical for Practitioners and*

Students (Philadelphia, 1896), p. 17. See also Florus F. Lawrence, "Pelvic Diseases in Young Women," *Journal of the American Medical Association* 11 (October 1903). On the history of women in medicine, see Regina Morantz Sanchez, *Sympathy and Science* (New York, 1985), and Virginia Drachman, *Hospital with a Heart: Women Doctors and the Paradox of Separatism at the New England Hospital, 1862–1969* (Ithaca, N.Y., 1984).

13. Herman E. Hayd, "Retrodisplacements of the Uterus in Young Girls and Unmarried Women—Their Frequency and Best Method of Treatment," *Transactions of the American Association of Obstetricians and Gynecologists* 14 (1901): 69–73.
14. Edwin M. Rosenthal, "Medical Treatment During the Adolescence Period of Girls," *American Journal of Surgery and Gynecology* 14 (1900–1901): 180.
15. Some typical textbooks with warnings are Baldy, *An American Textbook of Gynecology;* E. C. Dudley, *Diseases of Women* (Philadelphia, 1899); Gustavus M. Blech, *The Practitioner's Guide to the Diagnosis and Treatment of Diseases of Women* (Chicago, 1903); W. Blair Bell, *Principles of Gynecology* (New York, 1910); but they continue through J. Roswell Gallagher, *Medical Care of the Adolescent* (New York, 1960), and Somer Sturgis et al., *The Gynecologic Patient: A Psycho-Endocrine Study* (New York, 1962). Both Gallagher and Sturgis were worried about psychological effects rather than breaches of modesty. The quote is from a report by E. H. Miller, "Puberty—Its Benefits and Dangers," *Journal of the Missouri State Medical Association* 11 (May 1906): 735.
16. See, for example, the plates in William Easterly Ashton, *A Textbook on the Practice of Gynecology* (Philadelphia, 1908), and William Blair Bell, *The Principles of Gynecology* (New York, 1910).
17. Baldy, *An American Textbook of Gynecology,* fig. 178. African-American women are also used as models in Howard A. Kelly, *Gynecology* (New York, 1928). For more on nineteenth century medicine's attitudes toward race, see Todd L. Savitt, "The Use of Blacks for Medical Experimentation and Demonstration in the Old South," *Journal of Southern History* 48 (August 1982): 331–48. The doctor who is best known for his gynecological experiments on slave women is Alabaman J. Marion Sims; see Deborah Kuhn McGregor, *Sexual Surgery and the Origins of Gynecology: J. Marion Sims, His Hospital, and His Patients* (New York, 1989).
18. According to George Gelhorn, "Anatomy, Pathology and Development of the Hymen," *American Journal of the Diseases of Women and Children* 50 (August 1904): 144–79, it was hard to study the hymen "in as much as suitable post mortem material is not easily obtained and portions of tissue excised during life are not often at our disposal." Gelhorn was professor of obstetrics and gynecology and director of the department at St. Louis University School of Medicine. See also Fred J. Taussig, "The Development of the Hymen," *American Journal of Obstetrics and Gynecology* 11 (November 1921): 471–78. Taussig believed that the hymen was an evolutionary adaptation, important for protecting the vagina when the human race squatted on the ground. For discussion of the differential placement and density of hymens in African-American women, see Gelhorn, "Anatomy,

Pathology," p. 145, and Edward B. Turnipseed, "Some Facts in Regard to the Anatomical Differences Between the Negro and White Races," *American Journal of Obstetrics and Diseases of Women and Children* 10 (January 1877): 32–33; C. H. Fort, "Some Corroborative Facts in Regard to the Anatomical Difference Between the Negro and White Races," *American Journal of the Diseases of Women and Children* 10 (April 1877): 258–59; A. G. Smythe, "The Position of the Hymen in the Negro Race," *American Journal of the Diseases of Women and Children* 10 (January 1877): 638. The discussion of distinctions in hymens was part of a larger debate in nineteenth-century medicine about whether the anatomy of the races was homologous. See McGregor, *Sexual Surgery,* Chapter II, on this point. The authors cited here argued that in Negro women the hymen was placed farther in the vagina, and it was of greater density. This anatomical difference could be linked to racist ideas about the alleged superior size of black male sex organs and, also, the notion that women of color sought penetration in a way that was different from white women.

19. R. W. Shufeldt, "Popular and Medical Opinions in Regard to the Hymen," *Pacific Medical Journal* 49 (January 1906): 8.
20. *Cunningham* v. *People of Illinois* 71 N.E. 389; Odem, pp. 65, 114, 131, 144–45.
21. Reported by Carl Henry Davis, *Gynecology and Obstetrics,* vol. 3 (Hagerstown, Md., 1933), p. 32A.
22. See, for example, Gustavus M. Blech, *The Practitioner's Guide to the Diagnoses and Treatment of Diseases of Women* (Chicago, 1903); Henry Sturgeon Crossen, *Diagnosis and Treatment of Diseases of Women* (St. Louis, 1915); D. Todd Gilliam and Earl Gilliam, *A Textbook of Practical Gynecology* (Philadelphia, 1916); Brooke M. Anspach, *Gynecology* (Philadelphia, 1927); Davis, *Gynecology and Obstetrics;* J. P. Greenhill, *Office Gynecology* (Chicago, 1939).
23. A.H.F. Barbour and B. P. Watson, *Gynecological Diagnosis and Pathology,* 2nd ed. (Edinburgh, 1922), p. 20.
24. Dr. C. L. Bonifield, Cincinnati, reported in "Discussion," following Lawrence, "Pelvic Diseases in Young Girls," p. 954.
25. Because of anesthesia, gynecological surgery increased dramatically after 1870; pelvic exams of virgins probably did so as well. For information on the history of anesthesia, see Virginia Thatcher, *A History of Anaesthesia* (New York, 1953); Martin Pernick, *A Calculus of Suffering* (New York, 1985); Judith Walzer Leavitt, *Brought to Bed: Childbearing in America, 1750–1950* (New York, 1986); and John Duffy, "Anglo-American Reaction to Obstetrical Anaesthesia," *Bulletin of the History of Medicine* 38 (1964): 32–44. A literary approach, with a different perspective on doctors and patients, can be found in Mary Poovey, "Scenes of an Indelicate Character: The Medical 'Treatment' of Victorian Women," in *The Making of the Modern Body,* Catherine Gallagher and Thomas Laqueur, eds. (Berkeley, 1987), pp. 137–68.
26. Lawrence, "Pelvic Diseases in Young Girls," p. 951.
27. Ibid., p. 955.

28. On the sexual revolution of the 1920s, see Paula Fass, *The Damned and the Beautiful: American Youth in the 1920s* (New York, 1977); Mary Ryan, "The Projection of a New Womanhood: The Movie Moderns in the 1920s," in *Our American Sisters: Women in American Life and Thought,* 2nd ed., Jean E. Friedman and William G. Shade, eds. (Boston, 1976), pp. 366–84; John D'Emilio and Estelle Freedman, *Intimate Matters: A History of Sexuality in America* (New York, 1988).
29. The quotations that follow are from the diaries of Yvonne Blue, 1928–30, Schlesinger Library, Radcliffe College.
30. See Alfred C. Kinsey et al., *Sexual Behavior in the Human Female* (Philadelphia, 1953), pp. 310–36. In *Middletown: A Study in Contemporary American Culture* (New York, 1929), Robert Lynd and Helen Merrell Lynd confirmed the "normality" of petting in high schools and colleges in the 1920s. On the history of courtship in the United States, see Ellen Rothman, *Hands and Hearts: A History of Courtship in America* (New York, 1984); John Modell, *On One's Own: From Youth to Adulthood in the United States, 1920–1975* (Berkeley, 1989); and Beth Bailey, *From Front Porch to Back Seat: Courtship in Twentieth-Century America* (Baltimore, 1988). For a popular booklet of the time, published by the Associated Press, see Max Exner, *The Question of Petting* (New York, 1926). The title page said that the publication was a "response to an urgent demand." *New Girls for Old* (New York, 1930), by Phyllis Blanchard and Carlyn Manasses, also discusses petting among teenage girls in the 1920s.
31. Kelly, *Gynecology,* pp. 65–66; Robert Latou Dickinson, *A Thousand Marriages* (New York, 1932), p. 12; D'Emilio and Freedman, *Intimate Matters,* p. 268.
32. Greenhill, *Office Gynecology,* p. 391.
33. On the ideal of companionate marriage, see Ben R. Lindsey and Wainwright Evans, *The Revolt of Modern Youth* (New York, 1925); Charles Larson, Introduction to Ben R. Lindsey and Wainwright Evans, *The Companionate Marriage* (reprint, New York, 1972); Stephen Mintz and Susan Kellogg, *Domestic Revolutions* (New York, 1988), pp. 112–17. Obviously, writing by Sigmund Freud and Havelock Ellis also played a role in the new attention to female sexuality. See D'Emilio and Freedman, *Intimate Matters,* Chapter 5.
34. Kelly, *Gynecology,* p. 218.
35. Greenhill, *Office Gynecology,* p. 391; Arthur Hale Curtis and John Huffman, *A Textbook of Gynecology* (Philadelphia, 1950), p. 158.
36. On the history of the tampon, see Robert Latou Dickinson, "Tampons as Menstrual Guards," *Journal of the American Medical Association* 7 (June 16, 1945): 490–94; Madeline J. Thornton, "The Use of Vaginal Tampons for the Absorption of Menstrual Discharges," *American Journal of Obstetrics and Gynecology* 46 (1943): 259–65; Laura Kidd Klosterman, "Menstrual Technology in the United States, 1854–1921," unpublished Ph.D. dissertation, Iowa State University, 1994.
37. See *Official Guide Book. New York World's Fair* (New York, 1939), p. 152.
38. Dickinson, "Tampons as Menstrual Guards," pp. 490–94.

39. See Goodrich Schauffler, *Pediatric Gynecology* (Chicago, 1942), pp. 7–15, and *Guiding Your Daughter to Confident Womanhood* (Englewood Cliffs, N.J., 1964); Edward D. Allen, "Gynecological Problems of the Adolescent Girl," *Medical Clinics of North America* 27 (1943): 17–25, and "Examination of the Genital Organs in the Prepubescent and in the Adolescent Girl," *Pediatric Clinics of North America* (February 1958): 19–34. For my understanding of clinical practice with adolescents in the postwar period, I am indebted to Heather Munro Prescott's unpublished paper, "Virginity Is a State of Mind, Not an Anatomical Condition: Changing Attitudes Towards Pelvic Examinations of Adolescents, 1900 to the Present," American College of Obstetricians and Gynecologists, May 1995.
40. J. Roswell Gallagher, *Medical Care of the Adolescent* (New York, 1960), p. 195. Gallagher was a pioneer in the field of adolescent medicine; see Heather Munro Prescott, *A Doctor of Their Own: The Emergence of Adolescent Medicine as a Clinical Subspecialty, 1904–1980* (forthcoming).
41. Andrew Kelly, *A Catholic Parent's Guide to Sex Education* (New York, 1962), p. 71; *Seventeen*, May 1964, p. 202.
42. *Today's Health* 50 (1974): 9.
43. Jeanne Brooks-Gunn and Diane Ruble, "Psychological Correlates of Tampon Use in Adolescence," *Annals of Internal Medicine* 96 (June 1982): 962–65.
44. Diary of Ellen Anderson (pseud./poa), June 1976; Karen Hein, "The First Gynecologic Exam," *Diagnosis* 3 (January 1981): 38.
45. Hugh R. K. Barber, "Her First Pelvic Exam: When and How to Do It," *Consultant* 19 (July 1979): 33–37. Barber talked about using the "Huffman adolescent speculum" introduced in the late 1960s by John W. Huffman, a professor of obstetrics and gynecology at Northwestern University. See John W. Huffman et al., *The Gynecology of Childhood and Adolescence*, 1st ed. (Philadelphia, 1968).
46. The quotations that follow are from the diary of Laura Ramirez (pseud./poa), 1969–1970.
47. See, for example, Alfred M. Bongiovanni, *Adolescent Gynecology: A Guide for Clinicians* (New York, 1983); Karen Hein, "The First Pelvic Examination and Common Gynecological Problems in Adolescent Girls," in *Health Care of the Female Adolescent*, ed. Sharon Golub (New York, 1984), pp. 47–63; S. Jean Emans, "Pelvic Examination of the Adolescent Patient," *Pediatrics in Review* 4 (April 1983): 307–12.
48. See *Family Planning Perspectives* in the late 1960s for use of this term. For a discussion of the term *ruined*, see Joan Jacobs Brumberg, " 'Ruined' Girls: Changing Community Responses to Illegitimacy in Chemung County, New York, 1890–1920," *Journal of Social History* 18 (Winter 1984): 247–72.
49. Ralph Lopez, "Menstrual Irregularities in Teenage Girls," *Drug Therapy* 2 (April 1981): 40. In the clinical literature, there is some debate about how to ask the critical question. In Alvin Goldfarb's "The Initial Encounter," in Alfred M. Bongiovanni's guide for clinicians, the author advises against asking this question "directly" (*Adolescent Gynecology*, p. 3).
50. Huffman, *Gynecology of Childhood and Adolescence*, p. 410.

51. W. Haas, *Teenage Sexuality* (New York, 1979); Susan F. Newcomer and J. Richard Udry, "Oral Sex in an Adolescent Population," *Archives of Sexual Behavior* 14 (1985): 41–46.
52. Harold Leif, "Sexual Behavior in Adolescence," p. 59, in Bongiovanni, *Adolescent Gynecology.*
53. See Harriet Pilpel and Nancy Weschsler, "Birth Control, Teenagers, and the Law," *Family Planning Perspectives* I (Spring 1969): 29–36; L. Wilkins, "Children's Rights: Removing the Parental Consent Barrier to Medical Treatment of Minors," *Arizona State Law Journal* (1975): 31–92; Heather Munro Prescott, "Legislating Family Values: An Historical Commentary on the Parental Consent Requirement in the Casey Decision," *Trends in Health Care, Law, and Ethics* 8 (Summer 1993): 32–36.
54. See Prescott, *A Doctor of Their Own: The Emergence of Adolescent Medicine As a Clinical Subspeciality* (forthcoming).
55. Robert Masland, Personal Correspondence, 7/1/71–6/30/72, Children's Hospital Archives, Boston, Mass. This letter was brought to my attention by Heather Munro Prescott.
56. Huffman, *Gynecology of Childhood and Adolescence,* p. 408.
57. Separating teenage girls from their mothers became virtually universal practice. See Huffman, *Gynecology of Childhood and Adolescence,* p. 410; Karen Hein, "The First Gynecological Exam: Putting Yourself and Your Patient at Ease," *Diagnosis,* January 1981, p. 39; Sheridan Phillips et al., "Teenagers' Preferences Regarding the Presence of Family Members, Peers and Chaperones During Examination of Genitalia," *Pediatrics* 68 (November 1981): 665–69; Goldfarb, "The Initial Encounter," p. 3. According to a 1986 survey, 37 percent of the male membership of the Society for Adolescent Medicine performed pelvic examinations without any chaperone present. This was done, the doctors said, because of patient preference. See Richard M. Buchta, "Use of Chaperones During Pelvic Examinations of Female Adolescents: Results of a Survey," *American Journal of Diseases of Children* 141 (1987): 666–67. For a sensitive discussion of the importance to patient and doctor of the first penetration of vaginal space, see Philip Sarrel, "Indications for a First Pelvic Examination," *Journal of Adolescent Health Care* 2 (1981): 145–46.
58. Hein, "The First Gynecological Exam," p. 35.
59. Judy Blume, *Deenie* (New York, 1973). By the 1980s, popular magazines for teens were also more accepting of masturbation. See, for example, Kathy McCoy, "Masturbation: Normal or Not?," *Seventeen,* October 1984, pp. 12–14, and "Straight Talk About Masturbation," *Seventeen,* November 1988, p. 36, which reported that over 90 percent of American women masturbated by age twenty-one. See fn. 7, chapter 3.
60. Boston Women's Health Collective, *Our Bodies, Ourselves* (New York, 1973).
61. In her diary, Lou Henry (Hoover) described her infatuation with different young female teachers, what they looked like, and what they said to her. Her interest was

not unusual in diaries of that era. For discussions of women's relationships in the nineteenth century, see Nancy Sahli, "Smashing: Women's Relationship Before the Fall," *Chrysallis* (1979): 17–27; Carroll Smith-Rosenberg, "The Female World of Love and Ritual: Relations Between Women in Nineteenth-Century America," in *Disorderly Conduct: Visions of Gender in Victorian America* (New York, 1985); Anna Mary Wells, *Miss Marks and Miss Wooley* (Boston, 1978); Leila J. Rupp, "Imagine My Surprise: Women's Relationships in Historical Perspective," *Frontiers* 5 (Fall 1980): 61–70; Helen Horowitz, *The Power and Passion of M. Carey Thomas* (New York, 1994).

62. For historical accounts of the social and economic conditions that made lesbianism a more viable option, see Lillian Faderman, *Odd Girls and Twilight Lovers: A History of Lesbian Life in Twentieth-Century America* (New York, 1991), and D'Emilio and Freedman, *Intimate Matters.* For the narratives of contemporary gay teenagers, see Kurt Chandler, *Passages of Pride: Lesbian and Gay Youth Come of Age* (New York, 1995); for analysis of their psychological development, see Rich Savin-Williams, *Gay and Lesbian Youth: Expressions of Identity* (New York, 1990), and A. Damien Martin, "Learning to Hide: The Socialization of the Gay Adolescent," *Annals of the American Society for Adolescent Psychiatry* 10 (1982): 52–65. There is an insightful analysis of "coming-out stories" in Ken Plummer, *Telling Sexual Stories: Power, Change and Social Worlds* (New York, 1995).
63. The quotations that follow are from the diaries of Ellen Anderson (pseud./poa), 1969–76.
64. Robert Masland, "Sex Education," in *Pediatric and Adolescent Gynecology,* 2nd ed., S. Jean Herriot Emans and Donald Peter Goldstein, eds. (Boston, 1982), p. 330.
65. Leif, "Sexual Behavior in Adolescence," p. 61.
66. The quotations that follow are from the diary of Deborah Perry (pseud./poa), 1981–82.
67. Emans, "Pelvic Examination of the Adolescent Patient," p. 10. Heather Munro Prescott makes the point that the clinical approach implied that parents and children could not resolve generational conflicts over sexuality without expert intervention.
68. In addition, pelvic inflammatory disease, a well-known cause of infertility, is ten times more likely to appear in the adolescent than the adult population. See Sandra Blakeslee, "An Epidemic of Genital Warts Raises Concern But Not Alarm," *The New York Times,* January 22, 1982; Janet E. Gans et al., *America's Adolescents: How Healthy Are They?* (Chicago, 1990).
69. Five- and six-year-old girls are another vulnerable age group. Donald E. Greydanus and Robert B. Shearin, *Adolescent Sexuality and Gynecology* (Philadelphia, 1990), p. 245.
70. Jennifer Steinhauer, "Study Cites Adult Males for Most Teen-Age Births," *The New York Times,* August 2, 1995, p. A10; Ellen Goodman, "Adult Men Must Not Be Left Out of the Teenage Pregnancy Question," *Ithaca Journal,* February 9, 1996. In *Going All the Way: Teenage Girls' Tales of Sex, Romance and Pregnancy* (New

York, 1995) and "Putting a Big Thing in a Little Hole: Teenage Girls' Accounts of Sexual Initiation," *Journal of Sex Research* 27 (August 1990): 341–61, Sharon Thompson provides narrative accounts of sexual activity that reveal the sexual pressure contemporary girls feel.

71. Chuck Sudetic, "Seven Are Arrested in Groping of Girl in Pool," *The New York Times,* July 24, 1995. A well-known case of sexual harassment by middle-class teenage boys involved the Spur Posse, a California group that made sexual conquest and brutality central to their identity; see Jill Smolowe, "Sex with a Scorecard," *Time,* April 5, 1993, p. 41.
72. The quotations that follow are from the diary of Sarah Compton (pseud./poa), 1981–82. It is no accident that the American Association of University Women entitled its 1993 report, *Hostile Hallways: The AAUW Survey on Sexual Harassment in the School* (New York, 1993). For an analysis of the different forms of unwanted public attention from men, see Carol Brooks Garner, *Passing By: Gender and Public Harassment* (Berkeley, Calif., 1995).
73. *Seventeen,* August 1992, p. 120; May 1995, pp. 68, 84.
74. Carol Tavris and Susan Sadd, *The Redbook Report on Female Sexuality* (New York, 1977); Alfred Kinsey et al., *Sexual Behavior in the Human Male* (Philadelphia, 1948); Morton Hunt, *Sexual Behavior in the 1970s* (New York, 1974). In the 1970s, oral sex was also taught through popular books, intended for adults, such as Bernhardt Hurwood, *Joys of Oral Love* (New York, 1975).
75. On oral sex among adolescents, I have relied on Susan F. Newcomer and J. Richard Udry, "Oral Sex in an Adolescent Population," *Archives of Sexual Behavior* 14 (1985): 41–46; Arthur B. Shostak, "Oral Sex: New Standard of Intimacy and Old Index of Troubled Sexuality," *Deviant Behavior* 2 (1981): 127–44; Michael Young, "Attitudes and Behavior of College Students Relative to Oral-Genital Sexuality," *Archives of Sexual Behavior* 9 (1980): 61–67; Janet Lever, "Lesbian Sex Survey," *Advocate,* August 22, 1995, pp. 22–30. In *Coming of Age in New Jersey: College and American Culture* (New Brunswick, N.J., 1989), Michael Moffat suggests that oral sex among college students eventually became mutual and pleasurable for those who become "established couples."
76. See Maureen A. Pirog-Good and Jan E. Stets, *Violence in Dating Relationships: Emerging Social Issues* (New York, 1989); J. E. Koval, "Violence in Dating Relationships," *Journal of Pediatric Health Care* 3 (1989): 298–304; Andrea Parrot, "Acquaintance Rape Among Adolescents: Identifying Risk Groups and Intervention Strategies," *Journal of Social Work and Human Sexuality* 8 (1989): 47–61; Peggy Sanday, *Fraternity Gang Rape: Sex, Brotherhood and Privilege on Campus* (New York, 1990); "Adolescent Acquaintance Rape," *American College of Obstetricians and Gynecologists Technical Bulletin* 122, May 1993.
77. Debra Kent, "Sex & the Body," *Seventeen,* June 1994, p. 84.
78. See, for example, American Professional Society on the Abuse of Children, *Practical Guidelines: Descriptive Terminology in Child Sexual Abuse Medical Evaluations* (Chicago, 1995); Abbey B. Berenson et al., "Appearance of the Hymen in Prepubertal

Girls," *Pediatrics* 89 (March 1992): 387–94; John McCann et al., "Genital Findings in Prepubertal Children Selected for Nonabuse: A Descriptive Study," *Pediatrics* 86 (September 1990): 428–39; Astrud Heger and S. Jean Emans, *Evaluation of the Sexually Abused Child: A Medical Textbook and Photographic Atlas* (New York, 1992); Angelo P. Giardino et al., *A Practical Guide to the Evaluation of Sexual Abuse in the Prepubertal Child* (Newbury Park, Calif., 1992); Robert M. Reece, *Child Abuse: Medical Diagnosis and Management* (Philadelphia, 1994).

CHAPTER SIX

Girl Advocacy Again

1. Jane Hirshmann and Carol Munter, *When Women Stop Hating Their Bodies* (New York, 1995).
2. Ellen Goodman, "Adult Men Must Not Be Left Out of the Teenage Pregnancy Equation," *Ithaca Journal*, February 9, 1996.
3. Elkind proposes that we raise some kind of protective structure once again, a suggestion that echoes conservative critics, who want to restrict the freedom of girls and return to the moral universe of yesteryear. But even progressive "girl advocates," such as Carol Gilligan, think we should try to elongate preadolescence in girls in order to give them more time to be nurtured, develop their identity, and solidify the self. David Elkind, *Ties That Stress: The New Family Imbalance* (Cambridge, Mass., 1994); Lyn Mikel Brown and Carol Gilligan, *Meeting at the Crossroads* (Cambridge, Mass., 1992).
4. Although the overall number of teens becoming parents has decreased slightly since 1993, births to girls under fifteen has actually increased. See E. Jones et al., *Teenage Pregnancy in Industrialized Countries* (New Haven, Conn., 1987); Laurence Steinberg, *Adolescence*, 3rd ed. (New York, 1993); C. Hayes, ed., *Risking the Future: Adolescent Sexuality, Pregnancy and Childbearing* (Washington, D.C., 1987); K. Moore, *Facts at a Glance* (Washington, D.C., 1991).
5. According to one theory, early physical maturation and motherhood are caused by stress, such as the absence of the father and poverty, which allegedly stimulates young women to hurry up, reproduce, and have children while they can. In this scenario, the teenage mother is "opportunistic" in an evolutionary sense. See Jay Belsky, Laurence Steinberg, and Patricia Draper, "Childhood Experience, Interpersonal Development, and Reproductive Strategy: An Evolutionary Theory of Socialization," *Child Development* 62 (1991): 647–70, for the controversial argument that early pregnancy may be an evolutionary advantage, as well as critical replies, in the same issue, by Robert Hinde and Eleanor Maccoby. The absence of fathers is also considered in Judith S. Musick, *Young, Poor and Pregnant: The Psy-*

chology of Teenage Motherhood (New Haven, Conn., 1993); Jeanne Brooks-Gunn and Frank Furstenberg, "Adolescent Sexual Behavior," in *Adolescent Behavior and Society*, ed. Rolf E. Muuss (New York, 1990), pp. 243–55; Jeanne Brooks-Gunn, "Pubertal Processes and Girls' Psychological Adaptation," in *Biological-Psychosocial Interactions in Early Adolescence: A Life-Span Perspective*, R. Lerner and T. T. Foch, eds., (Hillsdale, N.J., 1987), pp. 123–53. The best recent book on unwed teenage mothers is Kristin Luker, *Dubious Conceptions: The Politics of Teenage Pregnancy* (Cambridge, Mass., 1996).

6. If they did not marry, the white unmarried mother was sent off to a Florence Crittenden Home for unmarried mothers, and she probably gave her baby up for adoption; unmarried black women were excluded from this possibility and raised their babies within the African-American community; on this history, see Rickie Solinger, *Wake Up Little Susie: Single Pregnancy and Race Before Roe v. Wade* (New York, 1992).
7. William Julius Wilson, lecture at Cornell, November 12, 1995.
8. Data on racial differences in menarche from U.S. Department of Health and Human Services, Natality Statistics, published in (Jacksonville, Fla.) *Times Union*, June 28, 1995, p. D1. For studies that consider the expectations of girls, see Naiobi Way, "Can't You See the Courage, the Strength That I Have? Listening to Urban Adolescent Girls Speak About Their Relationships," *Psychology of Women Quarterly* 19 (1995): 107–28, and Sharon Thompson, *Going All the Way: Teenage Girls' Tales of Sex, Romance and Pregnancy* (New York, 1995).
9. Musick, *Young, Poor, and Pregnant*, pp. 84–87; D. Boyer and D. Fine, "Sexual Abuse as a Factor in Adolescent Pregnancy and Child Maltreatment," *Family Planning Perspectives* 24 (1992): 4–11, 19; Joy Dryfoos, *Adolescents at Risk: Prevalence and Prevention* (New York, 1990); Frank Furstenberg, Jeanne Brooks-Gunn, and P. Morgan, *Adolescent Mothers in Later Life* (New York, 1987); H. Gershenson et al., "The Prevalence of Coercive Sexual Experience Among Teenage Mothers," *Journal of Interpersonal Violence* 4 (1989): 201–19; A. Handler, "The Correlates of the Initiation of Sexual Intercourse Among Young Urban Black Females," *Journal of Youth and Adolescence* 19 (1990): 159–70; Goodman, "Adult Men Must Not Be Left Out."
10. In "Putting a Big Thing in a Little Hole," *Journal of Sex Research* 27 (August 1990): 341–61, Sharon Thompson notes the difficulties most girls have acknowledging their own sexual volition. Hayes, *Risking the Future;* George Cvetkovich et al., "On the Psychology of Adolescents' Use of Contraceptives," *Journal of Sex Research* 11 (1975): 256–70.
11. See, for example, Charles E. Irwin and Susan G. Millstein, "Biopsychosocial Correlates of Risk-Taking Behavior During Adolescence," in Muus, *Adolescent Behavior and Society*, pp. 339–55.
12. Steinberg, *Adolescence*, p. 380. Kristin Anderson Moore, David E. Meyers, et al., "Age at First Childbirth and Later Poverty," *Journal of Research on Adolescence* 3 (1993): 393–422.

13. On the confidence gap, see Peggy Orenstein, *School Girls: Young Women, Self-Esteem and the Confidence Gap* (New York, 1994), and American Association of University Women, *How Schools Short-Change Girls* (New York, 1995).
14. Dioclesian Lewis, *Our Girls* (New York, 1871), p. 10. Lewis was in favor of higher education and careers for American women, but his essential concern was preparing them for successful motherhood. In this respect, he was different from Stanton.

INDEX

B

Permissions

Grateful acknowledgment is made to the following for permission to use illustrative material.

Frontispiece: (*clockwise from top*) Permission of Leise Bronfenbrenner; permission of the author; permission of the author; permission of Megan Tobias; permission of Duke University, Special Collections, Cowherd Collection; permission of Joel Kerlan.

Title page: (*left*) Permission of the author; (*right*) permission of Ellen Grebinger and Natalie Rifkin.

Photo insert: 1. Permission of Stanley Weintraub; 2. permission of the author; 3. William Easterly Ashton, *A Textbook on the Practice of Gynecology* (1905); 4. permission of the author; 5. *The Ladies' Home Journal* (1904); 6, 7, 8. Division of Rare and Manuscript Collections, Cornell University Library; 9. Standard Sanitary Manufacturing Company catalog (1912); 10. *The Ladies' Home Journal* (1898); 11. James Harvey Sequeira, *Diseases of the Skin* (1911); 12. National Bellas Hess Company catalog (1917); 13. *Retail Druggist* (1923); 14. *The Ladies' Home Journal* (1897); 15. *The Ladies' Home Journal* (1907); 16. *The Ladies' Home Journal* (1903); 17. *The Ladies' Home Journal* (1902); 18. *The Ladies' Home Journal* (1909); 19. permission of the author; 20. *The Ladies' Home Journal* (c. 1900); 21. *The Ladies' Home Journal* (1903); 22. permission of the author (c. 1910); 23. permission of the author (1910); 24. permission of the Dewitt Historical Society of Tomkins County (1911); 25. permission of the author (1905); 26. permission of the author (c. 1924); 27. *The Ladies' Home Journal* (1927); 28. permission of the author (1920s); 29. *The Ladies' Home Journal* (1927); 30. *Delineator* (1924); 31. *The Ladies' Home Journal* (1927); 32. permission of UPI/Corbis-Bettmann (1927); 33. permission of UPI/Corbis-Bettmann (1920s); 34. permission of Ann Lane (1945); 35. *Seventeen* (1944); 36. *Seventeen* (1945); 37. *Seventeen* (1944); 38. permission of UPI/Corbis-Bettmann (1956); 39. *American Girl* (1949); 40. *Seventeen* (1951); 41. *American Girl* (1958); 42. *Life* (1958); 43. permission of Ann Russ; 44. permission of Donna Dempster-McClean; 45. permission of Ada Albright; 46. permission of Jan Jennings; 47. *Optometric Weekly* (1961); 48. photo by Arthur Rothstein, *Look* (1954); 49. permission of Donna Dempster-McClean; 50. permission of Jon Reis/Photolink, Ithaca, N.Y.; 51. permission of Helen Johnson; 52. permission of Krista Rowe and Ted Milardo, photographer; 53. *Seventeen* (1990); 54. Delia catalog (1995); 55. permission of Beth Timmons; 56. permission of Kathleen Poe; 57. *Sassy* (1990); 58. permission of Lynley Shulman and Jon Reis/Photolink, Ithaca, N.Y.; 59. *Sassy* (1990); 60. permission of Adam Brumberg.